An Introduction to

The Nature and Functions of Language

HOWARD JACKSON and PETER STOCKWELL

Howard Jackson is Professor of English Language and Linguistics and
Peter Stockwell is Lecturer in Sociolinguistics and Stylistics in the
School of English at the University of Central England in Birmingham

STANLEY THORNES (PUBLISHERS) LTD

Investigating English Language

First published in 1996 by:
Stanley Thornes (Publishers) Ltd
Ellenborough House
Wellington Street
CHELTENHAM GL50 1YW
England

A catalogue record for this book is available from the British Library.

ISBN 0–7487–2580–6

98 99 00 / 10 9 8 7 6 5 4 3

Typeset by Tech-Set, Gateshead, Tyne and Wear
Printed and bound in Great Britain at Scotprint Ltd, Musselburgh, Scotland

Acknowledgements

The author and publishers wish to thank the following for permission to use copyright material:

Blackwell Publishers for material from P. Fletcher, *A Child's Learning of English*, 1985; Everyman's Library Ltd for an extract from 'Sir Gawain and the Green Knight' from A. C. Cawley and J. J. Anderson, eds, *Pearl, Cleanness, Patience, Sir Gawain and the Green Knight*, Everyman edition; Fuji Photo Film (UK) Ltd for text from advertising material; The Controller of Her Majesty's Stationery Office and the National Curriculum Council for an extract from 'Evolution of the Implementation of English in the National Curriculum at Key Stages 1, 2, 3 (1991–1993)'; Oxford University Press for 'Northumbrian Caedmon's Hymn' and 'West Saxon Caedmon's Hymn' from H. Sweet, *An Anglo-Saxon Reader in Prose and Verse*, 15th edition revised by D. Whitelock, Clarendon Press, 1967; W. W. Norton & Company Ltd for E.E. Cummings, 'anyone lived in a pretty how town' from *Complete Poems 1904–1962* by E. E. Cummings, ed. by George Firmage. Copyright © 1940, 1968, 1991 by the Trustees for the E. E. Cummings Trust; Penguin UK Ltd for adapted Table 10 from Peter Trudgill, *Sociolinguistics: An Introduction to Language and Society*, Penguin Books, 1974, revised 1983, p. 109. Copyright © Peter Trudgill, 1974, 1983.

Front cover picture: *L'Encre Invisible* 1947, Kurt Schwitters © DACS 1996, Private Collection/Visual Arts Library.

Every effort has been made to trace all the copyright holders but if any have been inadvertently overlooked the publishers will be pleased to make the necessary arrangements at the first opportunity.

CONTENTS

Introduction

This book is intended to introduce students to a range of subjects within linguistics. It presents a theoretical approach to language, although this is rooted in a descriptive approach to real examples as they exist in the world. It is aimed primarily at students and teachers following the Advanced Level in English Language. However, it represents a broad introduction to linguistics and would be very useful preparatory reading for students about to begin undergraduate courses in English Language and Literature. It is complementary to Urszula Clark's *Connecting Text and Grammar: An Introduction to Stylistic Text Analysis*.

Very little knowledge of language study is assumed in this book. We have set out to explain and illustrate fundamental concepts, and to build on this in presenting a more sophisticated discussion in later chapters. We first survey the field of linguistics, in order to orientate the student who is new to this important area. In Chapter 2, we provide a detailed account of the structure of the English language system, introducing many concepts and terms that will be useful later on.

In Chapter 3, we present a survey of how English developed from its very beginnings, through its ancestry to the present day. We discuss the nature of language change and show why English looks and acts like it does today. From the development of the language of a society, in Chapter 4 we trace the development of language in the individual. We link the acquisition of language in young children with their cognitive development, and we consider related issues of schooling and bilingualism.

The field of sociolinguistics is surveyed in Chapter 5. Here we look at varieties of English and how differences in social structure accompany different forms of language. We continue this concern with the contemporary usage of English in the final chapter, where we outline how meaning is generated and perceived through language.

The book aims to cover the whole syllabus of language theory at A-level. However, we have tried to make the chapters self-contained and coherent, and so different topics placed into different areas by the examination boards are here presented according to their linguistic disciplines. We feel this makes for a better understanding of the interconnectedness of the whole subject.

Although each chapter can be read on its own, it would be sensible to follow and grasp the content of Chapters 1 and 2 first. This is because they introduce key concepts of linguistic description that are used in the discussions of subsequent chapters.

We include sections of Activities throughout the book. These can be followed to check your progress (as in the early chapters) and to help you to think more deeply about the ideas introduced (in later chapters). Activities often include examples and passages that illustrate the ideas mentioned in the chapter. They can be used independently for interest by the student, or as resources for classroom discussion.

At the end of each chapter, we include suggestions for further reading. These partly comprise the published source material for the chapter. It is always a good idea, having grasped the outline of an area by reading the chapter, to go and read the original material. This will greatly extend your understanding, as well as helping you to become accustomed to the appropriate style of professional academic books and articles. It is useful, too, to see at first hand the fine points of disagreement between linguists writing on the same subject.

Included at the end of each chapter are also some suggestions for project work and extended study. We identify the key features involved in researching that particular area, and we suggest a few specific lines of inquiry. These, of course, are only guidelines. The intention overall is to encourage you to develop your own interests and to investigate language for yourself.

Throughout the text, important terms are highlighted in **bold** type. Those terms that are printed in **<u>bold underlined</u>** type are described in more detail in the Glossary at the end of the volume.

Language and its description

1.0 Introduction

The aim of this chapter is to set the scene. It previews in general terms the topics that we want to explore in this book. The detail is filled in by the following chapters. It investigates the nature of language and outlines the discipline of linguistics, which provides the academic framework for investigating and talking about language.

1.1 What is language?

We need to distinguish first of all between 'language' and 'a language'. We use the term **language** to refer to the general faculty, which enables human beings to engage in the verbal exchange of information. The exchange may take place by means of speech, writing, signing or Braille. And it may be in any one of the world's 4000 or so languages.

We are now using 'language' in our second sense: to refer to 'a language'. A language is the particular form of verbal communication used by a group of speakers. It is defined in part by the particular characteristics of its pronunciation, grammatical structure and vocabulary. It may be defined, too, by the fact that its speakers understand each other but are not understood by, and do not themselves understand, speakers of other languages. However, a language is often also defined in political or national terms: for example, Hungarian is the language spoken by the people of Hungary. Both of these definitions are gross generalisations, as we shall see later. But for now, they serve to make the distinction between 'language' and 'a language'.

1.1.1 Speech and writing

Speech and writing are the 'expression' side of language, the media by which we disseminate our verbal messages. Of these, speech is the primary **medium** of expression. We acquire the ability to speak first; we are not taught to speak, as we are taught to write. All languages have a spoken form, but not all are written, and no natural language has existed in a written form before being a spoken language.

When we speak, we produce a succession of speech sounds. When we write, we produce a succession of letters, the counterpart in writing to the sounds of speech. The sounds of speech are accompanied by the rhythm and pitch features of **intonation**. The letters of writing are organised by the devices of spacing and **punctuation**. Intonation includes variation in pitch over a sequence of sounds, and variation of emphasis or stress, as well as features of continuity and pausing. Punctuation includes the use of spaces to separate groups of letters, as well as marks such as the full stop, question mark, exclamation mark, comma and colon, and single and double quotation marks; and perhaps even, with word-processed text, the use of bold, underlining and italics. All of this suggests that language has structure.

1.1.2 Words and sentences

What are the sounds of speech and the letters of writing expressing? Speech is not just a sequence of sounds, nor writing just a sequence of letters. The spaces in writing indicate that letters form larger units: **words**. And the punctuation indicates that there are larger units still: a full stop marks a **sentence**, while commas and semi-colons may mark phrases and clauses. These structural units are more obvious in writing than in speech, because writing reflects not just pronunciation, but aspects of grammatical structure as well. Words and sentences, as units of structure, are expressed, though, by speech as well as by writing.

We rarely communicate in single sentences, however. In the dialogue of conversation, the utterances of the participants build up into a **discourse**. In writing, whether in a newspaper article or a 500-page novel, the sentences combine to form a **text**. Discourses and texts are also units of language, with their particular forms of organisation and structure.

1.1.3 Language is...

From what we have said so far, we can describe language as the human faculty that enables us to exchange meaningful messages with our fellow human beings by means of discourses and texts, which are structured according to the rules and conventions of the particular language that we share with them.

ACTIVITY 1

1 Make a recording from the radio of an interview or other live speech. Transcribe about one minute of it, noting down as many features of what you hear as you can, including hesitations, mumblings and the like.

2 Take a brief article from a newspaper.

3 Compare your transcription of the spoken data with the written text, and note down all the differences that you can observe. Are speech and writing very different from each other?

1.2 Language is contextualised

None of us speaks and writes our language (or languages) in exactly the same way. We are all individuals when it comes to language, as we are in other aspects of our behaviour – for example, our mannerisms, or the way we dress or style our hair. An individual's language is called their **idiolect**: the form *lect* derives from a Greek word meaning 'speak', and *idio* derives from the Greek word for 'private'.

For any discourse or text that we produce, a number of factors contribute to our individuality as language users. First, there are psychological factors: our individual history as language users. Second, there are geographical factors: where we come from or have lived during childhood and adolescence. Third, there are social factors: the social milieu in which we were brought up and the social groups to which we belong. And fourth, there are factors relating to the purpose of a discourse or text. We will look at each of these different types of context in turn.

1.2.1 Psychological factors

We normally begin our acquisition of language during the first year of life within the context of a family, where we are spoken to by other family members – parents, sisters and brothers, aunts and uncles, grandparents. From them we learn our early vocabulary. We model our speech on their speech. Eventually, we can participate in their conversations.

In due course we go to school. Our language learning continues apace and now brings in the written medium: we learn to read and write. Not only that, but we probably come across different styles of speaking. The teacher's way of speaking may differ from our own; some of our peers may speak differently. New models may be presented for us to imitate. We may learn to speak in a different way at school from how we speak at home. It may even be the case that the language of school and the language of home are two different languages: English and Bengali, say. In this case, we begin to acquire a second language and to become **bilingual**.

As our schooling progresses, and especially as we learn to read and write, we become aware of the operation of language itself: the relation between sounds and letters, the notion of a sentence. If we go on to learn a foreign language in school, we may have our attention drawn to differences between that language and English. We begin to develop what is called **metalinguistic** knowledge: that is, knowledge about language.

Already, on entering school, we find ourselves taking on different roles: the role of child to our parents, that of sister or brother to our siblings, that of friend to our peers. In school, we take on the role of pupil to our teachers. As we go on in life, the roles that we assume may become more numerous and varied. For each one, we may adjust our language, our style of speech or writing, even if only very slightly. It may be that some roles may require a different language: consider the religious use of Hebrew for Jews, Arabic for Muslims or Punjabi for Sikhs. Our language ability as adults spans a number of varieties, which we use according to the context in which we are speaking or writing.

1.2.2 Geographical factors

One of the ways in which a language varies is regionally. We refer to a regional variety of a language as a **dialect**. Dialect variation may affect the words we use (vocabulary), the structures we use (grammar) and the sounds we use (pronunciation). If the variation concerns pronunciation alone, then we refer to **accent** rather than dialect. Regional variation may be a matter of the difference between national varieties; for example, British English, American English, Australian English and Indian English. Or it may be a matter of variation within a national variety, with varying degrees of specificity; for example, West Midlands accent/dialect, Black Country accent/dialect and Dudley accent/dialect.

The accent or dialect that we use in any particular context will be determined by a number of factors. Our dialect is formed initially when we model our speech on that of our family and then perhaps also on that of our peers at school. It conforms to the dialect of the area in which we live. If we move away from that area – say, for university education or for work – we may modify our accent/dialect to make ourselves more understandable or acceptable to people from other areas of the country. When we go back home, we may well resume speaking in our local dialect. Indeed, we may find that we have become **bi-dialectal**, speaking two dialects, choosing the appropriate one for the people with whom we are talking. We may not do this consciously, but it shows that we can adapt our language to the context in which we are interacting.

1.2.3 Social factors

We have noted already that, as individual speakers, we adopt a number of social roles, which may require us to vary the language that we use. The role that we have in a particular context is only one of the social factors that influences our use of language. The other people involved in the interaction, whether as partners in a conversation or as an audience for a spoken monologue or a written text, may require us to adapt our language to the context. Our relationships with these people, both in terms of familiarity and in terms of relative social status, are obviously important determinants and affect the **formality** of our language. The more diverse and unknown the audience, the less we should be able to use features of our local dialect, for instance.

The physical context may combine with other social factors to influence our language. A conversation in the common-room or on the bus may be couched in different language from discussion of the same topic in the classroom or in a tutor's study. The presence of the tutor may be seen as influential here, though, which brings us back to the people involved in an interaction.

Both what we talk or write about – the topic of our message – and the type of interaction in which it takes place (sermon, interview, chat-show, newspaper article, and so on) are also part of the context and have an influence on the variety of the language that we employ.

1.2.4 Purpose factors

The context in which a discourse or text is produced includes its purpose. Some language, especially in informal conversation, has the sole purpose of maintaining social relationships, rather than conveying any information. Much of our conversation about the weather is of this kind.

While some discourse/text has the purpose of getting things done, giving instructions or directing people, other discourse/text has a persuasive purpose, attempting to convince people of the rightness of a belief or idea. Or a discourse/text may have entertainment as its purpose, by means of telling a story, cracking a joke or playing cleverly with language itself.

A distinction is sometimes made between language that is **interactional** and language that is **transactional**. Interactional language has as its main focus the social relationships between participants when they speak to each other. Transactional language has as its main focus the message that the language conveys: it is language for doing things.

What becomes clear is that, as language users, we have command over a wide variety of language, whether just in one language, or in two or more. We adjust our language to the context in which we are talking or writing. The corollary of this is that no language has one 'standard' form, but that each has a multiplicity of forms. As users of a language, we have to choose from this multiplicity what is appropriate to any given context.

ACTIVITY 2

1 For a typical day in your life, keep a diary of all the times during that day when you use language, either as a speaker or writer, or as a listener or reader.

2 Make a note of which role you have (speaker, listener and so on), who the other participants were, what the purpose of the use of language was, and the physical context.

3 Note also whether you noticed yourself adapting your language to the context – the people, the situation or the purpose.

4 At the end of the day, review your use of language during that day – and prepare to be astounded!

1.3 Describing language: the linguistic disciplines

From the previous two sections of this chapter we have established that language has both structure and enormous variety. What a linguist tries to do is to investigate that structure and that variety, and propose ways of describing them that will illuminate them and give insight into their workings.

It is worth emphasising that a linguist is interested in what speakers and writers do linguistically, not in what they ought to do in order to produce 'correct' or 'proper' language. Linguistics is fundamentally **descriptive** rather than **prescriptive**. Linguists take the data of speech and writing (see Section 1.4) and make an analysis of it, with the purpose of providing descriptions of a language in all its diverse manifestations and of making sense of human beings' language faculty.

To that end, a number of linguistic disciplines have been developed, which deal with various aspects of language and its usage. We will now review some of these, to give you an idea both of the range of linguistic phenomena that there is to investigate and of the scope of the academic discipline of linguistics.

1.3.1 Describing sounds

There are two related linguistic disciplines concerned with the description of sounds: **phonetics** and **phonology**. Phonetics deals with human speech sounds in general: what constitutes a human speech sound, the way in which speech sounds are produced (their articulation), the range of speech sounds of which human beings are capable, and the physical (acoustic) qualities of speech sounds.

Phonology deals with speech sounds from the perspective of a particular language. It considers the selection that a language makes from the inventory of human speech sounds, and the contrasts that the language invokes for the purpose of distinguishing words. It also considers the ways in which sounds combine in a language into syllables and words, as well as features of intonation, stress and so on, which accompany speech.

1.3.2 Describing words

The words of a language are investigated and described by means of the disciplines of **lexicology** and **morphology**. Lexicology is concerned with establishing what a **word** is in a language: Is the word *ear* that refers to the organ of hearing the same word as the ear of a cereal plant (ear of wheat)? It is also concerned with how the meanings of words can be described, and with the history of words and their meanings. Lexicology also considers how words relate to each other in the vocabulary as a whole (for example, the meanings that they share). The insights of lexicology are applied in lexicography to the making of dictionaries, which are attempts to make descriptions of a language's word stock.

Morphology, which is sometimes regarded as a part of grammar, is concerned with the analysis of the structure of words. The word **morphology** is made up of two elements that derive from Greek: *morph* means 'form' and *logos* means 'word', 'reason' or 'study'. Morphology is the study of (word) forms. A word such as *denationalised* is composed of a number of elements (called **morphemes**):

> the root *nation*
> the *-al* **suffix** to make *national*
> the *-ise* suffix to make *nationalise*
> the *de-* **prefix** to make *denationalise*
> the *-(e)d* suffix to make the past tense or past participle form of the verb

Morphology describes these word-formation and word-structuring processes, and how words vary in form (by means of an **inflection**) for different grammatical purposes.

1.3.3 Describing sentences

The linguistic discipline that deals with the structure of sentences is **syntax**, which – along with morphology – constitutes grammar. The word 'syntax' derives from a Greek term that means 'putting together': it investigates how words are put together into sentences. This is not just a matter of possible word orders (for instance, *I have to write an essay on Hamlet* is a possible order in English, while *Have to I Hamlet on essay write* is not). It also concerns the differences in meaning that result from alternative possible orders: compare *Jim kissed Mary*, *Mary kissed Jim*, *Jim and Mary kissed*. And it considers all the various ways, simple and complex, in which sentences are structured.

Syntax is sometimes limited to the study of the structure of sentences. However, sentences themselves are 'put together' into texts and discourses. These, though, are structured rather differently from sentences and they have spawned their own linguistic disciplines (discourse analysis and text linguistics).

1.3.4 Describing discourses and texts

For some linguists, the term **discourse** includes both spoken and written 'discourses'. So, discourse analysis would be concerned equally with the dialogue of conversation and the written articles found in scientific journals. Other linguists use the term **text linguistics** to include both written and spoken 'texts'. It is perhaps more sensible, since both terms exist, to restrict 'discourse' to spoken language and 'text' to written language.

Discourse analysis is, then, the linguistic discipline concerned with the description of spoken interaction, whether in the dialogues of interviews and conversation or in the monologues of sermons and lectures. It investigates the ways in which participants in dialogue interact and how a conversation keeps going, as well as the mechanisms of controlling more structured interactions.

Text linguistics, or text grammar, is concerned with the study of written communication, mainly in the form of monologues, but also, occasionally, in the form of a dialogue, as in an exchange of letters. It investigates the features that allow a text to make sense as a whole, as well as the means by which texts are structured (for instance, paragraphs) and the various types of text that exist to fulfil the diverse functions that texts have in communication (for example, telling a story, arguing a point, describing a place, telling someone how to do something).

1.3.5 Describing meaning

Meaning is all pervasive in language. The other aspects of language – the sounds/letters, the morphology, the syntax – all serve the purpose of communicating meaningful messages between human beings. The study of meaning is the province of the linguistic discipline of **semantics**. Semantics deals with the meaning of words and of parts of words (**morphemes**), and so overlaps with the interests of lexicology and morphology. It also deals with the meaning of sentences, and so overlaps with the interests of syntax. Indeed, the term 'semantics' is sometimes qualified to reflect these different concerns; for example, lexical semantics or grammatical semantics.

1.3.6 Describing language and the individual

The way in which an individual acquires language and the investigation of what goes on inside a person's mind when they use language are studied within **psycholinguistics**. As the term implies, this is a discipline that spans the common interests of psychology and linguistics. Its interest is language as an aspect of human behaviour, including language in its normal functions and how individuals cope as bilinguals with acquiring and operating in two or more languages.

As well as investigating how human beings acquire a language and learn second and subsequent languages, psycholinguistics also studies language breakdown and loss in individuals, as a result of head injury, stroke or other trauma. An individual's language may provide evidence of the nature of the injury sustained.

1.3.7 Describing language and social variation

The ways in which language varies socially are the concern of **<u>sociolinguistics</u>**, which – as the term implies – lies at the intersection of linguistics and sociology. Many of the categories of sociology (for instance, social network) are used by sociolinguists to investigate the ways in which language reflects, maintains or even constitutes social distinctions and behaviour.

Sociolinguistics often investigates the correlation between a linguistic feature (for example, of pronunciation or grammar) and a social distinction (for example, gender or social class). It is also interested in how multilingual communities work, how linguistic minorities (such as the Welsh in the UK) manage, and how **lingua francas** such as **pidgins** and **creoles** develop.

1.3.8 Describing language in use

In recent years a linguistic discipline called **<u>pragmatics</u>** has developed: this draws on a number of the disciplines we have already mentioned, especially sociolinguistics and discourse analysis, in order to present an account of the ways in which language is used. The emphasis is on the contexts and purposes of language use. It is interested, for example, in how people use language to get things done, or to influence or to persuade others.

1.3.9 Summarising...

The core linguistic disciplines, those which study the system of language, are phonology (drawing on phonetics), morphology, lexicology, syntax and discourse analysis/text linguistics. Pervading them all to a greater or lesser extent is semantics.

Looking outward from language to the wider context of its use in human communication are the disciplines of psycholinguistics, sociolinguistics and pragmatics.

Language can be approached from a number of perspectives. It is as this is done that a picture of the variety and complexity of language begins to emerge. It is an exploration that seems to have barely begun. You can share in that exploration as you undertake work in language study.

ACTIVITY 3

1 Take any sentence from the material that you collected for Activity 1 (see page 2).

2 With one or two other students, attempt to make a description of the sentence from as many linguistic perspectives as you can. Consider its structure, its meaning and its use within the context. Your description will inevitably be incomplete, but it will begin to give you an impression of the great variety of things that there is to find out about language.

1.4 Language data

What are linguists describing? Where do they get their data from? Linguists claim to be 'describing' what people say and write, not 'prescribing' how they should do it. They are, therefore, not trying simply to identify best practice. Anything that is said or written in a language constitutes data that may be of interest to a linguist for some descriptive purpose or other.

1.4.1 Introspection

Some linguists believe that, as native speakers of a language, reflecting on their own knowledge of their language provides them with the data that they need. This is accessing linguistic data by introspection. For some purposes – for instance, testing how a linguistic theory works – this may provide adequate data. But it has the danger of producing only the data that the linguist needs to prove a particular point. Moreover, you cannot always be sure of what you do regularly say or write. If you repeat a sentence or phrase to yourself enough times, you can persuade yourself that this is really what you would say.

1.4.2 Elicitation

Such self-generated, subjective data is for most purposes quite inadequate. There are two other, more reliable, ways of obtaining data. If linguists are interested in investigating some particular aspect of language, they may need to collect some very specific data. To do that, they may construct a questionnaire to elicit the data that they are interested in, from a particular set of speakers of a certain language. This is, therefore, called the **elicitation** technique of obtaining data. It is a common technique in sociolinguistics, where linguists are studying the correlation between linguistic features and social categories. For example, a linguist may be interested in which preposition a given social group uses after the adjective *different* (*different from*, *different to* or *different than*). An elicitation technique would be the appropriate way in which to collect such data.

1.4.3 Corpora

Many linguists, who may be interested in rather broader areas of linguistic investigation, rely these days on a **corpus** of data. A corpus is a collection of texts and/or discourses, which a linguist uses to study aspects of a language. For investigations of the language system, the corpus will need to be quite extensive, and to include a representative sample of the range of discourses and texts that occur in a language community. If the interest is in vocabulary (that is, lexicological), then the corpus needs to be more extensive than if the interest is phonological or grammatical. Nowadays, the corpus is likely to be held on a computer.

One of the earliest and most famous corpora (or corpuses) is the **Survey of English Usage**, which is a corpus of some 750 000 words, two-thirds of which are spoken data. It was collected at University College London under the direction of Professor Randolph Quirk, and it has been used by many linguists to investigate various aspects of English. It was converted into computer form at the University of Lund and became the **London–Lund Corpus**. Another extensively used computer corpus is the one million word **Lancaster/Oslo–Bergen Corpus**, which contains some 500 text extracts of around 2000 words each from printed materials published in 1961. It was constructed under the direction of Professor Geoffrey Leech at the University of Lancaster, as a British English counterpart to a corpus of American English that had been constructed at Brown University in the USA in the 1960s – the **Brown Corpus**. A number of comparisons between British and American English have been made using these two corpora.

With the greater power and storage capacity of even desktop computers in recent years, and the development of highly accurate scanners and optical character-reading software, which can translate text into electronic form without the need for keying it in, linguists are looking to develop very large corpora. Corpora of around 100 million words are now under development; for example, the **British National Corpus** and the **International Corpus of English**. Quite sophisticated computer software to analyse, annotate and search corpora has also been developed and is continuing to be developed. The use of computer corpora is also revolutionising dictionary-making, beginning with the *Collins COBUILD Learner's Dictionary* (1987), developed at the University of Birmingham under Professor John Sinclair.

Much useful work in language study can be undertaken with a more modest corpus. Any collection of data, however limited, can reveal interesting things about language. But it is usually useful if you have some idea of what you are looking for. This is why you need to have a general knowledge and understanding of the linguistic system.

We turn to this in the next chapter.

ACTIVITY 4

1 Make a small collection of texts (say, half a dozen) of the same type; for example, advertisements, obituaries, book or film reviews.

2 Examine them and make a note of any features of the texts that you think are unique to or characteristic of the type. Such features would include the words that are used, how the text is organised on the page, punctuation, length of sentences and so on.

Further reading

A wide-ranging and readable introduction to the study of the English language is Crystal (1988). A more detailed, systematic and technical survey of the field is Gramley and Pätzold (1992).

The following are useful reference sources that can be mined for information on English and on language in general: McArthur (1992), Crystal (1987) on language in general, and Crystal (1995) on the English language.

The linguistic system of English

2.0 Introduction

In this chapter, we are going to explore how the English language works, from the point of view of its internal system. We begin with the smallest elements, sounds and letters. We then move on to the structure and meaning of words; after that, to the structure and function of sentences; and finally to the structure of discourses and texts.

2.1 Sounds and letters

The English alphabet – the word is derived from the names of the first two letters of the Greek alphabet: alpha α and beta β – contains 26 letters: abcdefghijklmnopqrstuvwxyz. They are used to write the words and sentences of English. Five of the letters are said to be vowels: aeiou. The remainder are consonants. The terms **consonant** and **vowel** are more appropriately used of the sounds which the letters represent.

We have already established (see Section 1.1.1) that speech is the primary medium of language. Letters are therefore the counterpart in writing of speech sounds. There are more speech sounds in English than there are letters in the alphabet – some forty altogether. The alphabet is thus inadequate for representing each sound with a unique symbol. Phoneticians have devised a notation, based on the Roman alphabet, with symbols from the Greek alphabet and elsewhere, in which each sound has a unique symbol; it is called the **International Phonetic Alphabet** or IPA. We shall be introducing the symbols as we discuss the speech sounds of English.

Speech sounds are produced as we breathe out. The column of air that we exhale is modified as it passes from the lungs out, past the glottis in the throat, and through the mouth or nose: it is given voice (noise) by the vocal cords in the glottis; individual sounds are shaped by the mouth, and especially the tongue (note the use of the word tongue as an archaic synonym of language).

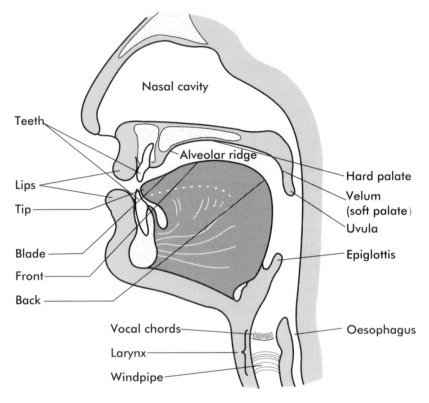

Figure 1 The organs of speech.

2.1.1 Vowels

Vowel sounds are voiced sounds: they are made with the vocal cords vibrating. What distinguishes vowels from consonants is that vowel sounds are made without any restriction in the mouth to the airflow. Different vowel sounds are made by the conjunction of three factors:

> how high or low the tongue and lower jaw are (high, mid, low)
> where in the mouth the sound is made (front, central, back)
> the shape of the lips (spread, rounded)

For example, a 'high front spread vowel' is the vowel in *seed* represented by *ee*; a 'high back rounded vowel' is found in *food*, represented by *oo*.

Front vowels

English has four front vowels, those in *seed, Sid, said, sad*, for which the IPA symbols are:

> *seed* /iː/ (the colon ':' indicates a long vowel) – long high front spread vowel
> *Sid* /i/ – short high front spread vowel
> *said* /e/ – short mid front spread vowel
> *sad* /a/ – short low front spread vowel (also symbolised by /æ/)

If you say these vowels in order, from high to low, you will perceive that your tongue is progressively lowered and your mouth becomes more open.

Note that it is conventional to put phonetic transcriptions between slash brackets '/ /'. Square brackets '[ ]' are also used, as we shall see later (in Section 2.1.4).

Central vowels

English has three mid vowels, those in *bird*, the first in *taboo* and in *bud*. The IPA symbols for these vowels are:

> *bird* /ɜː/ – long mid central spread vowel
> *taboo* (a) /ə/ – short mid central spread vowel
> *bud* /ʌ/ – short low central spread vowel

This last vowel /ʌ/ occurs typically in the speech of southern British English speakers. Speakers in the Midlands and the North use a high back rounded vowel /u/ instead.

Back vowels

English has five back vowels, those in *food*, *good*, *ford*, *God*, *guard*. The IPA symbols for these vowels are:

> *food* /uː/ – long high back rounded vowel
> *good* /u/ – short high back rounded vowel
> *ford* /oː/ – long mid back rounded vowel (also symbolised by /ɔː/)
> *God* /o/ – short low back rounded vowel (also symbolised by /ɒ/)
> *guard* /aː/ – long low back spread vowel

Many words that are pronounced in southern British English with the long low back spread vowel /aː/ are pronounced in the Midlands and the North with the short low front spread vowel /a/; for example, *ask*, *grass*, *laugh*, *path*. You will notice that the labels for vowel sounds follow a regular sequence:

length – height – place – lips – vowel

Diphthongs

All of the vowel sounds that we have considered so far are made with a single configuration of the mouth. Once having made the configuration, in terms of tongue height, place and lips, we can make the vowel sound for as long as we have breath to sustain it. You might notice that it is on the vowel sounds that singers are able to sustain notes. There are, however, some vowel sounds in English where the configuration of the mouth changes in the course of making the sound. They are called **<u>diphthongs</u>**. For example, the vowel in *made* is a diphthong: it begins as a mid front vowel and then tends towards a high front vowel; it is symbolised as /ei/.

English has three sets of diphthongs, according to the second vowel of the diphthong:

> those tending towards /i/
> those tending towards /u/
> those tending towards /ə/

The /i/ diphthongs are the vowel sounds in *sail*, *stile*, *soil*, which are represented by the following IPA symbols:

sail /ei/ – mid front to high front diphthong
stile /ai/ – low front to high front diphthong
soil /oi/ – mid back to high front diphthong

The /u/ diphthongs are the vowel sounds in *load*, *loud*, represented by the following IPA symbols:

load /ou/ – mid central to high back diphthong
loud /au/ – low back to high back diphthong

The /ə/ diphthongs are the vowel sounds in *fierce*, *scared*, *fuel*, which are represented by the IPA symbols:

fierce /iə/ – high front to mid central diphthong
scared /eə/ – mid front to mid central diphthong
fuel /uə/ – high back to mid central diphthong

There is some variation in the pronunciation of these diphthongs, and in some accents – for instance, Scottish – simple vowels may be used instead. In the case of *fuel*, for example, the vowel may, for many speakers, be /u:/ rather than /uə/.

We have now described the twelve simple vowels and the eight diphthongs of English. It is in the vowels that there is the greatest disparity between the number of sounds (twenty) and the number of letters (five), even taking into account combinations of letters (see also Section 2.1.5). It is also in the vowel sounds that we can detect most of the differences of accent among speakers of English (see also Section 2.1.8).

	Front	Central	Back
High	i　i:		u　u:
Mid	e	ə　ə:	ɔ:
Low	a	ʌ	ɒ　a:

Simple vowels

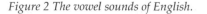

Diphthongs

Figure 2 The vowel sounds of English.

ACTIVITY 5

Give the IPA symbol for the vowel sounds in the following words. If you get stuck, you can seek help in an up-to-date dictionary: many of them (check in the edition's 'Guide to Using the Dictionary') use the IPA to indicate the pronunciation of words, but there may be some variation in the symbols used.

can	feel	cook	ladder
soup	bark	rope	choice
born	learn	lunch	palm
song	safe	tough	risk
send	peace	bought	affair

See page 63 for the answers.

2.1.2 Consonants

The pronunciation of <u>**consonants**</u> involves some interruption of the airflow, which is caused by articulators (tongue, lips, roof of the mouth) coming together, or into close proximity. There are three factors that determine the quality of a consonant sound:

whether the vocal cords are vibrating (<u>**voicing**</u>)

the place where the articulation takes place

the manner of the articulation – complete interruption of the airflow, as against partial interruption

Voicing

Whether or not the vocal cords are vibrating determines whether a consonant is **voiced** (with vibration) or **unvoiced** (without vibration). Many consonants in English are in unvoiced/voiced pairs; for example, in the final sounds of *lace* /s/ and *laze* /z/, /s/ is unvoiced while /z/ is voiced. To test this, put your fingers in your ears and say /s/ – /z/ in succession: the buzzing in your ears when you say /z/ indicates that your vocal cords are vibrating.

Place of articulation

Much of the articulation of consonant sounds occurs with some part of the tongue against some part of the roof of the mouth, but not exclusively. Starting from the front of the mouth, we can identify a number of <u>**places of articulation**</u> relevant to the pronunciation of English consonants (see Figure 1 in Section 2.1).

Labial articulation – involving the lips – is used for the initial sounds of *boast* /b/, *most* /m/ and *vast* /v/. The first two /b m/ have a **bilabial** articulation, using the upper and lower lip. The last one /v/ has a **labio-dental** articulation, using the lower lip and the upper front teeth.

Dental articulation – with the tongue tip against the back of the upper front teeth – is used for the initial sounds of *third* /θ/ and *those* /ð/.

Alveolar articulation – with the blade of the tongue against the bony, alveolar ridge just behind the upper front teeth – is used for the initial sounds of *tent* /t/, *door* /d/, *zoo* /z/, *near* /n/, *leaf* /l/.

Palatal articulation – with the front of the tongue against the hard palate – is used for the initial sound of job /dʒ/ – represented here by the letter 'j' – and of *shop* /ʃ/ – represented here by the letter combination 'sh'.

Velar articulation – with the back of the tongue against the velum (soft palate) – is used for the initial sound of *girl* /g/ and for the final sound of *bang* /ŋ/ – represented here by the letter combination 'ng', except in some accents (for example, in the West Midlands) where 'ng' is pronounced /ŋg/.

Glottal articulation – using the glottis – is used for one sound in English, the unvoiced /h/ at the beginning of *horse*.

Manner of articulation

The **manner of articulation** describes the way in which the articulators come together. It provides a useful way in which to categorise consonant sounds. We can identify five classes of consonant according to their manner of articulation: stop (or plosive), fricative, nasal, lateral and approximant.

Stop consonants   This class of consonant includes /b/ at the beginning of *bird*, /d/ at the beginning of *dirt* and /g/ at the beginning of *girl*. They are called **stop** consonants because the articulators come together to stop the airflow completely. The subsequent release of the stopped airflow is often accompanied by plosion, which gives them their other name of **plosive**.

The following unvoiced/voiced pairs of stop consonants occur in English:

bilabial /p b/, initially in *pin, bin*
alveolar /t d/, initially in *tin, din*
velar /k g/, initially in *come, gum*

We might note here the **glottal stop** /ʔ/, made by bringing the vocal cords together in the glottis. Although associated with the speech of East London (Cockney), it is used by many people, particularly adolescents, as a substitute for 't' in the middle of words such as *butter* or at the end of words such as *sit*.

English also has a pair of stop consonants at the palatal place of articulation, which are a little different from those just described. The release of the stop involves friction (see fricatives below), and they are sometimes called **affricates**. They are found initially in *choke* and *joke*: palatal /tʃ dʒ/ (compare alveolar stops above and palatal fricatives below).

Fricatives   In the pronunciation of **fricatives** the articulators come close together, but without completely stopping the airflow. As air is forced through the small gap between articulators, friction occurs. There are four unvoiced/voiced pairs of fricatives in English:

labio-dental /f v/, initially in *fan, van*
dental /θ ð/, initially in *thin, then*
alveolar /s z/, initially in *sap, zap*
palatal /ʃ ʒ/, finally in *ash* and in the middle of *azure*

The voiced palatal fricative has a limited distribution in English, occurring rarely word-initially or word-finally.

There is one further sound in English that is counted as a fricative: it is the unvoiced glottal fricative /h/, which occurs only at the beginning of a syllable: for instance, *heat*, *inhuman*.

Nasal Nasal consonants are like stops in that there is a complete closure of articulators in the mouth. However, the uvula, which normally blocks off the passage to the nose for other speech sounds, is lowered, and the airflow escapes instead through the nose. So, nasals are continuant sounds, like fricatives: they can be sustained or 'continued'. All nasals in English are voiced consonants, without voiceless counterparts. There are three in all:

bilabial /m/, initially in *mice*
alveolar /n/, initially in *nice*
velar /ŋ/, finally in *long*

The velar nasal /ŋ/ is restricted in its distribution: it does not occur at the beginnings of syllables/words. In some accents it is always followed by the voiced velar stop /g/, giving /loŋg/ rather than /loŋ/. When this is the case, it could be regarded as a variant of the alveolar nasal /n/ occurring before /g/ (see Section 2.1.4 on variants).

Lateral Like stops and nasals, <u>lateral</u> consonants involve a complete closure in the mouth, between the tongue and some part of the palate. However, air is allowed to escape over the sides of the tongue – thus 'laterally'. There is one lateral consonant in English, which is voiced:

alveolar /l/, initially in *lord*

Approximant There are three further sounds in English, which are counted as consonants. In articulation they are more like vowels in that they do not impede the airflow; however, they are like consonants in the kinds of articulation that they 'approximate' and in their function in the structure of syllables (see Section 2.1.3). These **approximants** are all voiced:

bilabial /w/, initially in *wet*
alveolar /r/, initially in *rat*
palatal /j/, initially in *yet*

All three approximants are restricted in their distributions in syllables and words:

bilabial /w/ generally occurs only initially, although it is used as a substitute for /l/ in the speech of some southern English and Scottish speakers; for example, in *film*, *kill*

alveolar /r/ occurs readily initially and between vowels (for example, in *hurry*), but variably, according to accent, in other positions

palatal /j/ occurs initially and in initial consonant combinations with /p/ (for example, *pure*), /b/ (*beauty*), /f/ (*few*), /t/ (*tune*), /d/ (*duke*), /k/ (*cure*), /n/ (*new*), and for some speakers /l/ (*lure*)

Place of articulation

	Bilabial	Labio-dental	Dental	Alveolar	Palatal	Velar	Glottal
Stop	p b			t d		k g	ʔ
Affricate					tʃ dʒ		
Fricative		f v	θ ð	s z	ʃ ʒ		h
Nasal	m			n		ŋ	
Lateral				l			
Approximant	w			r	j		

(Manner of articulation)

Figure 3 The consonant sounds of English.

ACTIVITY 6

Give a phonetic transcription of the following words. When you check your transcription with that in a dictionary using the IPA, you should remember that the dictionary is notating a particular accent, namely southern British English. If this is not your accent, there may be some legitimate variation in transcription. It is interesting to see whether the dictionary confesses that its pronunciation is for only one accent.

piece	cream	youth
fad	shore	happy
lurch	clothe	binge
mouth	good	frequent
joy	stretch	station
wrong	weave	thankful

See page 63 for the answers.

2.1.3 Syllables

Sounds do not occur in isolation, except as expressions of surprise, pleasure, frustration or annoyance (*Oh! Mm! Eh! Aargh!*). Sounds combine together into (spoken) words and sentences. The ways in which sounds combine can best be described, however, if we recognise the **syllable** as a unit of phonological organisation smaller than a word. Some words are composed of only one syllable (for example, *plum*, *pear*): they are **monosyllabic**. Others are composed of more than one syllable (for example, *lemon*, *strawberry*): they are **polysyllabic**.

A syllable has a vowel sound as its central element. The vowel may be preceded by up to three consonants and followed by up to four consonants. There are restrictions on which consonants may occur in which positions. For example, if three consonants precede a vowel, the first one must be /s/, the second may be either /p/, /t/ or /k/, and the third may be either /l/ (if the second consonant is /p/), /w/ (if the second consonant is /k/) or /r/ (with any of the second consonants). Thus the possible syllable-initial three-consonant combinations are: /spl/ (*splash*), /spr/ (*spray*), /str/ (*stray*), /skr/ (*screw*), /skw/ (*square*). Clearly, there is a much greater number of possible two-consonant combinations, and every consonant may occur singly in syllable-initial position, with the exception of /ŋ/.

The possible combinations of consonants are those that occur naturally in monosyllabic words. In polysyllabic words it is not always easy to determine where the boundaries between syllables fall, but the permissible consonant combinations give some fair guidance. For instance, in *acute* /əkjuːt/ there are two syllables, with the vowels /ə/ and /uː/. The question is: To which syllable do the consonants /k/ and /j/ belong? The /k/ could belong to the first syllable, but the /j/ could not, because /kj/ is not a possible syllable-final combination. The /j/ could belong to the second syllable; so could the /k/, since /kj/ is a possible syllable-initial combination (for example, *cure* /kjuə/). So, the syllables in *acute* could be divided either as /ək – juːt/ or as /ə – kjuːt/. The decision between these two rests on judgements about likelihood, based on how frequently occurring the alternative patterns are found to be in English words.

How many syllables may a word contain? Clearly, there are many monosyllabic words in English (*scratch, flask, squashed*). Two- and three-syllable words are also quite common (*fla-grant, nui-sance; im-por-tant, af-ter-noon*). Then, as the number of syllables in words increases, the pattern occurs less frequently, and the words become more obscure:

> four-syllable – *me-lan-cho-ly, un-de-ci-ded*
> five-syllable – *pri-vi-ti-sa-tion, ad-mi-nis-tra-tive*
> six-syllable – *in-dis-tin-gui-sha-ble, sen-ti-men-ta-li-ty*
> seven-syllable – *in-des-truc-ta-bi-li-ty*

ACTIVITY 7

Work out the syllable structure of the following words. The spelling is not necessarily a reliable guide: you should make a phonetic transcription first, so that you can see the sounds that you have to deal with.

standard	screamed	newspaper	premillennial
decision	television	procedure	sparkling
police	vanquished	circular	planetary
asteroid	envelope	entertainment	

See page 63 for the answers.

2.1.4 Variation

A particular sound may not always have exactly the same pronunciation every time that it occurs. Sounds vary according to the context of the other sounds that surround them. The variation is of several kinds. Some sounds vary on a regular basis according to their position in a syllable or word. Certain sounds, when they come at the end of a word, are liable to vary in the direction of a sound with which the following word begins: /d/ of *bad* assimilates to the /b/ of boys in *bad boys* /bab boiz/. Some sounds are liable to be omitted in certain contexts: the /t/ of *mint* may drop in *mint sauce* /min so:s/.

Allophones

The technical term given to a speech sound of a language is a **phoneme**. We have been discussing the phonemes of English, how they are articulated and how they combine into syllables and words. A phoneme is a sound segment which enters into the structure of syllables and words, and which, when replaced by another phoneme, makes a different word. For example, the substitution of /t/ for /d/ in /din/ makes a different word in English, /tin/; so does the substitution of /m/ for /n/ – /dim/. Clearly, then, /t/, /d/, /m/ and /n/ are different phonemes in English.

Now consider the pronunciation of /l/ in *lip* /lip/ and in *pill* /pil/. These two occurrences of /l/ are articulated slightly differently: in the case of /lip/, the tongue blade contacts the alveolar ridge, but the rest of the tongue is fairly flat in the mouth – the so-called **clear l**. In the case of /pil/, however, while the tongue blade contacts the alveolar ridge as before, the back of the tongue is raised towards the velum (soft palate) – the so-called **dark l**. Note that the substitution of one type of /l/ for the other would not make a different word, but merely a slightly strange pronunciation. This variation is not 'phonemic', but **allophonic**, and it is entirely predictable: the clear 'l' **allophone** of /l/ occurs before vowels, while the velarised or dark 'l' allophone occurs before consonants (*help*) and word-finally (*full*). When transcription is at the detailed level of phonetic (allophonic) variants it is put between square brackets, for example, clear [l], dark [ɫ], to distinguish it from the more general, phonemic, level.

Another major case of allophonic variation occurs with the unvoiced stops /p t k/. In initial and final positions, these unvoiced stops, when they are released, are accompanied by a puff of air called **aspiration**. Hold your hand in front of your mouth and say *pie* and you will feel the aspiration. However, when these stops occur after /s/ (for instance, in *sport, stork, score*), they are unaspirated. So, the unvoiced stops have an aspirated allophone [pʰ tʰ kʰ] and an unaspirated allophone [p t k], the occurrence of which is predictable from their phonological context.

We also noted earlier (in Section 2.1.2) that in accents where nasal /ŋ/ is always followed by /g/, it could be considered to be a variant of /n/: it is an allophone of /n/ before /g/.

Assimilation

What is happening in the case of /ŋ/, when regarded as a variant of /n/, is that the alveolar nasal /n/ is 'assimilating' to the velar articulation of the following /g/. **Assimilation** also occurs at word boundaries, when a word-final alveolar consonant (for example, /t/, /d/, /n/) may assimilate to a following word-initial bilabial or velar.

Say the following phrase out loud to yourself several times at a normal speed, and notice in particular the pronunciation of the final consonant of the first word: *loud bangs*. Two things are happening here: first, the /d/ of *loud* assimilates to the initial /b/ of *bangs* and becomes /b/; second, this /b/ is not released, but the closure is held for the /b/ of *bangs*, where it is then released.

Here are some further examples of where assimilation is likely to occur at the end of a word in fluent speech:

> *short course* – /t/ to /k/
> *light bulb* – /t/ to /p/
> *good girl* – /d/ to /g/
> *lean meat* – /n/ to /m/
> *fine car* – /n/ to /ŋ/

Assimilation is illustrated here with word-final alveolar stops and nasals, since they appear to be more susceptible to change than most. Other types of assimilation do occur – for instance, /s/ to /ʃ/ in *nice shop* – and you will no doubt notice more as you begin to listen carefully to the way people around you speak.

Elision

Another process that happens when words are connected in speech is **elision**, which is the term applied when a sound that is present in the pronunciation of a word in isolation is omitted. We are all familiar with the dropped 'h': *orrible* instead of *horrible*. It is a feature, to a greater or lesser degree, of the casual speech of most English speakers.

Elision occurs, perhaps less perceptibly but more commonly, at word boundaries. A word-final alveolar stop /t d/ may be elided in fluent speech when it is preceded by a consonant and the following word begins with a consonant. For example, in the phrase *last bus*, the /t/ of *last* is elided; in *round top*, the /d/ of *round* is elided.

After elision has taken place, the consonant preceding the elided /t/ or /d/ may then be subject to assimilation. For example, in *lined paper*, the /d/ of *lined* is elided, and then /n/ assimilates to bilabial /p/ of *paper* and becomes /m/: /laim peipə/. In *signed confession*, the /d/ of *signed* is elided, and the /n/ assimilates to the initial /k/ of *confession* and becomes /ŋ/.

ACTIVITY 8

Make a transcription of the words in the following phrases as though they were pronounced in isolation. Then consider whether any of the types of variation that we have discussed in this section – allophones, assimilation or elision – could occur.

slot machine	ten past four
wine bottle	sent by post
lead weight	on this shelf
list price	a slight cold in the head
wet but happy	don't lose your way

See page 63 for the answers.

2.1.5 Letter–sound correspondence

We have noted already that there is a disparity between the number of letters in the alphabet (twenty-six) and the number of phonemes in English (about forty).

But there is another disparity: a letter (or group of letters) does not always correspond with the same phoneme; and a phoneme is not always represented by the same letter.

Let us consider an example of each of these. How is the letter 's' pronounced in the following words: *soon, rise, mansion, leisure*? It corresponds to four different phonemes: /s/, /z/, /ʃ/ and /ʒ/. How is the phoneme /o:/ spelt in the following words: *cord, fall, four, sword, caught, bought, floor, broad*? If we count 'w' in *sword* and 'gh' in *caught* and *bought* as silent letters, we have the following spellings for /o:/: or, a, our, au, ou, oo. You will notice that this single vowel sound (not a diphthong) corresponds in some of these words to two letters (called a **digraph**).

The reason for the extensive lack of correspondence between spelling and pronunciation in modern English is historical (see Chapter 3). English spelling represents the pronunciation of over 500 years ago: in the intervening time, pronunciation has changed considerably, but the spelling has changed little.

ACTIVITY 9
It would take too long to outline all the letter–sound correspondences in modern English, but you can explore this for yourself. Here are some key sounds to investigate, for the letters that they may be represented by:

consonants – /k/, /f/, /ʃ/, /j/
vowels (much more variable!) – /i/, /e/, /a:/, /u:/, /ə:/, /ə/, /ei/, /ou/, /ai/

As examples of what you may find, consider: /k/ – c in *cow*, k and ck in *kick*; /i/ – ee in *beef*, ea in *leap*.

2.1.6 Stress and intonation

Sounds (phonemes) combine together into syllables and syllables into words (see Section 2.1.3), and words into the utterances of connected speech. In a word of more than one syllable (a polysyllabic word), one of the syllables is uttered with more prominence than any of the others. For example, in the two-syllable word *carpet*, the first syllable is more prominent than the second, whereas in *secure* the second is more prominent than the first.

This is the pattern in the pronunciation of English words, that one syllable receives **main stress**, but not the same syllable in every word. In a word with several syllables, one of the other syllables may also receive *secondary stress*; for example, in *calculation*, the main stress is on the third syllable 'la' /lei/, while the first syllable 'cal' /kal/ receives secondary stress. The remaining syllables are said to be *unstressed*.

Syllables that are unstressed frequently contain the mid central vowel /ə/ (also called the 'schwa' vowel) or the /i/ or /u/ vowels; for instance, the second and fourth syllables of *calculation*. Some words that do not have a schwa vowel when spoken in isolation have their usual vowel replaced with a schwa in connected speech: compare *and* /and/ with *fish and chips* /fiʃəntʃips/ (note also elision of /d/); *of* /ov/ with *cup of tea* /kʌpəvti:/.

Prominence is, then, a feature of the pronunciation of words in the form of stress. It is also a feature of utterances in connected speech, as part of **intonation**. Intonation refers to the variations in tone, the **tunes**, which accompany speech. For example, a question such as *Would you like a drink?* would probably be uttered with a 'rising' intonation, whereas a statement such as *I'd like some coffee, please* would be uttered with a 'falling' intonation.

Also, one word (strictly speaking, the stressed syllable of that word) is more prominent in the intonation tune than the others. It is called the **nucleus** of the tune and it falls on the most newsworthy item in the utterance; *drink* in the first example in the previous paragraph, and *coffee* in the second.

In the most neutral utterance, the nucleus is likely to be on the last or nearly last word in an intonation tune. However, it may be placed on almost any item, usually with emphatic effect. Notice the effect of making, in turn, *would*, *you* and *like* prominent in *Would you like a drink?* Prominence, and other resources of intonation, enable us to express a variety of attitudes to what we are saying: sincerity, irony, sarcasm and so on.

ACTIVITY 10

1 Where does the main stress fall on the following words when spoken in isolation?

safety	satisfaction	sensational
safari	saxophone	sentimental
salute	security	serenade
sandwich	segregate	sociology

2 Where, in a neutral utterance of the following sentences, would the nucleus of the intonation tune most likely fall?

a Please pass the salt.

b How far is it to the station?

c This is where we pick Aunty up.

d Have you completed the exercise?

e Keep off the grass.

Where else could you place the nucleus and what difference would it make to the hearer's understanding of the sentence?

See pages 63-4 for the answers.

2.1.7 Punctuation

In writing, we do not have the resources of stress and intonation in order to add colour and nuance to what we are communicating. Instead, we have **punctuation**: the comma (,), semi-colon (;), colon (:), full stop (.), question mark (?) and exclamation mark (!), and quotation marks (' '). However, intonation and punctuation are not equivalent. Punctuation does not fulfil in writing the same functions that intonation fulfils in speech.

The exclamation mark and question mark could perhaps be associated with features of stress and intonation. For example, an exclamation mark at the end of *She was a wonderful woman!* would incline you to read this with a rising nucleus on *WONderful*.

The comma, semi-colon and colon are used to mark structural units within a sentence, especially where there is likely to be ambiguity in reading it. In that sense, they may correspond with the boundaries of intonation tunes, but not necessarily. For example, in the previous sentence, the first comma marks off the initial phrase *In that sense* from the rest of the sentence, but in speech it would not need to have its own intonation tune but might well be incorporated with what follows. Equally, in speech there could be an intonation boundary between *boundaries* and *of*, which is not marked by a comma in writing.

It is better to regard punctuation as an independent system from intonation, one that has been fashioned especially for writing. There are no hard and fast rules for the use of punctuation. Fashions as to where to use commas, semi-colons and colons have changed over the years. We do not have time to go into the details here. You should consult a reputable style guide.

ACTIVITY 11

If you are interested in finding out more about the current conventions on punctuation, you could consult one of the following:

the guide to punctuation at the back of the *Concise Oxford Dictionary* (eighth edition, 1990)

the punctuation terms (comma, semi-colon and so on) in the *Chambers Pocket Guide to Good English* (1985)

Both of these give a sensible account of punctuation and its usage.

2.1.8 Accent and handwriting

One way in which we show our individuality as human beings is how we speak and write. You can recognise a person just from their voice on the telephone, or who the sender of a letter is from the handwriting on the envelope. The physical shape of our mouths, the distance between our glottis and our lips, and the size of our nasal cavity all contribute to making us sound as individual as we do when we speak. How we hold a pen or pencil, whether we are left- or right-handed and the angle of the pen to the paper all contribute to making our handwriting individual.

We also share features of our **accent** (the way we speak) with particular groups in society (see also Chapter 5). If we are Midlanders or Northerners of England, we will probably say /gras/ and /kup/ rather than southern /gra:s/ and /kʌp/. Some groups of people regularly substitute a glottal stop for /t/ in words such as *water* and *butter*. Women often have slightly different intonation patterns from men.

Similar characteristics are true of handwriting. We may have been taught a particular method of handwriting, when we first learnt to write, and we share the features inculcated by that method with others who were similarly taught. Women and men often have different styles of writing. There are those who believe that handwriting can give clues to personality and character, and some personnel managers use handwriting analysis as part of the selection procedure for new staff.

Just as we can change other aspects of our appearance and behaviour, so we can make an effort to change our accent and handwriting. In particular, we may unconsciously adapt our accent when we begin mixing with new groups of people – if we go away to university, for example.

The expression side of language, how we speak and how we write, are fascinating areas of study in themselves, not least because they reflect our individuality. But we have to remember that they serve primarily to convey the meanings that we want to communicate, which are encoded by the words and sentences of grammar. It is to words that we turn next.

ACTIVITY 12

1　Tape record yourself, if possible when you are speaking in normal conversation. (We often adjust our accent when we read.)

2　Listen to the recording, and make a note of what you think are the distinctive features of your accent.

3　Look at an example of your handwriting and compare it with someone else's. What are the differences in the way you form your letters – their size, shape, angle and so on? What is it that makes your handwriting individual to you?

2.2 Words

As experienced writers of a language, we readily have a notion of what a word is: a sequence of letters bounded by spaces. If we relate that back to speech, a spoken word is presumably a sequence of sounds; but there is nothing in speech corresponding to the spaces of writing. We do not pause between each word; although when we do pause, it is usually – but by no means always – at the end of a word.

Linguists who analyse languages that do not have a written form use a variety of criteria for determining what the words of the language are, such as: what constitutes the minimal response to a question; what sequences of sound re-occur with the same meaning in different contexts; how word stress operates; and how prefixes and suffixes are managed. What a linguist determines from these criteria becomes the basis of words in the written language. The words that we identify in writing in English, then, are not arbitrary sequences of letters but have validity in the grammar of the language.

This section is going to examine words in modern English. We will define what we mean by the term **word** in grammar, and we will look at the structure and meaning of words.

2.2.1 Words and homonyms

Let us begin for the moment with the definition of a word as a sequence of letters bounded by spaces. On this definition, is the sequence *tear* in the following sentences the same word?

A tear rolled down his cheek.
Your coat has a tear in it.

On the definition as given the answer must be 'Yes': the two instances have the same sequence of letters. But from our wider knowledge of English, we know that they are different words: for a start, they have different pronunciations – /tiə/ and /teə/.

Now consider the sequence *fan* in the following sentences:

The fan asked the footballer for his autograph.
Engines are fitted with a fan to keep them cool.

On this occasion, the spelling is the same, and so is the pronunciation – /fan/. So, a definition of words that takes account only of spelling and pronunciation is not adequate.

The two instances of *tear* and the two instances of *fan* differ in meaning. You will find that *tear* and *fan* both have two entries in a dictionary, corresponding to their different meanings.

Words which share the same spelling and pronunciation, such as *fan*, are called **homonyms** (from two Greek words, *homo* 'same' and *nym* 'name'). Words which share the same spelling but have a different pronunciation, such as *tear*, are called **homographs** (Greek *graph* 'writing').

The other possibility, which we have not mentioned yet, is where two words share the same pronunciation but have a different spelling. They are called **homophones** (Greek *phone* 'sound'). An example of a pair of homophones would be *cue* and *queue*, both pronounced /kju:/.

Clearly, a definition of 'word' needs to take into account the fact that different words may happen to be pronounced or spelt the same, as a result of historical changes. Meaning must be central to the definition of words. In order to be able to talk about words as sequences of letters or sounds, linguists sometimes use the terms **orthographic word** and **phonological word**, respectively. And they use the term **lexeme** to talk about a word from a semantic perspective, approximating to an entry in a dictionary. So, *tear* represents a single orthographic word but two phonological words and two lexemes; *fan* represents a single orthographic and phonological word but two lexemes.

ACTIVITY 13

English has quite a number of homonyms (different words spelt and pronounced the same): for instance, *base, compact, elder, host, last, mint, pen, spar*. Homonyms are considered to be different lexemes because they have a different origin.

1 Look these words up in a dictionary, to establish that they are homonyms, having a different meaning and a different origin. The origin or **etymology** of a word is usually given in square brackets at the end of a dictionary entry.

2 Now think of five further pairs of homonyms and check your guesses in a dictionary.

2.2.2 Word classes and inflections

We do not know how many **words** there are in English. The current (second) twenty-volume edition of the *Oxford English Dictionary* contains over half a million words. Some of those have fallen out of use and are obsolete; on the other hand, the OED does not have many modern words from areas such as science, technology, computing and pop culture, to name but four.

When linguists want to describe the way in which words operate in the structures of the language, it would be impossible to treat each word individually. In any case, many words operate in the same way. So, linguists assign words to **word classes**, and the description of grammar is then, in part, the description of the operation of these word classes.

An older term for 'word class' is 'part of speech', which modern linguists reject as a rather misleading or at least uninformative term. Words are assigned to a class on criteria of:

similar operation in syntax
similar variations in form (morphology – see Section 1.3.2)
a similar type of meaning

For English, some eight major word classes are established:

noun	pronoun
verb	determiner
adjective	preposition
adverb	conjunction

The class with the largest membership is that of **noun**. The verb, adjective and adverb classes also have large memberships. The remaining four classes have relatively small numbers of words, and their members are mainly used to provide grammatical connections within and between sentences.

We will look at each word class in turn.

Nouns

Here is a list of English nouns:

mother	*piece*	*hour*
architect	*triangle*	*bravery*
factory	*humour*	*theory*
spoon	*inquiry*	*suspense*

Nouns refer to the 'things' that we talk about. You will see from the small selection of nouns listed above that they refer to a wide variety of 'things': people, objects, abstractions and ideas.

In the syntax of sentences, nouns are the entities that are involved in what is going on, the subjects and objects (see Section 2.3.1) of sentences. For example:

The architect (subject) *designed a factory* (object).
My mother (subject) *ate the cake* (object).
Her theory (subject) *shows the relationship* (object) *of bravery and humour.*

It is a notable characteristic of many 'things' that they can be counted: three mothers, six architects, many factories, all theories. You can see that the nouns change their shape slightly: they add an **inflection** to mark the plural. Countable nouns thus have two forms: a **singular** form, which is the uninflected base form; and a **plural** form, which is the singular form with the addition of an inflectional suffix, in writing either *-s* or *-es*. 'Singular' and 'plural' are terms of the grammatical category of **number**.

Other nouns are uncountable: they refer to a mass and they do not have a plural inflection (for instance, *humour, bravery, suspense, flour, furniture, oil*). In order to refer to individual quantities of the mass, you have to use expressions such as *four types of humour*, *300 grams of flour* and *three pieces of furniture*.

Some nouns have a another inflection, which relates to possession. Look at these examples: *the violinist's instrument, the violinists' instruments.* You may have noticed that these two examples have the same pronunciation, which is also the same as the plural inflection *violinists*. In writing, however, we distinguish possession by a singular noun (*'s*) from possession by a plural noun (*s'*).

The use of *'s* or *s'* represents the possessive (or **genitive**) case. **Case** is a grammatical category associated with nouns (and pronouns), which signals a noun's relation to other elements in the sentence. English nouns have only two cases: the possessive case (with *'s* or *s'* inflection), and the common case (no inflection). Nouns in the possessive case signal a relationship of possession with another noun. Common case nouns are used in all other functions.

ACTIVITY 14

Not all plurals are marked by the *-(e)s* suffix. Look at the following plural nouns and relate them to their singulars. How is the plural formed from the singular in each case?

feet	men	indices
mice	children	corpora
oxen	cacti	
teeth	criteria	

See page 64 for the answers.

Verbs

Here is a list of English verbs:

throw	*lose*	*believe*	*be*
spread	*forget*	*contain*	
decide	*stand*	*seem*	
fall	*prefer*	*have*	

Verbs refer to:

what people do (actions; for example, *throw, decide*)
what happens (events; for example, *lose, forget*)
the way things are (states; for example, *contain, seem*)

In the syntax of a sentence, the **verb** tells you about the situation (action, event, state) that the 'things' (that is, nouns) are involved in. For example:

The architect threw the spoon to my mother.
That comedian has lost his humour.
The factory contains a lot of furniture.

Verbs have a number of inflections. Look at the following forms of the verb *decide*:

decide	*(to) decide*
decides	*deciding*
decided	*decided*

The forms in the first column, called the **finite** forms, show distinctions of the grammatical category of **tense**. The first two forms are **present tense**, and the third one is **past tense**. The base (uninflected) form is the present *decide*. *Decides*, which has a *-(e)s* inflection, is called the **third-person singular present tense** inflection (see the section on pronouns below). The past tense inflection is normally *-(e)d*.

The forms in the second column, called the **non-finite** forms, are: the **infinitive** (*to decide*), sometimes without *to*; and the two **participles** – the present participle with the *-ing* inflection, and past participle with the *-(e)d* inflection (like the past tense). For a few verbs the past tense and past participle have different inflections: for instance, *show, shows, showed, to show, showing, shown*. The past participle form is the one that comes after *have* in constructions such as: *I have decided to stay, I have stolen the crown jewels.*

One, very common, verb – *be* – has eight different forms:

am – first-person singular present tense
is – third person singular present tense
are – second-person and plural present tense
was – first- and third-person singular past tense
were – second-person and plural past tense
to be – infinitive
being – present participle
been – past participle

ACTIVITY 15

Quite a number of verbs do not follow the regular pattern for verb inflections given above. Give the third-person singular present, past tense and past participle forms for the following (base forms of) verbs. The first one is completed for you.

steal	steals	stole	stolen
sing			
see			
take			
bring			
tell			
stand			
wear			
think			
speak			

See page 64 for the answers.

Adjectives

Here is a list of English adjectives:

tall	*superb*	*yellow*
wide	*necessary*	*brave*
little	*round*	*fierce*
clear	*stable*	*comic*

An **adjective** refers to the 'qualities' of 'things'. It serves to classify and describe nouns: for example, *a wide road, a superb view, a stable relationship.*

In the syntax of English sentences, adjectives come either before a noun, or after a verb such as *be* or *seem* in relation to a noun as subject: for example, *You turn into the wide road, The road is wide.*

Many adjectives have inflections for **comparative** and **superlative** degree, marked by the suffixes *-er* and *-est*: for example, *wider, widest; smaller, smallest.*

Some adjectives mark the comparative and superlative with the adverbs *more* and *most*: for example, *more stable, most stable; more necessary, most necessary*. Whether the inflections *-er/-est* or the adverbs *more/most* are used depends in large part on how many syllables the adjective word has: single-syllable adjectives usually take *-er/-est*; adjectives with three or more syllables take *more/most*; and two-syllable adjectives vary.

Some adjectives are not **gradable** in this way and so do not have comparative and superlative forms: for instance, *round, yellow*. A 'thing' is normally either 'round' or some other shape (square, triangular, conical and so on); it is either 'yellow' or some other colour: there are no degrees of 'roundness' or 'yellowness'.

ACTIVITY 16

Give the comparative and superlative forms for the following adjectives – the list includes some of the small number of adjectives that form their comparative and superlative irregularly:

great	nasty	lovely
bad	good	handsome
attractive	free	timid
honest	cruel	

See page 64 for the answers.

Adverbs

Here is a list of adverbs in modern English:

slowly, superbly, carefully
now, often, always
out, off, up
however, therefore, thus

The class of **adverbs** contains a rather varied set of words. The above list contains examples of four subclasses:

'-ly' adverbs, derived from adjectives (*slow-ly, careful-ly, spontaneous-ly*), referring to the manner in which something happens or is done (*She walked slowly down the street*)

simple adverbs (*now, often*), referring mostly to time meanings, and so complementing the tense of the verb in the sentence

adverb **particles** (*out, up*), the main use of which is to combine with verbs to form **phrasal verbs**; for example, *speak out, give up*

conjunctive adverbs (*however, therefore*), which are used to join sentences together; for example, *The standard of the service was not very good. I cannot therefore recommend this restaurant.*

Some adverbs can be graded for degree, like adjectives, but only with the adverbs *more* and *most*, not normally with inflections: *more slowly, most carefully, more often*.

ACTIVITY 17

Identify the adverbs in the following sentences and say which subclass each of them belongs to:

1 He began his speech rather pompously.

2 You've done it again!

3 Their team has, moreover, won the match.

4 Her plane has just taken off.

5 You shouldn't give up so easily.

See page 65 for the answers.

Pronouns

The general function of **pronouns** is to stand for or replace nouns. This is the first of the small, grammatical classes of word that we mentioned in Section 2.2.2. It contains a diverse set of items, but what we mostly readily think of as pronouns are the personal pronouns:

> *I, me, mine*
> *we, us, ours*
> *you, yours*
> *he, him, his*
> *she, her, hers*
> *it, its*
> *they, them, theirs*

They are an interesting group of words, because they manifest some grammatical categories that are not evident anywhere else in English.

First of all, the category of **person** applies, and there are three terms in this category. First-person pronouns refer to the speaker: *I*, *we* and so on. Second-person pronouns refer to the person addressed: *you*. Third-person pronouns refer to the person/thing being talked about: *he*, *she*, *it*, *they* and so on.

Second, the category of **number** applies. Singular pronouns include: *I*, *he*, *she*, *it*. Plural pronouns include: *we*, *they*. The pronoun *you* may be used with either singular or plural reference; that is, to a single addressee or to an audience.

Third, the category of **case** applies. For the noun we saw that there was a 'common' case form and a 'possessive/genitive' case form. For the pronoun, there are three terms in this category: subjective, objective and genitive (or possessive). In the first-person singular pronouns, *I* is subjective case, *me* is objective case and *mine* is genitive case. With *you* and *it* there is no distinction between subjective and objective case. Subjective case forms are used when the pronoun has subject function in a sentence; objective case forms are used when the pronoun has object function in a sentence (see Section 2.3.1), or after a preposition; and genitive case forms are used when the pronoun refers to possession. For example:

> *I met her yesterday.*
> *She can have a go after me.*
> *The responsibility is yours.*

Fourth, the category of **gender** applies, but only in the case of the third-person singular pronouns. There are three terms: masculine, feminine and neuter. The masculine pronouns are *he, him, his*. The feminine pronouns are *she, her, hers*. The neuter pronouns are *it, its*.

Combining these categories, we have a system of personal pronouns in English as follows:

	First		Second		Third			
	Singular	Plural	Singular	Plural	Singular			Plural
					m	f	n	
Subject	*I*	*we*	*you*	*you*	*he*	*she*	*it*	*they*
Object	*me*	*us*	*you*	*you*	*him*	*her*	*it*	*them*
Genitive	*mine*	*ours*	*yours*	*yours*	*his*	*hers*	*its*	*theirs*

ACTIVITY 18

This is the personal pronoun system that operates in modern 'standard' English. There are many non-standard and dialect variations. Perhaps you can think of some in your own or your friends' language, or in the language of your area of the country.

In what ways might the use of personal pronouns in the following be considered 'non-standard'?

1 The teacher gave the book to Billy and I.

2 Me and Billy are going to tell on you.

3 Her's the one to blame.

4 I don't think them over there like us.

5 Give us a break!

See page 65 for the answers.

The remaining subclasses of pronoun are as follows:

Reflexive pronoun: *myself, ourselves, yourself, yourselves, himself, herself, itself, themselves*. These are used either in reference to the person under discussion (*She has hurt herself*) or for purposes of emphasis (*She congratulated me herself*).

Interrogative pronoun, used for questioning: *Who?, Whom?, Whose?* (subjective, objective and genitive case, respectively), *What?, Which?*.

Relative pronoun, used to introduce 'relative clauses' (see below): *who, whom, whose, which, that*.

Indefinite pronouns, used to refer to a non-specific person or thing. They are formed with *some, any, every* or *no* as a first part, and *body, thing* or *one* as a second part; for instance, *someone, nothing, everybody*.

Demonstrative pronouns, which have a pointing function: *this, these* (for close to speaker); *that, those* (for distant from speaker).

Determiners

The words in this grammatical class have the general function of accompanying nouns and 'determining' their status in an ongoing discourse or text. There are two broad subclasses of **determiner**: **identifiers** and **quantifiers**.

Identifiers   The subclass of identifiers includes:

Articles: *a/an* (indefinite), *the* (definite).

Possessives: *my, our, your, his, her, its, their*. Note the general difference in form between these determiners and the genitive pronouns (*his* and *its* are the same). Compare *My book is the red one* (possessive determiner) with *The red one is mine* (genitive/possessive pronoun). Note that pronouns replace nouns, while determiners accompany nouns.

Demonstratives: *this, these; that, those* (the same forms as the demonstrative pronouns). Compare *That pencil belongs to me* (determiner) with *That is my pencil* (pronoun).

Quantifiers   The subclass of quantifiers includes:

Numerals: the cardinal numbers (*one, two, three, ...*) and the ordinal numbers (*first, second, third, ...*) expressing specific quantities of things.

Indefinite quantifiers: *some, many, several, a lot, few*, and so on, which express non-specific quantities of things.

Prepositions

The word class of **prepositions** contains items such as the following:

about	*between*	*near*	*through*
after	*by*	*on*	*towards*
against	*during*	*opposite*	*under*
along	*from*	*over*	*until*
among	*into*	*since*	*with*

Prepositions are used to connect a noun, which follows the preposition, either to another noun or to some other element in the sentence. For example, in *The girl at the cashdesk*, the preposition *at* connects the noun *cashdesk* to the noun *girl*, explaining which girl you are talking about. In *Please put the money into the box*, the preposition *into* connects the noun *box* to the rest of the sentence, especially the verb *put*.

Prepositions often have a place or direction meaning (as do *at* and *into* in the above examples). Prepositions also have other meanings:

time – *after, before, during*
topic – *about, concerning*
instrument – *with*
agent – *by*
accompaniment – *with, without*
comparison – *like*
purpose – *for*
reason – *because of*

ACTIVITY 19

1 Make up sentences using the prepositions in the above list, to illustrate their meanings. Some prepositions can have more than one meaning (for example, *after* for place and time). Ensure that your example makes clear which meaning is intended.

2 How many of these prepositions can be used with more than one meaning? Check your guesses in a dictionary.

Conjunctions

This class of grammatical words has two subclasses: **coordinating conjunctions** and **subordinating conjunctions**.

Coordinating conjunctions include *and*, *but* and *or*. Subordinating conjunctions include *when*, *while*, *if*, *so that*, *because*, *although*, *where*, *as* and so on.

The main function of <u>conjunctions</u> is to connect two sentences, either as equal partners (coordinating) or with one subordinate to the other (subordinating). Coordinating conjunctions are also used to connect other kinds of element – for example, words:

> *The milkman brought the milk at 6 a.m. and the postman delivered the letters at 6.30 a.m.* (sentence coordination with *and*).

> *He delivers normal and skimmed milk* (word coordination with *and*).

Subordinating conjunctions introduce 'adverbial clauses' (see below), with a range of meanings (time, condition, purpose, reason and so on). For instance:

> *We can go when you are ready* (time subordinate clause with *when*).

> *We've changed the date so that you can come too* (purpose subordinate clause with *so that*).

ACTIVITY 20

Give the word class label to all the words in the following sentences. Dictionaries usually give the word class of a word, although they often include what we have called determiners in the class of adjectives. If you are unsure, you can check your guess in a dictionary. Remember that some words belong to more than one word class.

1 She ran along the river bank.

2 A strange sensation suddenly came over him.

3 They are always asking for clarification of our aims.

4 Our holiday has been an exhausting but delightful experience.

5 He can come for this interview if it can be held next Friday.

See page 65 for the answers.

2.2.3 Prefixes and suffixes

We noticed in the previous section that the plural inflection for nouns and the past-tense inflection for verbs are usually suffixes added to the base form of the word: *-s* or *-es* for the plural; *-d* or *-ed* for the past tense. A word such as *onions* is, therefore, composed of two elements: the base *onion* and the ending *-s*. The form *onion* is itself an independent word, but the ending *-s* only ever occurs in combination with a base.

In the linguistic discipline of morphology, which studies the forms of words (see Section 1.3), the base element of a word is called the **root** and the ending is called a **suffix**. An element that is added before a root is called a **prefix**; for example, *re-furbish*, *un-stable*. Prefixes and suffixes are collectively called **affixes**; and roots and affixes are collectively called **morphemes**.

The structure of a word is described in terms of morphemes. The minimal structure of most words is a root morpheme (we will note one or two exceptions later). To the root may be added affixes.

Affixes may have two functions in the structure of English words. First, as we have seen, they may have an **inflectional** function, expressing grammatical categories such as plural number, past tense and comparative degree. Inflections in English are, in fact, always suffixes; and if a word has more than one suffix, the inflection is always the last one.

The second function that affixes may have, and this applies to both prefixes and suffixes, is a **derivational** function. A new word is derived by the addition of an affix to a root. For example, the addition of the suffix *-al* to the root *nature* enables us to derive the adjective *natural*; the further addition of the prefix *un-* enables us to derive the negative or opposite adjective *unnatural*.

Derivational suffixes usually change the word class of the item to which they are added. For instance:

> verb → noun: *-ant* (*disinfectant*), *-ation* (*organisation*), *-ment* (*agreement*), *-al* (*refusal*), *-er/-or* (*baker*, *actor*)
>
> adjective → noun: *-ness* (*sickness*), *-ity* (*sterility*)
>
> noun/adjective → verb: *-ify* (*purify*), *-ise* (*terrorise*), *-en* (*soften*)
>
> noun → adjective: *-ful* (*careful*), *-less* (*fearless*), *-ly* (*friendly*), *-ish* (*foolish*)
>
> verb → adjective: *-able/-ible* (*stackable*, *digestible*)
>
> adjective → adverb: *-ly* (*superbly*, *honestly*)

Derivational prefixes do not normally change the word class of the item they are added to. For example:

> negative/opposite: *un-* (*unsure*), *dis-* (*discolour*), *in-* (*inexpert*)
>
> degree/size: *super-* (*supernatural*), *sub-* (*substandard*), *over-* (*overindulge*), *under-* (*underfed*), *hyper-* (*hyperinflation*)
>
> time: *pre-* (*prewar*), *post-* (*postmodernist*), *ex-* (*ex-policeman*), *re-* (*reinvent*)

The following prefixes do, however, change the word class of the item that they are added to:

> *be-* (*befriend*, *besiege*) – forming verbs
>
> *en-* (*encircle*, *endanger*) – forming verbs
>
> *a-* (*afloat*, *awake*) – forming adjectives

Because English has, in its history, taken so many words (and parts of words) from other languages, especially the classical languages – Latin and Greek – the structure of some words today cannot be discerned, except with considerable difficulty or a knowledge of the classical languages. For example, the word *legible* looks as if it contains the suffix *-ible*, which, as we have seen, changes a verb into an adjective (*digest-ible*). But if we remove the suffix from *legible* we are left with (presumably the root) *leg* (which has nothing to do with *leg* the limb). *Legible* means 'able to be read': *leg* is a Latin root meaning 'read'. Without that knowledge of Latin, *legible* is unanalysable, unless we call *leg* a bound root (that is, it cannot exist as an independent word), which occurs only in the structure *leg-* + *-ible*.

Another case of bound root is found in the word *disgruntled*, which occurs only in this negative form in modern English: the root *gruntle* is now obsolete.

ACTIVITY 21

Analyse the structure of the following words, identifying the roots, prefixes and suffixes. For each suffix, say whether it has a derivational or an inflectional function. Notice any changes in the spelling and pronunciation of morphemes (especially roots), and note any changes of word class that result from derivational suffixes.

adviser	generalisation	slavery
blamelessly	interminable	thankfulness
classifies	misspelt	unfortunately
ensnaring	postmodernists	vocalist

See pages 65-6 for the answers.

2.2.4 Compound words

Derivation, by means of prefixes and suffixes added to a root, is one way in which new words are formed in a language. Another way is to form **compounds**, which involves combining two root morphemes; for example, *bookmark, deadlock, hamstring, popcorn, seaweed, textbook, touchstone*.

Many compounds, as these examples show, are written 'solid', as a single orthographic word and without a hyphen. Other compounds are written with a hyphen between the two root morphemes, and some are 'open' compounds with the two roots as separate orthographic words; for instance, *cable-car, day-dream, fan-belt, ring-finger, time-switch; cable television, day nursery, fan heater, ring road, time bomb*.

Whether a compound is open, hyphenated or solid may be a reflection of the degree to which it has been accepted as a lexeme by speakers of the language. Dictionaries may differ on how they treat some compounds.

Most compounds are nouns. All the examples given so far have been nouns, with the exception of *day-dream*, which belongs to both the noun and the verb class. Compounds are found in word classes other than noun. For example:

verbs – *babysit, double-cross, dry-clean, gatecrash, proof-read*
adjectives – *down-hearted, long-term, newsworthy, public-spirited, soft-hearted*

Some of these adjectives illustrate an interesting word formation process in English: adjective + noun + *-ed* (the past-participle ending on verbs, but here added to an adjective + noun combination to form a compound adjective).

There is another kind of compound found in English which, strictly speaking, is not a combination of root + root, since the parts of the compound do not exist as independent words in English. This type of compound can be illustrated by the following examples:

astronaut	*biology*	*misogyny*	*xenophobe*
bibliophile	*geography*	*telephone*	

The two parts of the compound are roots in Latin or Greek, which have been borrowed and then combined to form a compound in English; for example, *astro* 'star' + *naut* 'sailor', *biblio* 'book' + *phile* 'lover', *tele* 'distant' + *phone* 'sound'. The compounds did not exist in classical Latin or Greek. In English, such combinations are called **classical compounds**, and their parts are called **combining forms**. They are often formed for the technical language of science, technology and medicine.

Finally, there are some compounds that are hybrids of the classical and normal types, where one element (normally the first) is a combining form and the other is a normal English root; for example, *biodegradable, Francophile, geophysics, retro-rocket, telecommunication*.

Note that in *Francophile* the word *France* has been made to look like a classical combining form.

ACTIVITY 22

1 Think of as many compounds as you can that have as their first element the roots:

hard	white
light	electro-
road	tele-
tea	

Check your intuition with a dictionary.

2 Classify the compounds by their spelling (open, hyphenated, solid) and by their word class (noun, verb, adjective).

2.2.5 Word meaning

The meaning of a word is composed of a number of elements

what it refers to in the world of our experience

its place in the vocabulary of the language and its relationship to other words

the regular company that it keeps when it is used in speech and writing

We will deal with the third of these under the heading of 'collocation' in Section 2.2.7. The second involves lexical relationships of sameness (**synonymy**) and oppositeness (**antonymy**) of meaning, which we will consider in Section 2.2.6. In this section we will be concerned with what we probably most readily think of as the meaning of a word: the relation of **reference**.

The most obvious example of the reference relation is when a word can be associated with a set of objects. An example might be *apple* or *chair*. When we begin to think about the range of objects that we might want to apply either of these words to, we realise how difficult it is to characterise the reference of a word. The kinds of features that we might include in our description would include: size and shape, colour, use or function, its parts or components, and what general class of objects it belongs to.

Dictionary definitions are attempts to describe the reference of words. *The Longman Concise English Dictionary* (1985) defines *apple* as 'the fleshy, edible, usually rounded, red, yellow or green fruit of a tree of the rose family'. So, *apple* belongs to the class of 'fruit', has a round shape, can be red, yellow or green in colour, is used for eating, is composed of 'flesh', and comes from a particular type of tree.

Words such as *apple* and *chair* are fairly straightforward to define. They refer to objects that can be seen, or at least easily pictured, and they have physical features that can be observed and described. They belong to the set of **concrete nouns**, of which these things are true. It is much more difficult to characterise words that have an abstract reference, such as – to remain with nouns – *justice*, *conscience*, *space*.

With no observable features to describe, words with abstract reference have to be defined by means of paraphrase. Consider the definition of *conscience* in the *Longman Concise*: 'the consciousness of the moral quality of one's own conduct or intentions, together with a feeling of obligation to refrain from doing wrong'. It is classified as a kind of 'consciousness' and 'feeling', which themselves have abstract reference.

With verbs and adjectives, there are some that allow definition in physical terms; for instance, verbs referring to physical actions (*climb, run, swim*) or adjectives referring to physical qualities (*opaque, triangular*). But the great majority refer to abstract entities, where paraphrase is used for defining.

In the case of the grammatical word classes, many words do not have meaning in terms of the reference relation. Prepositions may refer to different kinds of spatial or temporal relation (*into, on*; *after, during*). Conjunctions may refer to various circumstantial meanings (*when* – time, *if* – condition, *because* – reason). Pronouns have a shifting reference: *I* refers to whoever the speaker happens to be; *you* to the addressee of the moment; and the third-person pronouns have reference to nouns previously mentioned in the discourse or text. Determiners also have a function largely internal to language, although quantifiers have some counterpart in the world of experience.

ACTIVITY 23

Some linguists view the reference of a word such as *cup* as some kind of ideal of the object. Others view the reference as a prototype: the prototypical cup will have certain features – a narrower base than top, for putting on a saucer; a handle; made from ceramic material; for holding liquids and drinking from; and so on.

Attempt a description of the reference of the following words by listing the features that you think are prototypical:

book   telephone
door   tree
suitcase

Check your description with the definitions in, preferably, more than one dictionary.

2.2.6 Synonyms and antonyms

The meaning of a word is determined not only by the reference relation that it enters into but also by the relations that it contracts with other words in the vocabulary, called **sense relations**. Two of those relations are **synonymy** (sameness of meaning) and **antonymy** (oppositeness of meaning).

Two or more words are said to be **synonyms** if their meanings overlap to a considerable extent and they could be substituted for each other in appropriate contexts. Such synonym pairs might include:

quick–rapid	*cry–weep*	*conceal–hide*	*lavatory–toilet*
small–little	*discover–find*	*buyer–purchaser*	*story–tale*

English is particularly rich in synonyms, because its vocabulary comes from two different primary sources: **Anglo-Saxon** (or Old English), the language of the Germanic invaders in the fifth and sixth centuries; and French/Latin, through the Norman Conquest of the eleventh century and the influence of classical Latin following the fifteenth-century Renaissance. Many pairs of synonyms have one word of Germanic origin and one of Latinate origin; for example, *quick–rapid*, *weep–cry*, *find–discover*, *hide–conceal*, *buy–purchase*. Often the Germanic word is more colloquial and the Latinate word more formal or technical.

Sometimes the members of a synonym pair have a different social cachet. This is the case with *toilet* and *lavatory*. (Which do you say?) Synonym pairs also arise from regional variation – for example, between British and American English:

biscuit–cookie   *lift–elevator*   *pavement–sidewalk*

Similar cases occur also within, say, British English:

plimsoll–sandshoe–pump–dap   *butty–sandwich*

Antonymy works rather differently from synonymy. Only some words have **antonyms**. You cannot ask, for example, 'What is the opposite of *yellow*?', because *yellow* does not have an antonym. *Yellow* is defined by its place in a series of colour words that are mutually exclusive: *yellow* is *yellow* because it is not *green*, *red*, *blue* and so on.

We can distinguish three different kinds of antonymy. One kind is illustrated by gradable adjectives such as *narrow–wide*, *short–long*, *cowardly–brave*, *cheap–expensive*, *dry–wet*. They are called gradable antonyms. Their reference is relative to the object being described: a narrow road is still wider than a narrow plank of wood. And when the quality is being questioned, only one of them is normally used; for example, *How wide is the road?* rather than *How narrow is the road?* The latter implies that you have already determined that the road is narrow. In such questions, and in giving measurements, it is always the 'larger' of the antonyms that is used; for example, *How long is it?*, *The road is 3 metres wide*.

A second kind of antonym can be illustrated by the pairs *true–false*, *alive–dead*, *open–shut*, *on–off*, *occupied–vacant*. Here the relationship is an either/or one. A door may be either *open* or *shut*; it cannot be more one than the other. The assertion of one quality is the denial of the other: if a statement is *true*, that implies that it is *not false*. Such antonyms are called **complementary** antonyms.

The third kind of antonym can be illustrated by the pairs *borrow–lend*, *buy–sell*, *give–receive*, *husband–wife*, *above–below*. These antonyms are called **converses** or **relational opposites**. They represent two sides of a relation. For example, if Bill is

Hilary's *husband*, then Hilary is Bill's *wife*; if Nathan *borrowed* £10 from Kirsten, then Kirsten *lent* £10 to Nathan.

Sense relations such as synonymy and antonymy contribute to defining the meaning of words. A third sense relation recognises that words may be related to each other in the generality of their reference. For example, *cutlery* is a more general way of referring to the more specific *knives*, *forks* and *spoons*. This sense relation is called **hyponymy**: *knife*, *fork* and *spoon* are hyponyms of *cutlery*.

ACTIVITY 24

1 Find synonyms for the following words:

| keep | money | yell |
| voter | hubris | commence |

Why might you choose one member of each pair rather than the other (for instance, dialect, formality or social connotation)?

2 Find antonyms for the following words:

| sharp | quiet | superior |
| parent | guilty | opaque |

What kind of antonymy do they represent (gradable, complementary or converse)?

3 List hyponyms (more specific words) for the following:

| furniture | crockery | fish |

See page 66 for the answers.

2.2.7 Collocations and idioms

We suggested earlier (in Section 2.2.5) that the meaning of a word is in part determined by the regular lexical company that the word keeps. For example, part of the meaning of *muggy* is its association with *weather*.

The adjective *false* is associated in one way with nouns such as *passport*, *banknote*, *number plates* (where it is synonymous with *counterfeit*), in a second way with nouns such as *assumption*, *hope* (where it is synonymous with *unwarranted*), and in a third with nouns such as *teeth*, *leg*, *eyelashes* (where it is synonymous with *artificial*). The **collocations** of *false* provide a basis on which to identify the different 'meanings' or 'senses' of the word.

From these two examples, *muggy* and *false*, it is clear that words differ in their range of collocation. *Muggy* has a rather restricted range of collocation; *false* has a somewhat broader range; and an adjective such as *good* has a very wide range, so much so that collocation does not contribute to the characterisation of its meaning.

At the more restricted end of collocational range, words may become so mutually predictable in a particular context that they form into a **fixed expression**: for example, *break a habit*, *a bad habit*. If such expressions become overused, they become clichés or stereotypical phrases; for instance, *desirable residence* (in estate agents' blurb), *once upon a time* (in fairy stories), *golden opportunity* (in advertising).

When such fixed expressions no longer have their literal meaning, or where the meaning of the expression is more than the sum of its parts, then we talk of an idiom; for example, *keep one's nose clean, poke one's nose into, turn one's nose up at.* Such idiomatic expressions operate in language as prefabricated wholes. There is a range of such expressions, from the completely idiomatic (non-literal) to the almost literal. We have no space here to look at them in detail.

ACTIVITY 25

1 What nouns do you associate most readily with the following adjectives?

rancid	powerful
flat	safe
unkempt	

2 What nouns would you expect to follow the following verbs?

prune	deny
spread	spend
prosecute	

Check your suggestions for 1 and 2 with someone else. There may well be quite a number of possible answers for each one.

3 What idioms can you form that include the following words?

hand
first
stand

Check your answers with a good dictionary.

2.3 Sentences

We are familiar with the notion of a **sentence** from writing. It is a sequence of words: the first word begins with a capital letter; and the sequence terminates with an appropriate punctuation mark – a full stop (.), question mark (?) or exclamation mark (!).

In this section, we are looking at the notion of 'sentence' from the point of view of its syntactic structure: the ways in which words combine, the elements in sentences and their possible orders. Written sentences do not always correspond to sentences defined in structural terms.

We begin by considering some of the basic structural elements of sentences.

2.3.1 Subject, object and complement

The basic structure of a sentence is made up of a verb together with a number of nouns. Sentences such as the following illustrate the basic structure:

Birds fly.
Cows eat grass.
Grass gives humans indigestion.

The first sentence contains the verb *fly* and the noun *birds*, functioning as **subject**. The second contains the verb *eat*, the noun *cows* functioning as subject, and the noun *grass* as **object**. The third contains the verb *gives*, the noun *grass* as subject, the nouns *humans* and *indigestion* as objects. *Indigestion* is called a direct object, and *humans* an indirect object. The indirect object can often also be expressed by means of the preposition *to* with the noun: *Grass gives indigestion to humans*.

You will notice that the subject occurs to the left of the verb in each instance, and the objects to the right. The subject noun also interacts with the verb: if the noun is singular in number (for example, *grass*), the verb is in the third-person singular form in the present tense (*gives*); if the noun is plural (*cows*), the verb has the form appropriate to third-person plural (*eat*). The subject noun is said to 'agree' with the verb in number. In English the verb will change its form in this way only when the verb is in the present tense and the subject is a third person (that is, third-person pronoun or noun).

From these three examples, we can see that verbs combine with different numbers of nouns: *fly* with only one, *eat* with two and *give* with three. If only one occurs, it has subject function. If two occur, one has subject function and the other object. And if three occur, one is subject, one is indirect object and the third is direct object. A subject and a verb are always present in a basic sentence. How many objects occur depends on the verb.

Some verbs require, in addition to the subject, an element called a **complement**; for instance, *Banks are businesses, Strawberries taste delicious*. In these examples, the complements are the noun *businesses* and the adjective *delicious*. Complements differ from objects in that they reflect back on and describe the subject. They occur with a limited set of verbs, typically *be* and *become*. And they may be adjectives as well as nouns.

Some verbs require an object and a complement in addition to a subject; for example, *Students think grammar difficult, America elected Bill president*. Here the complements are the adjective *difficult* and the noun *president*. In these sentences, the complements describe the objects *grammar* and *Bill* respectively. Again there is a limited set of verbs that require this structure: *think, consider, find* (in one of their meanings) – equivalent to *be*; *elect, make* – equivalent to *become*.

From what we have discussed so far, we can identify a number of basic sentence structures in English:

> subject + verb (*Birds fly*)
> subject + verb + object (*Cows eat grass*)
> subject + verb + indirect object + direct object (*Grass gives humans indigestion*)
> subject + verb + complement (*Banks are businesses*)
> subject + verb + object + complement (*Students think grammar difficult*)

Verbs which take an object are called **transitive** verbs. Those which do not are called **intransitive**. Similarly, sentence structures that contain an object are called transitive, and those which do not are called intransitive.

Note that where nouns occur as subject, object or complement, pronouns can also occur.

ACTIVITY 26

Which basic structure is represented by each of the following sentences?

1   Brian scores runs.

2   Babies cry.

3   They send charities money.

4   Curry smells appetising.
5   Coffee stains carpets.
6   She finds language fascinating.
7   Opinions differ.
8   You are wonderful.
9   Inventions generate trade.
10 Work makes you tired.

See page 66 for the answers.

2.3.2 Noun phrases

In all of the examples in Section 2.3.1 we used single words (verbs, nouns/pronouns, adjectives) for the sentence elements. As a result, some of the sentences sound rather unnatural, because subjects and objects especially rarely consist of a noun by itself (pronouns, however, do usually occur alone). A number of items may accompany a noun and serve as its **modifiers**. The term given to a noun and any accompanying modifiers is **noun phrase**.

As our examples have illustrated, a noun phrase may be composed of just a noun (or, more likely, just a pronoun). A noun is usually modified by at least a determiner; for instance, the definite or indefinite article, a possessive or a quantifier (see Section 2.2.2):

> *A journalist is interviewing the president.*
> *Our gain is your loss.*
> *This train is two hours late.*
> *Several people gave the beggar a few coins.*

Only one identifier (article, possessive, demonstrative) may occur in a noun phrase, but some combinations of quantifiers are possible, for example: *They sold us their last few stamps.*

Notice that any quantifiers follow the identifier, except that *all* and quantifiers including the word *of* precede an identifier; for example, *all the five songs*, *plenty of our friends*.

Another common modifier of nouns is an adjective, either with or without a determiner; for example, *the five green bottles*, *clear glass*.

More than one adjective may occur in a noun phrase; for example, *the large, red, plastic bag*. When multiple adjectives occur in a noun phrase, a principle of ordering operates. In this example, the size adjective (*large*) precedes the colour adjective (*red*), which in turn precedes the material adjective (*plastic*).

Some nouns may also act like adjectives and modify other nouns: they are known as 'noun modifiers' – for example, *a nasty ear infection*, *the famous history professor*. The noun modifiers in these examples are *ear* and *history*. If a noun modifier and noun become regularly associated, there is a chance that the combination will develop into a compound noun.

We have identified a number of elements that make up a noun phrase. The minimal structure contains the *head* noun (or pronoun). This may be preceded by modifiers in the following order:

identifier – quantifier(s) – adjective(s) – noun modifier

Besides these modifiers that may precede a noun, there are modifiers that may follow a noun in the structure of a noun phrase. Most of these are longer than a single word. Here is a list of them, with an example; we shall come back to most of them later on:

> adverb (*the road back*)
> prepositional phrase (*the road to the beach*)
> relative clause (*the road which leads to the beach*)
> present participle clause (*the road leading to the beach*)
> past participle clause (*the road taken by most holidaymakers*)

It is unusual for more than one type of modifier after the noun to occur, so they are not ordered in the same way as the modifiers before the noun. Combining both types of modifier can generate some quite complex noun phrases. How complex the nouns phrases are in a text is often a measure of the type of text it is, as well as of personal style: journalistic texts and formal/technical texts tend to have more complex noun phrases than, say, personal letters and popular fiction.

Noun phrases function in sentence structure as subjects, objects and complements.

ACTIVITY 27

Analyse the noun phrases in the following sentences by giving a label to each of their constituents – they contain only modifiers before the noun:

1 The famous brass band played a slow military march.

2 Your younger sister broke these valuable old records.

3 The first six people boarded the red London bus.

4 I told the police officer the whole truth.

5 They found Spielberg's latest film overwhelming.

See page 67 for the answers.

2.3.3 Verb phrase

We have noted that the verb element is central in a sentence (Section 2.3.1). The verb element is always a **verb phrase**. The minimal form of a verb phrase is a **lexical** (or **main**) verb. For example:

> *says*   *regret*   *proposed*   *took*

You will notice that these verbs show a distinction between **present** and **past** tense: *says* and *regret* are present tense, while *proposed* and *took* are past tense. All finite verb phrases show tense, either present or past, and it is the first word in the verb phrase that shows the tense.

Simple past-tense verbs (such as *proposed, took*) usually refer to a situation that occurred in past time. Simple present-tense forms (such as *regret, says, know*), however, usually refer either to something that is always the case (first example below), to something that occurs regularly (second example), or to a current state of mind (third example):

> *We regret that refunds cannot be given.*
> *She says grace before every meal.*
> *He knows that he is a danger to other drivers.*

Simple present-tense forms refer to the present moment in time only in commentary – for example, on sport:

Smith passes to Jones, and Jones shoots. It's a goal!

Further subtleties in relation to time are expressed by means of **auxiliary verbs**, which come before the main verb in a verb phrase. The **progressive aspect** is expressed by means of *be* as an auxiliary verb together with the present participle form of the main verb (see Section 2.2.2 under 'Verbs'). For example:

is cutting
are playing
was passing
were visiting

You will notice that the tense is now shown by the auxiliary *be*, as the first item in the verb phrase.

Progressive aspect focuses on a situation as being in progress or lasting over time. The progressive is not normally possible with main verbs referring to states, but only with those referring to actions or events. The present progressive is the most usual form for referring to something going on at the (present) moment of speaking. For example, to the question *What are you doing?*, the response is *I am cutting the hedge*.

The past progressive is often used to set the scene for a story. For example:

The sun was shining. The birds were singing. The trees were swaying in the breeze. People were going about their daily business.

The story itself will then normally be told in the simple past tense:

Lydia opened the front door and stepped out onto the pavement. She walked purposefully to the baker's and entered the shop.

English has a second aspect: the **perfect** (or **perfective**) **aspect**. It is formed with *have* as an auxiliary verb, together with the past participle of a main verb – for example:

has stayed
have found
had moved

Again the tense is shown in the auxiliary verb, as the first item in the verb phrase.

Perfect aspect relates to the distribution of a situation in past time. The present perfect refers either to a situation that began in the past and is still current at the time of speaking (first example below), or to a situation that occurred at an unspecified time in the past (second example):

He has lived in Birmingham since the war.
They have found their lost cat.

The past perfect refers to a situation that preceded another past-time situation, so it is a 'past in the past':

They had moved to their new house before Lydia was born.

A third auxiliary verb relates to a quite different grammatical category: **voice**. Voice distinguishes **active** and **passive** verb phrases (and sentences). The normal sentence structure is in the active voice. **Passive voice** is expressed by *be* as an auxiliary verb together with the past participle of a main verb – for example:

> *is claimed*
> *are performed*
> *was decided*
> *were written*

Passive voice involves not only an appropriate form of the verb phrase but also a rearrangement of the elements of the sentence. Compare the first, active example below with the second, passive example:

> *The pharmaceutical company claims a major breakthrough in pain relief.*
> *A major breakthrough in pain relief is claimed by the pharmaceutical company.*

The object (*breakthrough*) of the active sentence becomes the subject of the passive sentence; and the subject of the active sentence becomes a *by*-phrase. We have so far described three auxiliary verbs that may occur in a verb phrase:

> *have* + past participle (perfect aspect); for example, *has taken*
> *be* + present participle (progressive aspect); for example, *is taking*
> *be* + past participle (passive voice); for example, *is taken*

They may occur in combination, in which case they occur in the relative order:

> perfect auxiliary – progressive auxiliary – passive auxiliary – main verb

It is always the verb that immediately follows an auxiliary (whether another auxiliary or the main verb) which is in the participle form appropriate to the auxiliary (that is, present participle after progressive auxiliary *be*, and so on). For example:

> *has been taking*: *has* (perfect auxiliary) – *been* (progressive auxiliary in past participle form after perfect *have*) – *taking* (main verb in present participle after progressive *be*)

> *is being taken*: *is* (progressive auxiliary) – *being* (passive auxiliary in present participle after progressive *be*) – *taken* (main verb in past participle after passive *be*)

> *has been being taken*: *has* (perfect auxiliary) – *been* (progressive auxiliary in past participle after perfect *have*) – *being* (passive auxiliary in present participle after progressive *be*) – *taken* (main verb in past participle after passive *be*)

There is one further type of auxiliary verb that may occur in a verb phrase: a **modal auxiliary verb**. It precedes any other auxiliary. Here is a list of the main modal auxiliary verbs:

> *can/could*   *may/might*   *shall/should*   *will/would*   *must*

Modal auxiliaries are followed by the base form of the verb (the infinitive without *to*), for example:

> *can swim*   *might sleep*   *should have been speaking*   *must be being interviewed*

As the first item in the verb phrase – which they are whenever they occur – modal auxiliaries show present/past tense (the past of *must* is *had to*). However, individual present and past forms of modals have different meanings: *might*, for example, is not a direct past of *may*. Compare:

> *This story may amuse you./This story might amuse you.*
> *You may now begin writing./You might now begin writing*

In the first pair of examples, *might* expresses a less certain, more tentative statement than *may*. In the second pair, *may* gives permission, while *might* offers a suggestion (again more tentative than *may*).

We begin to see the kinds of meanings that the modal verbs express: on the one hand, the speaker's assessment of the possibility, probability or certainty of the situation; on the other hand, the subject's involvement in terms of ability, permission and obligation. For example:

> possibility/certainty –
> *The trains might be running on time.*
> *The trains could be running on time.*
> *The trains must be running on time.*
>
> ability/permission/obligation –
> *She can drive a car.*
> *You can/may drive her car.*
> *You should drive her car.*
> *You shall drive her car.*
> *You must drive her car.*

We will leave you to puzzle over the subtle differences in meaning conveyed by the modal auxiliary verbs in these examples.

You will have noticed that we have not mentioned a 'future' tense, only a present and a past tense. That is because English does not have a future tense as such: there is no suffix added to the verb to make the future, like the past tense suffix *-ed*. Appropriately, because of the uncertainty of the future, English uses the modal verb *will* (which has a 'prediction' meaning in many contexts) as one major means of referring to future time. Other means include the quasi-auxiliary *be going to*, as well as the simple present and present progressive tenses (usually with adverbs with a future reference). For example:

> *We will meet at six in the restaurant.*
> *We're going to meet in the restaurant.*
> *We meet at six.*
> *We are meeting Hilary and Bill at six.*

You may notice subtle differences of meaning in these different ways of talking about the future.

There is one last item found in a verb phrase that needs to be mentioned, which is not an auxiliary verb. It is the negative word *not*, which we use to make a verb phrase – and ultimately the sentence – negative rather than positive. *Not* comes after the first auxiliary verb in a verb phrase, and in colloquial styles it may be shortened to *n't* and, in writing, joined to the auxiliary that it follows. For example:

> *can't see   mustn't be seen   wasn't being looked after   haven't protested*

If there is no auxiliary verb in a verb phrase, but only a main verb, then a **dummy auxiliary** is used (*do*) to provide an auxiliary for *not* to follow. For example:

> *pays – does not pay/doesn't pay*
> *bought – did not buy/didn't buy*

You will notice that the *do* auxiliary carries the tense, as the first item in the verb phrase, and the main verb is in the base form.

Summarising, a verb phrase consists minimally of a main verb, which may be preceded by up to four auxiliary verbs and negative *not*, as follows:

> modal auxiliary – perfect auxiliary – progressive auxiliary –
> passive auxiliary – main verb

with *not* after whichever is the first auxiliary, or after *do* if no other auxiliary is present.

ACTIVITY 28

Identify the verb phrases in the following sentences. What is the tense of the verb phrase – present or past? Analyse the verb phrases by labelling each item.

1　We are operating in this area.

2　I don't need any replacement windows.

3　We have been pestered by double-glazing people.

4　Our next-door neighbour is talking to one at the moment.

5　We could have paid a lot of money.

6　Many such firms will be calling in the receiver.

See page 67 for the answers.

2.3.4 Adverbials

In Section 2.3.1, we looked at the major roles played by elements in a sentence – subject, object and complement – and at the basic structures that they compose. Subjects and objects represent the entities (persons/things) involved in the situation (action, event or state) represented by the (main) verb; complements represent attributes of entities.

In this section, we consider one further type of sentence element, which has the syntactic role of adverbial. **Adverbials** are normally optional elements in sentence structure: they are not required, by the verb, to make the sentence grammatical. Adverbial elements represent circumstantial information relating to a situation, such as place (where something happened), time (when), manner/means (how) and reason/purpose (why). For example:

> *I was doing my homework on the bus.*
> *Brian fell asleep after dinner.*
> *The bell tolled monotonously.*
> *We are cancelling the concert because of the lead singer's illness.*

On the bus is an adverbial of place; *after dinner* an adverbial of time; *monotonously* an adverbial of manner; and *because of the lead singer's illness* an adverbial of reason.

Adverbials are often expressed, as in these examples, by adverbs and prepositional phrases. The adverb here is *monotonously*, which is derived by means of the *-ly* suffix from the adjective *monotonous*. Manner adverbials are typically expressed by such *-ly* adverbs. Other adverbs express time; for instance, *now, soon, then, tomorrow, shortly, often, annually*.

A prepositional phrase consists of a preposition (*on, after, because of*) followed by a noun phrase (*on + the bus, after + dinner*). They are a common means of expressing all kinds of adverbials; for example, *before school* (time), *behind the shed* (place), *by a trick* (means), *for a laugh* (purpose).

A sentence may contain more than one adverbial; for example, *Sally won the race yesterday* (time) *in Helsinki* (place) *in record time* (manner). In this example, all three adverbials come at the end of the sentence. An adverbial may, however, be placed at the beginning of a sentence, or indeed in the middle (usually single-word adverbs). For instance:

> *On Friday evenings* (time) *we go with our friends* (manner) *to the cinema* (place).
> *During the summer* (time) *we have often* (time–frequency) *gone camping in the Cotswolds* (place).

Adverbials are usually optional elements: we can choose whether or not to give information about the time, place, manner, and so on of a situation. Subjects, objects and complements are not normally optional elements of sentence structure in this way. However, with some verbs, an adverbial (usually of place) may be more or less obligatory: to leave it out would create a structural gap in the sentence. For example:

> *Lydia has gone to the library.*
> *I left my umbrella on the bus.*

Someone has to go somewhere, so the place adverbial *to the library* is more or less obligatory. *Lydia has gone* does make sense on its own, although if the verb form is changed from present perfect to simple past (*Lydia went*), there is a greater sense of incompleteness. Again, with the second example, *leave* (like *lose* and *find*) implies somewhere; so *on the bus* is a more or less obligatory adverbial in this sentence. It is arguably more obligatory than *to the library* in the first example, since even *I have left my umbrella* is incomplete.

ACTIVITY 29

Identify the adverbials in the following sentences. What meaning – place, time, manner, reason and so on – does each one have? What form – adverb or prepositional phrase – does each one have?

1 We return from holiday tomorrow.

2 She carefully put the letter into the postbox.

3 Due to the rail strike no classes will be held until Monday.

4 On Saturday they are giving a concert for charity.

5 We travelled by coach from Santander along the coast to San Sebastian.

See page 67 for the answers.

2.3.5 Clauses

The units of syntactic structure that we have talked about so far have included word, phrase and sentence. Words combine together into phrases; for instance, noun phrase, verb phrase or prepositional phrase. A (simple) sentence is made up of a verb (phrase) together with the subject, object and complement (noun or adjective) phrases that the verb requires, as well as any adverbial (adverb or prepositional) phrases. Thus each **simple sentence**, as we have described it, contains a single main verb (plus any auxiliaries).

Simple sentences consist of one clause. A **<u>clause</u>** is a syntactic unit consisting of a verb together with its associated subject, objects/complement and adverbials. Complex sentences consist of more than one clause. Clauses combine into complex sentences in two ways: by **<u>coordination</u>** and by **<u>subordination</u>**. Two clauses are coordinated when they are joined by one of the coordinating conjunctions *and*, *but* and *or*. For example:

> *The bus was late and she missed her connection.*
> *You can take the train, but the fare is higher.*
> *You can travel direct or you can go via London.*

Coordination joins clauses that are essentially independent. Consider *The bus was late. She missed her connection.*, where the first of the above examples has been separated into two simple sentences. The other examples can be similarly separated. What the coordinating conjunction does is to make explicit the meaning connection between the two clauses; various kinds of 'addition' for *and*, 'opposition' for *but* and 'alternative' for *or*.

Subordination joins a subordinate clause to a main clause. A subordinate clause functions within the main clause as subject, object, complement or adverbial. It cannot be separated from the main clause, leaving the two clauses to stand alone as simple sentences. Here are some examples of complex sentences containing a subordinate clause:

> *What you are telling me is an old story.* (Subject clause, *What you are telling me* + verb, *is* + complement noun phrase, *an old story*). The main clause is *X is an old story*; the subordinate clause, *What you are telling me*, fills *X*, the subject slot, in the main clause.

> *I did not know that you could speak German.* (Subject pronoun, *I* + verb, *did not know* + object clause, *that you could speak German*). The main clause is *I did not know X*; the subordinate clause, *that you could speak German*, fills *X*, the object slot, in the main clause.

> *The hardest task is remembering the vocabulary.* (Subject noun phrase, *The hardest task* + verb, *is* + complement clause, *remembering the vocabulary*). The main clause is *The hardest task is X*; the subordinate clause, *remembering the vocabulary*, fills *X*, the complement slot, in the main clause.

> *You can come here after you have been to the bank.* (Subject pronoun, *you* + verb, *can come* + adverbial (place) adverb, *here* + adverbial (time) clause, *after...*). The main clause is *You can come here (X)*; the subordinate clause, *after you have been to the bank*, fills *X*, the optional adverbial slot in the main clause.

Subordinate clauses that function as subject, object or complement replace noun phrases, and so they are called **<u>nominal clauses</u>**. Those that function as adverbials replace adverbs/prepositional phrases, and they are called **adverbial clauses**. There are also clauses that function as modifiers of nouns, within a noun phrase, which do the same job as an adjective: they are called **adjectival clauses**. Adjectival clauses include relative clauses (see Section 2.3.2 and below); for instance, *an interesting proposal, which we will discuss at our next meeting*. Nominal clauses include the following types (all illustrated in the following examples in object position in the main clause, where nominal clauses are found most commonly):

The *that*-clause, introduced by the conjunction *that*, which is sometimes, however, omitted (for example, *I think (that) you know each other*).

The *wh*-clause, introduced by a *wh*-word (for example, *who, what, why, whether*). Unlike the *that* of *that*-clauses, the *wh*-word is an element (subject, object and so on) of the *wh*-clause (for example, *You haven't told me what you did on holiday*. Here *what you did on holiday* is the *wh*-clause object of *told*, and within the *wh*-clause *what* is the object of *did*).

The *-ing*-clause, introduced by a present participle form of the verb and often lacking a subject (for example, *I don't remember seeing him at the theatre*. Here the *-ing*-clause, *seeing him at the theatre*, is object of *remember*, and it has no subject. In this case, the subject is assumed to be the same as that the main clause, so *I*. If the subject of the subordinate *-ing*-clause is different from that of the main clause, it is often possible to supply one; for example, *my daughter* in *I don't like my daughter staying out late*, where *my daughter staying out late* is object of *like*.

The inf-clause, introduced by an infinitive form of the verb, and often without a subject; for example, *We have decided to offer you the job*. Here, the subordinate inf-clause, *to offer you the job* is object of *decide*, and it has no subject: it is the same as the subject of the main clause, *we*. If the inf-clause is direct object in a sentence with an indirect object (for instance, with the verb *tell*), then the subject of the inf-clause is assumed to be the same as the indirect object; for example, *I told Lydia to close the door behind her*. As with -*ing*-clauses, a subject may be supplied where appropriate; for example, *the fee* in *She requested the fee to be paid into her account*. Sometimes an introductory *wh*-word precedes the inf-clause, as in *We haven't decided where to go on holiday*: this is called a *wh*-inf-clause.

Adverbial clauses are usually introduced by a subordinating conjunction, which gives some indication of the adverbial meaning of the clause. For example, *when/before/after/while* (time), *because/since* (reason) or *if/unless* (condition):

When the buzzer sounds, you should press this button.
We are unable to fulfil your order, because the items are out of stock.
If you call into the office, the forms can be signed.

Minor types of adverbial clause include the following:

The inf-clause, introduced by an infinitive form of the verb and with the meaning of 'purpose'; for example, *I have to call in at the post office to buy some stamps*. Note that the subject of the purpose inf-clause (*to buy some stamps*) is the same as the subject of the main clause (*I*). If the subject is different, it is introduced by the preposition *for*; for instance, *I had to call in for Bill to sign the form*.

The *ing*-clause, containing a present participle form of the verb, sometimes introduced by a subordinating conjunction, and with a 'time' meaning; for instance, *I found this gold ring, (while) looking for shells on the beach*; *After visiting the cathedral, they went to a cafe for a coffee*. In this case the subject of the *-ing*-clause is always the same as the subject of the main clause.

Adjectival clauses, which all function as modifiers after the noun (see Section 2.3.2), include the following types:

The relative clause, introduced by a relative pronoun. Like the *wh*-word in *wh*-clauses, the relative pronoun has a function (subject, object, complement and so on) within the relative clause: for example, in *the song which she sang*, the relative pronoun *which* is object of *sang*; in *the song which comes next on the record*, *which* is subject of *comes*. If the relative pronoun is functioning as object in the relative clause, it may be omitted; for instance, *the song she sang, the friend (whom) she met at the party*.

The *-ing*-clause, introduced by a present participle form of the verb; for example, *the song topping the charts at the moment*. The *-ing*-clause does not have a subject; it is assumed to be the same as the noun being modified (*song* in this example).

The *-ed*-clause, introduced by a past participle form of the verb; for example, *the exam failed by most students*. As with the *-ing*-clause modifier, there is no subject in the *-ed*-clause; it is assumed to be the same as the noun being modified (*exam* in this example).

Coordination and subordination of clauses introduces considerable complexity into the syntax of sentences, and such sentences often take considerable unravelling to understand how the structure is working. Complexity of syntactic structure is also a reflection of how elaborate our language can become, especially when we write, which is where most of the more complex subordination occurs.

ACTIVITY 30

Here are a few sentences for you to try and unravel:

1 Who could have told you that remains a mystery.

2 You should read the instructions before you operate the machine.

3 The shock for me was winning the poetry prize.

4 Sites which have lain derelict for years are now being built on.

5 I would like to help you.

Identify the subordinate clause in each of the sentences.

Is the subordinate clause functioning as subject, object, complement or adverbial, or is it adjectival? There is one of each.

See page 67 for the answers.

2.3.6 Sentences

When we use a **sentence** in communication, it fulfils for us one of four purposes or functions: it makes a statement, asks a question, gives a command or expresses an exclamation.

Compare the following:

statement – *We have visited all the capital cities of Europe.*
question – *Have you visited all the capital cities of Europe? What have you visited?*
command – *Visit the capital cities of Europe!*
exclamation – *What a lot of cities to visit!*

You will notice that the different functions are reflected in different forms (order of words). The statement, usually considered the basic type of sentence, has the elements in the order subject – verb – object.

There are two types of question. The 'yes/no' or polar question (*Have you visited...?*) expects either *yes* or *no* as an answer. It differs from the statement form in that the first auxiliary of the verb phrase inverts with the subject (*You have... – Have you..?*). The *wh-* or information-seeking question (*What have you visited?*) begins with the *wh-*word, which specifies the type of information being sought, and then subject/auxiliary inversion takes place, unless the *wh* word is itself the subject (*Who came yesterday?*).

A command sentence has no subject, and the verb is in the base form (infinitive without *to*). A person can be nominated – *Sally, pass me the salt, please* – but they are not the subject of the sentence.

An exclamation is introduced by either *what* or *how*. *What* is followed by a noun phrase: *What an amazing sight! How* is followed by an adjective or adverb: *How beautiful your eyes are! How charmingly she spoke to us!*

Sentences rarely occur in isolation, except, for example, in notices (*Passengers must cross the line by the bridge.*). A sentence usually forms part of an ongoing discourse or text, and as such it may be adapted in various ways to the other sentences in its immediate context. That is the topic of the next section.

ACTIVITY 31

Divide the following sentences into their constituent elements – subject, verb, object, complement and adverbial:

1 The foreign students did not understand their teacher's humour.

2 These bottles are empty and we are taking them to the bottle bank.

3 The traffic warden told me to park on the other side.

4 Have you finished making fun of them?

5 I stupidly forgot that she had gone away.

What category of element fills each slot (for example, pronoun, noun phrase, prepositional phrase, adverb, *that*-clause, *-ing*-clause and so on)?
See page 68 for the answers.

2.4 Discourse and text

Sentences combine into discourses and texts, which are investigated with the tools of discourse analysis or text linguistics (see Section 1.3). Some linguists use the term **discourse** to refer to both spoken and written acts of communication; others use the term **text** for the same purpose. Since both terms are available, it seems sensible to use them for the type of communication that they suggest: 'discourse' for spoken communication, and 'text' for written communication.

In a sense, there is no clear dividing line, but rather a certain amount of overlap. There is text that is written to be spoken: such as news broadcasts, speeches, drama and poetry. There is discourse that has the formality of much written text: such as oath taking and other law-court rituals, aspects of debating, and announcements. There is text that shares some of the features of ordinary conversation: such as personal letters, diary entries, and notes and messages.

However, the distinction remains – discourses are transmitted through the medium of sound, originated by a speaker and received by a hearer, while texts are transmitted through the medium of writing, originated by a writer and received by a reader. At one time, you would add to the previous statement, in respect of written text, 'received by a reader, possibly remote in time and in space'. With the development of broadcast media and of sound recording, that could now be equally true of spoken discourse.

2.4.1 Dialogue and monologue

Spoken discourses may involve either a single speaker with one or more hearers (monologue), or multiple speakers who also function as hearers (dialogue). Written text is inevitably monologue, since writer and reader are remote from each other; unless you regard an exchange of letters as a kind of dialogue.
Examples of spoken monologue would include: speeches, lectures and sermons (which will usually have some kind of written basis); commentary (a guided tour or a radio sports commentary); and a reading (of a story) or recitation (of poetry) – which are directly from a written text.

Spoken discourse is found essentially in dialogue, where each participant acts in turn as speaker and hearer. There are many fascinating features of dialogue to explore, which we do not have space to discuss here. Let me mention just two: turn-taking and topics.

One of the surprising features of conversation is how smoothly it flows, how little overlapping speech occurs, and how few silences occur between one speaker and the next. A hearer seems able to anticipate when it is appropriate to 'take the floor' and become the next speaker. Sometimes the existing speaker will 'nominate', either directly or indirectly, the next speaker; for example: *I'm not in favour of wholesale privatisation. What do you think, Sarah?*

More usually, the hearer will react to clues given by the speaker which indicate that they are about to complete their turn. Such clues include: an intonation pattern that signals completion, the syntax moving towards a point of completion; and body language, such as renewal of eye contact, gestures and so on. At such points of possible change of speaker, a hearer is able to take the floor smoothly, without it being experienced as an interruption. A hearer may choose not to take the floor, and the existing speaker may continue.

An existing speaker may indeed wish to prolong their turn. They can attempt to do this by refusing to give the appropriate clues: using a non-completion intonation, not making eye contact, or making sure the syntax is incomplete, if only by adding *and* or *but*. You may notice how people (such as politicians) interviewed on the radio, where time is often limited, will often ensure that they can make their point by prefacing their turn with expressions such as *I want to make three points* or *There are two sides to this question*, or simply *First*, implying that there is at least a *Second*.

ACTIVITY 32

1 Listen to an ordinary conversation in your family or among your friends, and then listen to a chat-show or interview on the radio or television.

2 What are the differences in the turn-taking procedures? For example, is there more direct nomination in interviews, or more interruption in conversation? Or are there more question and answer exchanges in interviews?

Another aspect of dialogue that has been investigated is the way in which topics are introduced and change in the course of a conversation. In some kinds of dialogue, sometimes called **transactional** dialogue, the introduction of topics is controlled by one of the participants; for instance, the interviewer in all kinds of interviews, or the chair of a committee. In ordinary conversation, which is **interactional** rather than transactional (that is, the focus is on the personal relationships rather than on the business to be done), participants may have their agendas – topics that they want to be dealt with – but conversation often slides from one topic to another. A topic may be introduced explicitly: *How is your mother these days?* Or a topic may arise from some association with the topic that has already been under discussion.

ACTIVITY 33

1 Attempt to record an ordinary conversation. Alternatively, record a chat-show or discussion programme from the radio.

2 Make a list of the topics covered in the conversation. Note how the transition is made from one topic to the next. How is the conversation eventually brought to a close?

2.4.2 Cohesion

Some of the essential features that make a collection of sentences into a discourse or text are that they fit together (in some logical order), make sense (are 'coherent') and are linked together. The links between sentences are the topic of **cohesion**.

There are explicit ways of making links, by means of conjunctive adverbs such as *however, moreover, therefore, consequently*. These adverbs are often used in a text that is presenting a closely argued case. An adverb such as *then* connects sentences referring to successive events in a story. The sequence *first, second, third, ...* presents steps in an argument or a set of instructions.

Other forms of cohesion are less explicit and may also be part of the means of making language more economical. Such cohesion is achieved by third-person pronouns. Consider the following example: *She gave them to him.* You cannot interpret this sentence unless you know the nouns or noun phrases to which the pronouns *she*, *them*, *him* refer. To find out which those nouns are, you have to refer back in the text to a previous sentence in which they are mentioned. Because of this referring back, third-person pronouns have a cohesive function. But pronouns are also an economical device, because they save repeating the noun or noun phrase.

Another device of cohesion and economy is **ellipsis**, which is a particular feature of discourse. Ellipsis is the omission from a subsequent sentence of an item or items contained in some sentence of a discourse or text. Consider the following pair of utterances:

> *Where did you put the milk?*
> *Back in the fridge.*

The person giving the answer does not need to repeat *I put the milk*; that can be recovered from the question. But what this means is that you can interpret *Back in the fridge* only by referring back to the previous sentence in the discourse in order to supply the ellipted words. Ellipsis thus serves also as a cohesive device.

The types of cohesion that we have considered so far are often referred to as **grammatical** devices, to distinguish them from **lexical** devices of cohesion. Lexical devices include the repetition of words, the use of synonyms or near-synonyms, and the use of collocations.

The simple repetition of a word acts as a cohesive link between one sentence and another – for instance, of *tyre* in the following:

> *As the tyre burst he almost lost control of the car. When he finally stopped at the side of the road, the tyre was in shreds.*

In the following example, *call* is used as a synonym of *telephone* to form a cohesive link:

> *Unable to undo the wheel-nuts, he decided to telephone for assistance. When he called the AA, they said they would be with him within the hour.*

In the following example, the cohesion is formed by *casing* as a collocate of *tyre*:

> *When the AA patrolman saw the state of the tyre, he said they were very fortunate not to have crashed. The casing had completely disintegrated.*

ACTIVITY 34

1 Take a news article and an editorial from a newspaper. In both texts, examine every sentence after the first one and determine how it is linked cohesively with the previous sentence. Is the cohesion grammatical or lexical?

2 Does the news article or the editorial have the tighter cohesion? Grammatical cohesion is generally tighter than lexical, and explicit links (with conjunctive adverbs) are tighter than cohesion by means of pronouns or ellipsis. Generally, the more explicit and overt the cohesion, the more tightly structured a text appears to be.

2.4.3 Fronting and postponement

A sentence is a linear sequence of elements arranged in a particular order. The basic order for a statement (see Section 2.3.6) is:

subject – verb – object/complement – (adverbial)

The initial element in a sentence, usually the subject, is the one that normally creates a link with the previous sentence in a text or discourse, so creating the logical order that we mentioned in Section 2.4.2. For example:

The 200 metres hurdles was won by Sally. She easily outpaced her rivals.

She in the second sentence picks up the *Sally* of the first. Subjects are often pronouns for this reason. They represent **given** information mentioned in the previous sentence.

The subject is often the **topic** of the sentence, about which the rest of the sentence (the **comment**) says something **new**, with the most significant or newsworthy information coming at the end of the sentence.

The initial and final positions in a sentence are thus very significant, and for this reason there are devices for ensuring that the appropriate element appears in these positions.

The choice of verb will influence which item occurs as subject. Compare the choice of *give* and *get* in the following:

Hilary gave Bill the idea.
Bill got the idea from Hilary.

The use of a passive can bring into subject position an item that would be object in the active sentence. Compare the following:

Sally won the 200 metres hurdles.
The 200 metres hurdles was won by Sally.

If an element other than the subject takes up initial position in a sentence, in order to make the connection with the previous sentence, then we say that the element has been subjected to **fronting**. Consider the following examples:

Some races Sally can win easily. (object *some races* fronted)
Tired I am not. (complement *tired* fronted)
Across the bridge the refugees streamed. (adverbial of place *across the bridge* fronted)

Here the fronting is achieved by simply rearranging the elements in the sentences. The sentences may sound a little strange in isolation, but within a context much less so.

The opposite of fronting is **postponement**, where an element is moved from its usual position to the end of a sentence, because it is the most newsworthy item in the sentence. Sometimes the position that such an element vacates is filled by *it*. This is particularly the case if the element being moved is the subject. For example:

It was a surprise to find you already at home.
I call it an outrage that the library is shut on Saturdays.

In the first example, the subject infinitive clause (*to find you...*) is postponed, and in the second, the object *that*-clause (*that the library...*) is postponed. In both cases the vacated position in the sentence is filled by *it*, which functions by holding the place for the postponed subject or object. Nominal clauses, especially as subject, are often postponed in this way.

An element is sometimes postponed because it is the longest in the sentence. A long (or 'weighty') element is often also the most newsworthy. For example: *We reported to the police the theft of his bicycle from the school cycle rack.* Here the direct object (*the theft* ...) is postponed to after the indirect object prepositional phrase (*to the police*).

The rearrangement of elements in a sentence, to achieve fronting or postponement, serves the purpose of enabling the sentence to fit appropriately into a developing text or discourse. The message of the text or discourse is thus more clearly and smoothly elaborated and conveyed.

ACTIVITY 35

1 Take a text that discusses or explains some topic, or that argues a point (for instance, a feature article or editorial in a 'serious' newspaper).

2 Examine each sentence. Does it have its normal order of elements ('subject – verb – object/complement' for a statement sentence, and so on)? If not, how have they been rearranged (fronting, postponement) – and for what purpose (connection to previous sentence, most newsworthy information at end)?

2.4.4 Text types

Text linguistics and discourse analysis investigate both the ways in which texts and discourses are structured, as we have been doing so far in this section, and how those features of structure correlate with the purposes and functions that discourses and texts fulfil. We have already noted a distinction between **transactional** and **interactional** discourses (Section 2.4.2), which is reflected in the way in which turn-taking occurs.

There are several approaches to the analysis of the functions of texts and discourses. For example, you could seek to identify all the different kinds of text that occur and examine their particular features. Take a newspaper, for instance, and classify the kinds of text that you find there; news stories, feature articles, editorials, weather forecasts, book and film reviews, stock exchange listings, advertisements and so on. You will end up with rather a large number of classes.

An alternative approach is to identify more general **text types**, the features of which are found in a number of kinds of text. One such text type might be **narrative**, which you find manifested in all kinds of stories; news stories in newspapers, novels, anecdotes in conversation, history writing, biography and so on. All these 'kinds' of text share features of the narrative text 'type', such as simple past-tense verbs, adverbials of time, and actions and events organised in a temporal sequence. The narrative function (that is, telling a story) is reflected in linguistic features of the text.

Further text types might include descriptive, expository, persuasive and instructional:

> The **descriptive** text type is found in all kinds of descriptions of the physical features of objects, people and places – travel guides, encyclopaedias, technical manuals, textbooks and so on. Its linguistic features include use of

state verbs (*be*, *have*), adverbials of place, and prepositions of spatial relationship (*in*, *on*, *under*).

The **expository** text type is found in all kinds of explanations of ideas and concepts – textbooks, encyclopaedias, political speeches, newspaper feature articles and so on. Its linguistic features include state verbs of relation (*have*, *contain*, *resemble*), prepositions of abstract relationships (*of*, *for*), and use of simile (that is, comparisons with *like* or *as*).

The **persuasive** text type is found in all kinds of argument and opinion – debates, advertising, sermons, newspaper editorials, reviews (of books, theatre and films) and so on. Its linguistic features include verbs of opinion (*think*, *consider*, *argue*), conjunctive adverbs of logical connection (*however*, *therefore*, *nevertheless*), and adverbials of reason (*because*), purpose (*so that*) and condition (*if*, *unless*).

The **instructional** text type is found in all kinds of instructions and directions – rules for games, installation and operating manuals for machinery and equipment, do-it-yourself manuals, legal documents and so on. Its linguistic features include command sentences with imperative verbs, modal verbs of obligation (*shall*, *must*, *have to*), and conjunctive adverbs of logical order (*first*, *second*, *finally*).

ACTIVITY 36

1 Find an example of a text that manifests each of the text types (narrative, descriptive, expository, persuasive, instructional).

2 Look for linguistic features (such as those mentioned above) that seem to be typical of each text type, and make a list of them.

3 Compare your list with those of your colleagues.

2.5 Variability and correctness

In this chapter we have been discussing the linguistic system of English, examining the rules and conventions that we follow when we speak and write English. In describing language, we often give the impression that there is a closed system of rules, rather like a computer program, which we have to follow if we want to speak or write a language 'properly' or 'correctly'.

This section intends to correct that impression, to show that there is considerable variability and open-endedness in the linguistic system of English, as indeed of any language. Some of the points mentioned here will be explored more fully later, especially in Chapter 5.

2.5.1 Idiolect and dialect

Clearly, British English is only one of a number of 'national' varieties of English, including American English, Australian English, Indian English, West African English, and so on. But, within the British Isles, English has many regional variations – **dialects** (see Section 1.2). Dialects are mostly restricted to the spoken medium; with most written, or at least printed, text in the prestigious 'standard' dialect of public communication.

Sometimes the variation is solely one of pronunciation – accent. The grammar and vocabulary are from the standard dialect, and only the pronunciation has regional features. In that sense, we all speak with an accent, either one that betrays our regional origins (Yorkshire, Cornwall, Home Counties) or our social origins (so-called Received Pronunciation, promoted particularly in the private education system).

We also have features of our language that mark us out as individuals – our **idiolect**. It may be a word or phrase that we overuse. Students used to count how many times a former colleague used the phrase *in fact* in a lecture. It may be an idiosyncratic pronunciation. Notice how the Conservative politician Michael Howard pronounces 'l' at the end of a word, or how John Major pronounces the vowel in *want*. Or we may have a tendency to use a particular syntactic structure. Notice, for example, how some politicians, trade union leaders and the like frequently use the construction *What... is...* (in other words, *What I would say to you is...*).

English varies in pronunciation, grammar and vocabulary according to where you live, the education you have received, your past linguistic experience, and the kind of person that you are – including your personality, interests, and so on. Not only that, but you vary the way that you speak – and write – according to the context in which you are speaking or writing, and the people to whom you are speaking. What is 'correct' or 'proper' depends on the context in which the language is being used.

ACTIVITY 37

1 Listen carefully over a period of time to members of your family speaking. Make a note of features of their idolects.

2 Do you share some features as a family?

3 What is typical of the accent/dialect of the region in which you live?

2.5.2 Changing language

Language is constantly changing (see Chapter 3). This inevitably means that the language system is open and unstable. At any time, some change is taking place, perhaps imperceptibly to the current speakers, but evident in the longer term.

Change is most obviously seen in vocabulary. For example, the words of approval used by your parents or grandparents are not those that you would use. A recent word of approval has been *cool*, corresponding to your parents' *great*, perhaps, and to your grandparents' *capital* or *A1*. What word do you use now to signal approval? Not only do exisiting words change their use, but new words are also constantly being coined in the language and old ones become obsolete, as the interests and preoccupations of the generations change.

Pronunciation also changes, as does the status of accents; for example, those that are considered acceptable in public broadcasting. If you hear a news reader (or should it be 'newscaster'?) of thirty years ago, you will find their accent quite different from those of the news readers of today. The prestigious 'Received Pronunciation' accent does not sound the same as it did two or three decades ago (compare, for example, Michael Portillo with Edward Heath). New accents arise: there has been discussion recently about the rise and increasing acceptability of 'Estuary English' in the London area, a kind of adaptation of RP to the Cockney accent of East London (for example, the Labour politician Ken Livingstone, and the radio personality Steve Wright).

Nor does grammar remain immune from change. There are areas of disputed grammatical usage, which probably represent a change taking place. One such concerns the preposition used after the adjective *different*: Is it *from*, *to* or *than*? The conservative one is *from*, but *to* is probably more widely found in present-day English; *than* is still largely frowned upon.

Another grammatical change, which is not particularly a matter of dispute, is in the usage of the relative pronoun *whom*. In fact, this pronoun is falling out of use and disappearing from the class of relative pronouns. The reason for this is probably that most speakers do not understand the subject/object distinction, which governs the use of *who/whom*.

In part, a lack of understanding of the subject/object distinction is also the reason for another current grammatical change: the *between you and I* phenomenon. After a preposition, a personal pronoun normally takes the object form: *for me*, *after her*, *from us*, *about them*. However, if there are two pronouns after a preposition, joined by *and*, and the second one is a first-person singular, then a current tendency is to use *I* rather than *me*: so *between you and I* instead of *between you and me*.

Another cause of much confusion in modern English usage is the apostrophe. This is partly a matter of punctuation (and so orthography), but it is also largely a matter of grammar, since an understanding of grammar (for example, of the possessive/genitive) is needed in order to use the apostrophe appropriately. Will the apostrophe finally die?

ACTIVITY 38

1 Find out what the rules are for the use of the apostrophe (for instance, in the appendix on punctuation in the *Concise Oxford Dictionary*, eighth edition).

2 Look out for missing or wrongly used apostrophes – in shopkeepers' signs, personal and official letters, handbills, and so on.

3 Would it be better if we dropped it altogether?

2.5.3 Creative language

It should be clear by now that a language is neither a closed system (it allows considerable variation) nor in a static state (it is constantly changing). The openness and instability are most obviously seen in the expansion of the vocabulary, as new words are coined in the language to deal with changes in culture and society – new discoveries and inventions in science and technology, and new concerns and fashions; for example, in respect of the environment or in youth culture. But, as we have seen, there is variability and change in pronunciation and grammar as well, and incidentally in the construction of texts and discourses.

One of the consequences of this openness and instability is that we are able to play with language and to be creative with it. We do this in the playground in primary school; it is often the basis of jokes, or of a comedian's repartee; and poetry is sometimes an experimentation with language. Here are two examples. The first comes from Lewis Carroll's poem *Jabberwocky*:

> *'Twas brillig, and the slithy toves*
> *Did gyre and gimble in the wabe:*
> *All mimsy were the borogroves,*
> *And the mome raths outgrabe.*

The effect here is achieved by lexical innovation (nonsense words), but the grammar is conventional. You could assign a word class label to each word quite easily: *brillig* – adjective, *gyre* – verb, *raths* – plural noun, and so on.

The second example is from e e cummings:

> *anyone lived in a pretty how town*
> *(with up so floating many bells down)*
> *spring summer autumn winter*
> *he sang his didn't he danced his did.*

Here the poet is playing with the grammar. Many words are reassigned to a different word class and used in unusual syntactic positions: *anyone* is used as a proper noun, *how* is used as an adjective, *didn't* and *did* are used as nouns, and so on. And what do you make of *up so floating many bells down*?

ACTIVITY 39

Try and work out what is happening to the grammar in the following further extract of verse by e e cummings:

> *when by now and tree by leaf*
> *she laughed his joy she cried his grief*
> *bird by snow and stir by still*
> *anyone's any was all to her*

Answers to Activities

Activity 5

can /a/	feel /i:/	cook /u/	ladder /a/ + /ə/
soup /u:/	bark /a:/	rope /ou/	choice /oi/
born /o:/	learn /ə:/	lunch /ʌ/ or /u/	palm /a:/
song /o/	safe /ei/	tough /ʌ/ or /u/	lisk /i/
send /e/	peace /i:/	bought /o:/	affair /ə/ + /eə/

Activity 6

piece /pi:s/	cream /kri:m/	youth /ju:θ/
fad /fad/	shore /ʃo:/	happy /hapi:/
lurch /lə:tʃ/	clothe /klouð/	binge /bindʒ/
mouth /mauθ/	good /gu:d/	frequent /fri:kwənt/
joy /dʒoi/	stretch /stretʃ/	station /steiʃən/
wrong /roŋ/	weave /wi:v/	thankful /θaŋkfəl/

Activity 7

standard /'stan-dəd/	newspaper /nju:z-pei-pə/
decision /di-si-ʒən/	procedure /prə-si:-dʒə/
police /pə-li:s/	circular /sə:-kjə-lə/
asteroid /a-stə-roid/	entertainment /en-tə-tein-mənt/
screamed /skri:md/	premillennial /pri:-mi-le-njəl/
television /te-lə-vi-ʒən/	sparkling /spa:-kliŋ/ or /spa:k-liŋ/
vanquished /van-kwiʃt/	planetary /pla-nə-tə-ri/
envelope /en-və-loup/	

Activity 8

slot machine /slot məʃi:n/ – /slop məʃi:n/
wine bottle /wain botəl/ – /waim botl/
lead weight /led weit/ – /leb weit/
list price /list prais/ – /lis prais/
wet but happy /wet bət hapi:/ – /wep bət api:/
ten past four /ten pa:st fo:/ – /tem pa:s fo:/
sent by post /sent bai poust/ – /sem bi poust/
on this shelf /on ðis ʃelf/ – /on diʃ ʃelf/
a slight cold in the head /ə slait kould in ðə hed/ – /ə slaik kould in ði ed/
don't lose your way /dount lu:z jo: wei/ – /doun lu:z jə wei/

Activity 10

1

safety /'seifti:/	security /si'kjuriti/
safari /sə'fa:ri:/	segregate /'segrəgeit/
salute /sə'lu:t/	sensational /sen'seiʃənəl/
sandwich /'sandwitʃ/	sentimental /senti'mentəl/
satisfaction /satis'fakʃən/	serenade /serə'neid/
saxophone /'saksəfoun/	sociology /sousi'olədʒi/

2   **a** SALT
     b STAtion
     c AUNty
     d exerCISE
     e GRASS

Activity 14

feet: change of vowel from /u/ to /i:/

mice: change of vowel from /au/ to /ai/

oxen: addition of -en suffix

teeth: change of vowel from /u:/ to /i:/

men: change of vowel from /a/ to /e/

children: addition of -en (perhaps -ren) suffix, and change of pronunciation of root /tʃaild/ to /tʃild/

cacti: change of ending from -us to -i (Latin plural)

criteria: change of ending from -on to -a (Greek plural)

indices: change of ending from -ex to -ices (Latin plural)

corpora: change of ending from -us to -ora (Latin plural)

Activity 15

sing	sings	sang	sung
see	sees	saw	seen
take	takes	took	taken
bring	brings	brought	brought
tell	tells	told	told
stand	stands	stood	stood
wear	wears	wore	worn
think	thinks	thought	thought
speak	speaks	spoke	spoken

Activity 16

great: greater greatest
bad: worse worst
attractive: more/most attractive
honest: more/most honest
nasty: nastier nastiest
good: better best
free: freer freest
cruel: crueller cruellest
lovely: lovelier loveliest
handsome: handsomer handsomest or more/most handsome
timid: more/most timid

Activity 17

1   pompously (-*ly* adverb)
2   again (simple adverb)
3   moreover (conjunctive adverb)
4   just (simple adverb), off (adverb particle)
5   up (adverb particle), easily (-*ly* adverb)

Activity 18

1   'I' should be 'me': objective case after preposition 'to'
2   'Me' should be 'I': subjective case as subject of sentence
3   'Her' should be 'she': subjective case needed
4   'them' is used instead of the demonstrative 'those'
5   'us' usually used in such expressions as a singular, so 'me'

Activity 20

1   She (personal pronoun) ran (verb) along (preposition) the (definite article)
     river (noun) bank (noun)
2   A (indefinite article) strange (adjective) sensation (noun) suddenly (adverb)
     came (verb) over (preposition) him (personal pronoun)
3   They (personal pronoun) are (auxiliary verb) always (adverb) asking (verb)
     for (preposition) clarification (noun) of (preposition) our (possessive
     determiner) aims (noun)
4   Our (possessive determiner) holiday (noun) has (auxiliary verb) been (verb)
     an (indefinite article) exhausting (adjective) but (coordinating conjunction)
     delightful (adjective) experience (noun)
5   He (personal pronoun) can (modal auxiliary verb) come (verb) for
     (preposition) this (demonstrative determiner) interview (noun) if
     (subordinating conjunction) it (personal pronoun) can (modal auxiliary verb)
     be (auxiliary verb) held (verb) next (adjective) Friday (noun)

Activity 21

   adviser: advise (verb root), -er (derivational suffix, changes verb to noun)
   blamelessly: blame (noun root), -less (derivational suffix, changes noun to
   adjective), -ly (derivational suffix, changes adjective to adverb)
   classifies: class (noun root), -ify (derivational suffix, changes noun to verb),
   -es (inflectional suffix, third-person singular present tense)
   ensnaring: snare (noun root), en- (derivational prefix, changes noun to verb),
   -ing (inflectional suffix, present participle)
   generalisation: general (adjective root), -ise (derivational suffix, changes
   adjective to verb), -ation (derivational suffix, changes verb to noun)
   interminable: terminate (verb root), -able (derivational suffix, changes verb to
   adjective), in- (derivational prefix, negative)

misspelt: spell (verb root), mis- (derivational prefix, 'badly'), -t (inflectional suffix, past tense/past participle)

postmodernists: modern (adjective root), -ist (derviational suffix, changes adjective to noun), post- (derivational prefix, 'after'), -s (inflectional suffix, plural)

slavery: slave (noun root), -ery (derivational suffix, changes concrete to abstract noun)

thankfulness: thank(s) (noun root), -ful (derivational suffix, changes noun to adjective), -ness (derivational suffix, changes adjective into noun)

unfortunately: fortune (noun root), -ate (derivational suffix, changes noun to adjective), -ly (derivational suffix, changes adjective to adverb), un- (derivational prefix, negative)

vocalist: voice (noun root), -al (derivational suffix, changes noun to adjective), -ist (derivational suffix, changes adjective to agent noun)

Activity 24

1　For example –
keep: retain (formal)
voter: elector (formal)
money: bread (slang), dosh (informal)
hubris: pride (neutral)
yell: bawl (pejorative)
commence: start (less formal)

2　sharp: blunt (gradable)
parent: child (converse)
quiet: noisy (gradable)
guilty: innocent (complementary)
superior: inferior (converse)
opaque: transparent (gradable)

3　furniture: chair, table, sofa, stool and so on
crockery: dish, plate, bowl, cup, saucer and so on
fish: halibut, plaice, trout, salmon and so on

Activity 26

1　subject/verb/object
2　subject/verb
3　subject/verb/object/object
4　subject/verb/complement
5　subject/verb/object
6　subject/verb/object/complement
7　subject/verb
8　subject/verb/complement
9　subject/verb/object
10　subject/verb/object/complement

Activity 27

'da' = definite article, 'ia' = indefinite article, 'id' = identifier, 'poss' = possessive, 'dem' = demonstrative, 'qu' = quantifier, 'adj' = adjective, 'nm' = noun modifier, 'n' = noun, 'pron' = pronoun

1   the (da) famous (adj) brass (nm) band (n); a (ia) slow (adj) military (adj) march (n)

2   your (poss.id) younger (adj) sister (n); these (dem.id) valuable (adj) old (adj) records (n)

3   the (da) first (qu) six (qu) people (n); the (da) red (adj) London (nm) bus (n)

4   I (pron); the (da) police (nm) officer (n); the (da) whole (qu) truth (n)

5   they (pron); Spielberg's (poss.n) latest (adj) film (n)

Activity 28

1   are operating: present: are (progressive auxiliary), operating (main verb – present participle)

2   don't need: present: do (dummy 'do'), not (negative), need (main verb)

3   have been pestered: present: have (perfect auxiliary), been (passive auxiliary – past participle), pestered (main verb – past participle)

4   is talking: present: is (progressive auxiliary), talking (main verb – present participle)

5   could have paid: past: could (modal auxiliary), have (perfect auxiliary), paid (main verb – past participle)

6   will be calling in: present: will (modal auxiliary – with future meaning), be (progressive auxiliary), calling in (main verb (phrasal) – present participle)

Activity 29

1   from holiday (place: prepositional phrase); tomorrow (time: adverb)

2   carefully (manner: adverb), into the postbox (place: prepositional phrase)

3   due to the rail strike (reason: prepositional phrase), until Monday (time: prepositional phrase)

4   On Saturday (time: prepositional phrase), for charity (purpose: prepositional phrase)

5   by coach (means: prepositional phrase), from Santander (place: prepositional phrase), along the coast (place: prepositional phrase), to San Sebastian (place: prepositional phrase)

Activity 30

1   who could have told you that: subject of 'remains'

2   before you operate the machine: adverbial (of time)

3   winning the poetry prize: complement after 'was'

4   which have lain derelict for years: adjectival (relative clause modifying 'sites')

5   to help you: object of 'like'

Activity 31

s = subject, v = verb, o = object, c = complement, a = adverbial, np = noun phrase,
vp = verb phrase, adj = adjective, prep phr = prepositional phrase,
inf cl = infinitive clause, -ing-cl = present participle clause, adv = adverb,
that cl = that clause

1   The foreign students (s:np) did not understand (v:vp) their teacher's humour
     (o:np)

2   These bottles (s:np) are (v:vp) empty (c:adj) and (conjunction) we (s:np) are
     taking (v:vp) them (o:np) to the bottle bank (a:prep phr)

3   The traffic warden (s:np) told (v:vp) me (oi:np) to park on the other side
     (od:inf cl)

4   you (s:np) have finished (v:vp) making fun of them (o:-ing-cl)

5   I (s:np) stupidly (a:adv) forgot (v:vp) that she had gone away (o:that cl)

Further reading

A number of series of introductory books on language analysis and description
are beginning to appear; for example, the 'Learning about Language' series from
Longman and the 'Language Workbooks' series from Routledge.

   Knowles (1987) and Ashby (1995) deal with pronunciation. Katamba (1994) is an
introductory text on 'words'. Hofmann (1993), Jackson (1988) and Hudson (1995)
explore lexicology and semantics. Jackson (1990) and Fabb (1994) investigate
sentences and their structure. Stenström (1994) and Salkie (1995) look at the
analysis of spoken discourse.

   The 'standard' account of English pronunciation is by the late A. C. Gimson, the
latest edition of which (the fifth) is Cruttenden (1994).

   The 'standard' account of English grammar is Quirk *et al.* (1985). It contains
1790 pages. An abbreviated version, of 528 pages, is Quirk and Greenbaum
(1990). Other reference grammars of a more manageable size include COBUILD
(1990) and Leech (1989). Both of these were written primarily for foreign learners
of English, but they are usable equally by native speakers.

   Another useful and affordable series of introductory reference books about the
study of language is the 'Penguin English Linguistics' series, including Crystal
(1992), Roach (1992) and Leech (1992). These books are essentially extended
glossaries. The contents are a list of terms in the area of language study covered
by the book, with explanations, examples and cross-references.

Suggested projects

We have attempted to propose in this chapter a description of the linguistic
system of English. The intention has been to make you aware of how English
works and to provide you with the tools of analysis for uncovering the structures
of language that you find in the discourses and texts of everyday life.

   Topics for projects arising from this chapter would, perhaps, most appropriately
focus on the nitty-gritty of language; the sounds of someone's accent, the
grammatical structures used in a newspaper's editorial, or the vocabulary and
syntax of a children's reading book.

To undertake such a project you need to:

> decide what linguistic feature or features you want to find out about
> collect appropriate and sufficient language data
> analyse the data for your chosen features
> present your results and describe what you have found
> discuss the conclusions that you can draw from your results

Suggestions for investigating pronunciation

1   Make up a short passage that contains at least one of all the vowels and consonants of English. Ask four or five friends to read the passage, and record them doing so. Also record your friends engaged in ordinary conversation. Listen to your recordings. What differences in pronunciation are there: (a) between each individual's reading and their spontaneous conversation; (b) among your friends?

2   Record a favourite presenter from the radio. Make a detailed description of their pronunciation. Do they have any features of pronunciation that are peculiar to them?

3   Record and listen carefully to a number of news bulletins. What use does the news reader make of intonation in order to give meaning to the news? Can you tell, for example, that a news item is going to be a 'disaster' story before you have heard all the words? You can try the same investigation with football results: Can you tell if a particular result is a win, lose or draw for the home side before you hear the second score?

Suggestions for investigating words

1   Take a broadsheet newspaper (for example, the *Guardian* or *Independent*) and a tabloid (for example, the *Daily Mail* or *Daily Mirror*). Examine a news story, a feature article and an editorial from each for the complexity of the vocabulary in terms of: number and types of simple words; derived words (with prefixes and suffixes); and compound words. What differences emerge between the newspapers, and between the different types of article?

2   Take two different types of text – for example, a novel and a legal document – of equal length in terms of number of words (say, 2000). Sort the words in the text according to word class (noun, verb, preposition and so on). You may want to make subdivisions; for instance, to distinguish types of pronoun – personal, relative and so on. How do the two texts compare? Is there a difference in the number and types of grammatical word (determiner, pronoun, preposition, conjunction) that are used?

3   Collect all the compound words from an edition of a newspaper, noting the type of text (news story, advertisement and so on) that each comes from. Attempt a classification of the compounds; for example, according to word class, according to complexity (two, three or four roots), or according to whether neoclassical, from native roots or a combination. Are there any differences between types of text?

Suggestions for investigating sentences

1   Take any text or pair of texts and examine them for different types of sentence structure, including: the basic patterns (subject/verb, subject/verb/complement, subject/verb/object and so on); number, type and position of adverbials; and number, type (that-clause, -ing-clause and so on) and function (subject, object and so on) of subordinate clauses.

2   Take a newspaper news story, an extract from a novel and an article from an encyclopaedia. Examine the noun phrases, particularly the number and types of modifiers. Do any have more than one adjective in a noun phrase? What use is made of noun modifiers? Are there modifiers after the noun – relative clauses, prepositional phrases and so on?

3   Take any more extensive text and examine it for a particular grammatical feature; for example, prepositional phrases, adverbials, that-clauses, modal verbs or questions. How many and what types are used – and in what kinds of context and for what purpose?

Suggestions for investigating discourses and texts

1   Record a naturally occurring conversation or a chat-show from the radio. Observe how the conversation is managed: Does someone allocate the turns, and do they do it in an obvious way or by implication? How do transitions between speakers occur: what are the linguistic clues? How is the conversation structured: what topics are talked about and how do the participants move on from one topic to another?

2   Take two different types of text – for example, a newspaper editorial and an extract from a novel. Examine the cohesive devices used in the two texts and make a comparison. Does one use more grammatical types of cohesion? What use is made of pronouns?

3   Take a short story as an example of a narrative text and the *Highway Code* as an example of an instructive text. Compare them for linguistic features that reflect their text type and purpose; for example, tense of verbs, types of adverbials, use of subordinate clauses, modal verbs, adjectives and so on.

The changing English language

3.0 Introduction

As long as a language has living speakers (as do more than 4000 languages in the world today), then it is subject to change and development over time. For linguistic study, there are two aspects to this. The first concerns the formal, structural changes in the actual usage of the language, as far as these historical patterns can be deduced from the range of evidence available. The second aspect is concerned with the attitude of people throughout history towards the language that they and their ancestors spoke.

Both of these aspects are important for a thorough account of the history of English. Changes in the formal pattern of English have often provoked strong reactions amongst users of the language. And those reactions have often also had an effect on the shape of the language as it has come down to us at the turn of the second millennium. It is therefore necessary to consider both the actual changes and the attitudes to change together. This is the orientation of this chapter.

3.1 The prehistory of English

The language of English, distinct from its related Germanic languages, has been around for about 1500 years. The language of the Angles (*Englisc*) had its roots in the West Germanic communities which invaded the British Isles after the Roman occupying army had left (by about the year AD 400).

3.1.1 Linguistic detective work

Apart from the past hundred years, since recording equipment has enabled linguists to hear exactly how the language is spoken, our notion of English speech of the past 1500 years has largely been derived from documentary sources. Literary texts, with patterned rhyme, rhythm or alliteration, are very useful sources of evidence. The linguist can also be helped by contemporary grammar books, treatises on rhetoric or reflections on the speech of others across the country or in comparison with foreigners. Thus, poetry, travel accounts, prayers, sermons, saints' lives, church court records and chronicles can all provide clues to the state of the spoken language of the past. Using a few principles of language sound changes and these sources of data, the process of detective work can extrapolate backwards to the times from which there are few surviving written records.

3.1.2 Cognates

It is also possible to compile an idea of the languages that were around before even the earliest documentary manuscripts. For example, if the word for a common object is similar in two distant languages across the world, then it is likely that the two languages share a common ancestry and a common root word in an older language. Such related words are called **cognate** words, and cognates are the key to the reconstruction of old, unrecorded languages.

3.1.3 The earliest language

It is not known whether language originally developed close to the emergence of humanity in East Africa and the Middle East, spreading with the migration of people across the world, and diverging into regional or tribal variations to form different languages. Or perhaps the ability to use language developed almost simultaneously among different groups of humans, and different languages emerged over the centuries. It is unlikely that we will ever know the answer to this, and all of the earliest forms of spoken language are lost to us.

3.1.4 Language families

However, origins can be traced back into the relatively recent past. Modern languages which show similarities are grouped into language 'families', such as the Malayo-Polynesian languages of the Pacific, or the Dravidian languages of southern India, or Semitic, Japanese, Sino-Tibetan and Indo-European. Many of the modern languages of Europe belong to the Indo-European group of languages. Figure 4 shows the Indo-European group as a 'family tree', which is the most common form of presentation in linguistics textbooks.

3.1.5 The Indo-European group

As you can see, English belongs to the West Germanic group of languages, a branch which also includes High and Low German, Yiddish, Dutch, Flemish and Frisian. These are closely related to Gothic, Icelandic, Norwegian, Danish and Swedish. On another branch, Celtic languages include Scottish and Irish Gaelic, and Welsh. The Italic branch includes Latin, and its varieties of Portuguese, Spanish, French, Italian and Romanian. Greek belongs to the Hellenic line. Further distant relations of English include Polish, Russian, Persian, Sanskrit and its derivations Hindi and Bengali.

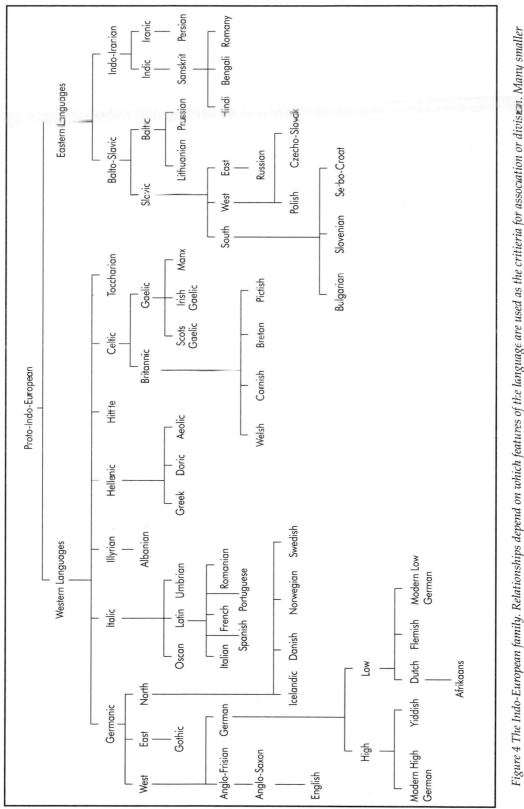

Figure 4 The Indo-European family. Relationships depend on which features of the language are used as the criteria for association or division. Many smaller languages have been omitted here: such language maps are determined as much by typesetting limitations as by linguistic factors.

The 'family tree' metaphor, however, can be very misleading. It implies that one language above another on the diagram pre-dates the second language and gave way to it, which is not necessarily the case. The diagram does not present contemporaneous periods as does a family tree. Moreover, the neat lines and branches imply a neat progression from one language into the next. In reality, as will be evident from this chapter, linguistic change is often a messy business, with different levels of the language, areas of the country and groups of speakers changing features at differing rates. Also, languages lower down the tree do not always replace those above; for example, high German coexists with Dutch in Europe today.

Finally, it would be wrong to assume the direct development from parent languages that the family tree suggests. In the case of English, for example, the basis is Germanic, but the language stands as it does today with strong influences from, among many others, Danish, French, Latin, Greek, Gaelic, and recently Hindi and Bengali. Perhaps lines should be drawn across the family tree to show that English is only Germanic in origin – and this is without accounting for influences from non-Indo-European languages on American English, Indian English, Australian English and the various African Englishes. Many of these influences will be discussed in the sections below.

3.1.6 Extrapolating from sound-change patterns

The unifying case for an Indo-European group of languages emerged at the beginning of the nineteenth century when linguists noticed similarities between European languages and Sanskrit, the ancient language of India. Very common words showed the most similarity: *father* (English), *vater* (German), *pater* (Greek) and *pitar* (Sanskrit). Jacob Grimm (the fairy-tale writer and linguist) showed how various sound changes across these languages operated on a regular and predictable pattern. Words originally with /p/, /t/, /k/ are altered to /f/, /θ/, /h/ in the Germanic languages. Latin and Greek retained the older voiceless stops in words such as *piscis* (fish), *tres* (three) and *centum* (with a hard /k/) (hundred). Furthermore, the sounds /b/, /d/, /g/ changed regularly in the Germanic languages to /p/, /t/, /k/. This supported the case that there was a common language, or set of closely related dialects, called Indo-European (sometimes called *Aryan* in older textbooks, but now avoided for obvious political reasons).

3.1.7 Extrapolating from lexical patterns

It is estimated that the primary branches (Celtic, Indo-Iranian and so on) of Indo-European were becoming established independently of each other by around 3000 BC. Archaeological and reconstructed linguistic evidence draws a picture of a settled, agricultural people. Technology was at the stage of using copper as a material, and tools and implements were used in subsistence farming. Common cognate words across various languages for *snow, winter, oak, beech, pine, deer, rabbit, bee* and many more put the Indo-European homeland in temperate central-eastern Europe. This is reinforced by the lack of common words for objects that would have been encountered and lexicalised later by migrating people: *elephant, rice, crocodile, monkey* and so on.

The existence of cognates and the predictive power of sound-change patterns allowed linguists to reconstruct a dictionary of Indo-European, and even a (more hypothetical) grammar. However, it is still unclear whether Proto-Indo-European was ever a single language of a coherent speech community, and it has even been suggested that it was originally a pidgin that allowed communication between nomadic peoples, and which subsequently developed into various fully realised native languages.

3.1.8 Early Celtic languages in the British Isles

It is unlikely that this version of Indo-European was ever spoken in the British Isles, the wild, far-flung and backward islands on the edge of the continent, where the Stone Age lasted until as late as 2000 BC. The language of these neolithic communities is lost, apart from some speculation that the language of the Basques in northern Spain is a remnant of it.

Celtic speakers spread into the British Isles from 1500 BC, and eventually displaced all trace of the native languages. The first wave came from northern Europe and their *Brythonic* dialect was spoken wherever these *Brythons* settled on the mainland. This dialect is now usually called *Britannic* Celtic, and the Britons are the ancestral speakers of later Cornish, Welsh, Breton and Pictish. Later, *Goidelic* Celts left southern France and settled in Ireland, and their dialect of Celtic came to be called *Gaelic*. It is the ancestor of Irish Gaelic, Manx, and of Scots Gaelic after a Celtic-speaking community called the Scotti left Ireland and settled in the northern mainland thereafter called Scotland.

Traces of the Celtic period of British history remain today in those parts of the islands that were the last to be influenced by the later Roman, Germanic and French invasions – the far north and west. Geographical terms from Celtic languages fill the landscapes of Scotland, Ireland, northern England, Wales and Cornwall. The hill (*tor*) at Torquay, churches (*llan*) in Llandudno and Llangollen, homesteads (*tre*) at Tredegar and Tralee, the river estuaries (*aber*) at Abergavenny and Aberdeen, the high forts (*dun/dum*) of Dundee and Dumfries, hill-tops (*pen*) at Pendle and Pen-y-ghent, deep valleys (*cwm/coombe*) in Cwmbran and Babbacombe – all of these keep their Celtic origins. The hard /k/ of *Kent* is one of the few traces that it was once a Celtic kingdom. The major British rivers often have names corrupted from the Celtic: the *Tamesa* still flows through London, the *Trinanton* crosses the East Midlands through Nottingham, and the *Tisa* still characterises the landscape of Teesdale. The names of the rivers *Esk*, *Exe*, *Usk* and *Avon* are themselves words meaning 'river'.

3.1.9 The effect of the Romans

The linguistic landscape of Britain began to change with 400 years of Roman occupation. Julius Caesar's initial raids around 55 BC were almost complete military disasters, but Claudius' invasion of AD 43 established a Roman occupying force, whose administrators spoke Latin, and whose army comprised Latin-speaking soldiers and auxiliary troops speaking a variety of contemporary European languages.

In the following four centuries, Celtic Britain became Romanised, although this occupation is unusual in that the effects were largely architectural and administrative rather than linguistic. There is no evidence that the mass of the population ever came to speak Latin, even as a poor second language. It seems that the Romans were concerned to keep their cultural knowledge to themselves. Latin was the language of control and government. The technology of systematic battle-plans, the geometrically precise and well-built road network, fortresses and defences, especially in the north, which remained a militarised zone, all represented control as well. It is significant that, after the Roman army left in 410, the Britons were unable or unwilling to maintain the masonry of the villas, baths and temples. The roads fell into disrepair, and buildings were looted for their stone. New villages developed beside old Roman towns. It seems that Roman knowledge and culture were lost with the occupying force; one later poem describes the remains of the Romans as 'the work of giants'.

The main effect of British Romanisation was in the establishment of what eventually came to be seen as an indigenous Christian religion. Although Celtic-speaking Irish monks and missionaries spread the Christian message in the north, they were largely able to do so because of the stability that the Roman administration provided in the south. Roman dominance was encouraged (and illustrated) by the decision of the Whitby Synod to follow Roman customs in monastic rule. The Church was left with Latin as its main ceremonial and organisational language. Even Bede's later (eighth-century) *Ecclesiastical History of the English People* was written in Latin (*Historia Ecclesiastica Gentis Anglorum*). However, Latin disappeared as a vernacular and secular language in Britain when the Roman army withdrew.

3.1.10 The Germanic influence

It is Bede who gives an account of the first Germanic invasions into the east of Britain in 449. Over the following two centuries, groups from what is now Holland, northern Germany and Denmark settled along the east coast and river estuaries of Britain, where the landscape of the country made it especially easy to invade and settle. These groups, the Jutes, Angles, Saxons and Frisians, spoke various regional dialects of West Germanic, and they brought their language to the respective areas in which they settled.

At first, the Celtic Britons called all the invaders 'Saxons', since it was this group that began settling even in the last years of the Roman occupation. The Saxons largely drove Britons off land along the south coast, establishing their own occupancy. Various resistance efforts, including a temporarily successful one led by a Romanised Celt called Arthur, were overcome by the Germanic invaders' superior numbers and war technology, and by greater and more recent experience of resistance to the Romans on the continent.

The Jutes claimed most of the south-east, and the Angles those parts of the east coast further to the north. Later, the Germanic settlers were characterised generally as Angles, and their language became collectively known as *Englisc* (pronounced as the modern word). Settlement of the southeastern half of what by 1000 was being called *Engleland* was so complete that the Germanic speakers could even refer to the native Britons as *wealas* (eventually *Welsh*), meaning 'foreigners'!

The picture by 700 is of a divided Britain. Generally, the Celtic Britons were driven out to Ireland, Brittany and the north and west of mainland Britain. The Midlands, east and south were colonised by West Germanic speakers. Specifically, these groups spoke dialects of **Anglo-Saxon**, depending on where on the continent they had come from. West Saxon was spoken across the south (in

Wessex and Sussex). Kentish was spoken where the Jutes had settled. North of the Thames, the Anglian dialects of Mercian and Northumbrian dominated. It is from this time that documentary evidence survives, and the dialects are sufficiently similar to be considered as comprising an English language.

3.2 Old English/Anglo-Saxon

Traditionally, linguistics has been concerned to present itself as a scientific discipline, and so it has deployed all the paraphernalia of objectivity and precise categorisation. The English language is thus regarded as an object in its own right, gradually but regularly changing over time, with all the changes being explainable. So Old English is said to have existed from the fifth century AD to 1100, and Middle English until 1500, followed by the early and late periods of Modern English. More recently, the increased emphasis on sociolinguistics (see Chapter 5) and awareness of the ideological basis of even scientific discourse (see Section 6.3) have changed the way in which language history is perceived. Speech communities are more important than courts; classes are more significant than kings; war and disease and migration affect language more than politics does. Not only does this make historical language study more complex, but it also means that there is a variety of possible explanations for specific changes. The rest of this chapter, for the sake of clarity, will first present an overview of changes in English, followed by discussion of some of the issues involved.

The Germanic dialects spoken by the settlers varied mainly in their word-endings (**inflections**) and in the vowels used in the middle of words. Over time, these differences disappeared, although the variations between Middle English dialects can be traced back to the original differences in Anglo-Saxon.

3.2.1 The case system

In contrast to Modern English, Anglo-Saxon was a **case** language. Whereas Modern English uses word-order and prepositions to indicate the function of words (for example, subject, object and so on) in a sentence, Anglo-Saxon used **inflections** (see also Section 2.2.2 for a reminder on this). Inflections are suffixes that identify the case of the noun, whether subject, object, possessive or indirect object/instrument. The cases associated with these functions are known respectively as the nominative, accusative, genitive and dative cases. All nouns had to have the right one of the 4 possible case endings. Additionally, Anglo-Saxon nouns had 3 grammatical genders: masculine, feminine and neuter. And (as in Modern English) it differentiated singular and plural. Nouns could thus have 24 ($4 \times 3 \times 2$) possible permutations, although in practice several of the permutations happen to have the same inflectional ending, making the **declension** table less complex than it might at first appear.

Adjectives had to 'agree' in form with the nouns they qualified for case, gender and number, as did definite articles. Thus, in the sentence, *Se ealda cyning clippeþ þā godan cwene* (*The old king kisses the good queen*), the Anglo-Saxon definite article *se* (for *the*), the adjective ending of *ealda* and the zero-inflection (no suffix) on *cyning* indicate that it is the king doing the kissing, rather than the queen. The inflections for *þā* (*the*), *godan* and *cwene*, all in the accusative, indicate that it is the queen that is the object of the kissing.

ACTIVITY 40
A crash-course in Old English grammar

The tables below show the declensions (that is, the possible permutations) for the words in *Se ealda cyning clippeþ þā godan cwene*. Every noun phrase must 'agree' grammatically (that is, be in the same case, number and gender).

Nouns:

		Masculine *king*	Feminine *queen*	Neuter *child*
Singular	Nominative	*cyning*	cwen	bearn
	Accusative	cyning	*cwene*	bearn
	Genitive	cyninges	cwene	bearnes
	Dative	cyninge	cwene	bearne
Plural	Nominative	cyningas	cwena	bearn
	Accusative	cyningas	cwena	bearn
	Genitive	cyninga	cwena	bearna
	Dative	cyningum	cwenum	bearnum

Adjectives (when with an article *the*) – *old* and *good*:

		Masculine	Feminine	Neuter
Singular	Nominative	*ealda*/goda	ealde/gode	ealde/gode
	Accusative	ealdan/godan	ealdan/*godan*	ealde/gode
	Genitive	ealdan/godan	ealdan/godan	ealdan/godan
	Dative	ealdan/godan	ealdan/godan	ealdan/godan
Plural	Nominative	ealdan/godan	ealdan/godan	ealdan/godan
	Accusative	ealdan/godan	ealdan/godan	ealdan/godan
	Genitive	ealdra/godra	ealdra/godra	ealdra/godra
	Dative	ealdum/godum	ealdum/godum	ealdum/godum

Articles – 'the':

		Masculine	Feminine	Neuter
Singular	Nominative	*se*	sēo	þæt
	Accusative	þone	*þā*	þæt
	Genitive	þæs	þǣre	þæs
	Dative	þǣm	þǣre	þǣm
Plural	Nominative	þā	þā	þā
	Accusative	þā	þā	þā
	Genitive	þāra	þāra	þāra
	Dative	þǣm	þǣm	þǣm

Verbs (this is a simplification of the several verb classes) – *clippan*, to kiss:					
Present	I	clippe	Past	I	clippede
	You (sg.)	clippest		You (sg.)	clippedest
	S/he	*clippeþ*		S/he	clippede
	We	clippaþ		We	clippedon
	You (pl.)	clippaþ		You (pl.)	clippedon
	They	clippaþ		They	clippedon

As you can see, there is much repetition of possible endings here (although this is a very simplified version of Old English grammar).
Use the tables to translate the following sentences:

1 The queen kisses the king.

2 The good child loves (infinitive *lufian*) the old queen.

3 The king's child was (verb *wæs*) good.

4 The queen brought (past *brohte*) the king to the children.

See page 100 for the answers.

Have a go at making your own sentences in Old English, using the words here. Remember that every word in the noun phrase (noun, adjectives and articles) must agree for gender, number and case.

You could have a look at some Old English poetry and prose. *The Voyage of Ohthere and Wulfstan* is easy prose reading. *The Dream of the Rood, The Wanderer* and *The Seafarer* are powerful short Anglo-Saxon poems, and *Beowulf* is the most famous long poem. Old English riddles (often pandering to the bawdy sensibilities of the times) are still entertaining. Parallel (that is, word-for-word) translations are available. Try and write a critical analysis of the literary text, focusing on the style of the piece.

The great advantage over Modern English is that this system does not rely on word-order for meaning. Thus, *Đa godan cwene clippeþ se ealda cyning* **still** means *The old king kisses the good queen*. The order in which the writer might want to place the words was much more flexible as a result, a feature which Anglo-Saxon poetry took full advantage of in arranging words stylistically to produce its characteristic powerful alliterative rhythm. This is illustrated by the texts in Activity 41 below.

3.2.2 Surviving remnants of the case system

Many of the variously declined articles and pronouns survived into later forms of English. Here are some of the survivors:

> *þā* (feminine accusative, plural nominative and accusative definite article) became *the*

> *ðæm* (dative plural article) became *them*

> *ðis* (demonstrative pronoun) became *this*

ic (nominative first-person pronoun) became *I*

wē (plural second-person pronoun) survived intact

mē and *ūs* (accusatives), and *mīn* and *ūre* (genitives) all remain in Modern English forms

ðū (singular nominative) became *thou* (singular)

ðē (singular accusative) became *thee*

ðīn (singular genitive) became *thine*

(these three remained until the sixteenth century and continue in some modern dialects)

gē (plural nominative) became *you* (plural)

ēow (plural accusative) became *you* (plural)

ēower (plural genitive) became *your*

(some regional accents of Modern English even preserve the earlier pronunciations)

Many inflectional endings left remnants in a final *-e* or *-a* well into the Middle English period, long after the case system had become archaic, and printing fossilised these spellings long after the final vowels had stopped being pronounced. One of the few remains of the genitive case surviving into Modern English is the singular masculine and neuter noun inflectional ending *-es*, which has been abbreviated with an apostrophe (*'s*) to show the omission of the *e*.

Anglo-Saxon verbs can be divided into two sets, which persist into Modern English. Weak (also called *regular*) verbs showed past tense by the addition of the suffix, *-ede*, *-od* or *-d*, to the stem. This becomes the Modern English *-ed*, as in *talk/talked*, *look/looked* and so on. Strong (or *irregular*) verbs express the past tense by altering the root vowel to show the perfect past and past participle forms. This remains in Modern English verbs such as *drive/drove/driven*, *sing/sang/sung*, *steal/stole/stolen*, *fall/fell/fallen* and so on. The strong form was probably the system used in Proto-Indo-European. The more modern weak system is the usual method of making past forms for new modern words (*rocketed*, *rubbished*, *rapped* and so on).

3.2.3 Word-formation in Old English

The formation of new words (or **lexicalisation**) is one of the most noticeable features of Anglo-Saxon, and one which illustrates its Germanic origins. Existing words were joined together, as **compounds** (see Section 2.2.4). Such lexicalisations in Old English are known as **kennings**, and these noun-compounds can be found especially in the poetry. Thus, *mere-stape* (sea-walker) signifies a *ship* and *mōdhord* (heart-treasure) is *understanding*. Prefix and suffix addition also extended the lexical range of the language: *mis-*, *of-*, *under-*, *ofer-* and *-ig*, *-full*, *-leas* (-less), *-lice* (-like). These remain major methods of lexicalisation in Modern English (as discussed in Section 2.2.3).

ACTIVITY 41
Old English texts

1   *The Lord's Prayer*

> *Fæder ūre,*
> *þū þe eart on heofonum,*
> *sy þīn nama gehālgod,*
> *Tōbecume þīn rīce.*
> *Gewurþe ðīn willa on eorðan swā swā on heofonum.*
> *Syle ūs tō daeg ūrne gedæghwamlican hlāf.*
> *And forgyf ūs ūre gyltas, swā swā wē forgyfað ūrum gyltendum.*
> *And ne lād ðū ūs on costnunge,*
> *ac ālȳs ūs of yfele.*
> > *Sōþlīce.*

Read aloud, this sounds more like the modern version than it looks. Try and identify some of the case-endings from the tables in Activity 40. Horizontal lines above vowels lengthen the pronunciation. ð and þ (and the capital Ð) are voiced and unvoiced *th*. The æ is called *ash* and is a short low /a/. The c is usually hard /k/, unless initially in a word, such as *cild* (as modern *child*). The *sc*, as in *Englisc*, is /ʃ/, as our modern pronunciation. Try to identify modern derivations of the words.

2   *Caedmon's Hymn*

This was originally composed in the Northumbrian dialect in the seventh century (by a shepherd in Whitby, according to Bede), but the first version here is from the late eighth century. The second is a copy written in the West Saxon dialect of the tenth century.

   Notice the dialectal differences and the later simplification of word-endings. Make a list of these and see if you can find their origins and meanings in an Old English dictionary.

   If you read it aloud you will also notice the powerful alliteration across the two halves of each line, which is allowed by the highly manoeuvrable syntax, and which gives Old English poetry its wonderful force.

   You could try to write a poem in Modern English in which both halves of the line alliterate with each other, to see how difficult this is in Modern English with its relatively fixed rules about word order.

> *Northumbrian Caedmon's Hymn*
>
> | *Nū* | *scylun* | *hergan* | *hefaenrīcaes* | | *uard* |
> | Now | should | to praise | of the heavenly kingdom | | guardian |
> | *metudæs* | *maecti* | *end* | *his* | *mōdgidanc* | |
> | of God | power | and | his | counsel | |
> | *uerc* | *uulderfadur* | | *suē* | *hē* | *uundra* | *gihuaes* |
> | work | of the glorious father | | as | he | of wonders | of every |
> | *ēci* | *Dryctin* | *ōr* | | *āstelidæ.* | |
> | eternal | Lord | beginning | | established | |
> | *Hē* | *ærist* | *scōp* | *aelda* | *barnum* | |
> | He | first | shaped | of men | for children | |
> | *heben* | *til* | *hrōfe* | *hāleg* | *scepen.* | |
> | heaven | as | a roof | holy | shaper | |

Thā   *middungeard*   *moncynnæs*   *uard*
Then   *middle-earth*   *of mankind*   *guardian*
ēci   *Dryctin*   *æfter*   *tīadæ*
eternal   *Lord*   *afterwards*   *established*
fīrum   *foldu*   *frēa*   *allmectig.*
for men   *earth*   *Lord*   *almighty.*

West Saxon Caedmon's Hymn

Nū scylen herian heofon-rīces weard
metodes meaht and his mōdgeþanc,
weorc wuldorfæder; swā hē wundra gehwæs
ēce Dryhten, ōr astellede,
Hē ǣrest scōp ielda bearnum
heofon til hrōfe, hālig scepen.
Đā middangeard, moncynnes weard,
ēce Dryhten, æfter tēode
fīrum folde, frēa ealmihtig.

Now we must praise the guardian of the heavenly kingdom,
for the power and counsel of God,
for the works of the father of glory; as he,
eternal Lord of wonders, created everything in the beginning.
He first made, for the children of men,
heaven as a roof, the holy Creator.
Then in this middle-place, the eternal Lord,
the guardian of mankind, afterwards established
the earth for men, Lord almighty.

3.2.4 The loss of inflections and Danish influence

Towards the end of the Anglo-Saxon period (ninth to eleventh centuries), the general trend was towards simplification of inflectional variation. Different suffixes tended towards a similar central vowel /ə/. Danish influence came from a series of Viking invasions and settlement along the east coast, and the large numbers of Danish speakers then in England affected the language. Many Danish words had the same root as the Anglo-Saxon, but different inflections, and so the inflectional endings came to be assimilated to aid communication. At the same time, the area of the Danelaw (the north and east) began to bear elements of Danish in place-names. The word *by*, meaning *town*, is suffixed to many English places, and survives in *by-laws*. Isolated land (*thwaites*), small territories (*tofts*) and villages (*thorps*) scatter East Anglia, the East Midlands and the North.

ACTIVITY 42
Linguistic archaeology
Using a map of Britain with detail of village place-names, plot the areas of linguistic influence: the extent of the Danelaw, the Celtic strongholds, and the types of habitation across the country. Remember that the spellings of towns and villages may have varied during the intervening millennium.

Celtic

cwm/combe/cum – valley
dun/dum – hill fort
bal – hamlet
tre – homestead
lan – church
pen – summit
afon – river
aber – river-mouth
bre/bar/tor – hill
crag – cliff
pill – tidal inlet
brocc – badger

Anglo-Saxon

ton/tun – enclosure
wic/wick – dairy farm
ham – village
ing – follower
rod/rode – cross
(From Roman Latin:)
port – sea-landing
burg/brough/bury/
  berry – fort
caster/cester/chester/
  castle – walled town

Scandinavian/Danish

toft – house
vik – inlet (hence, 'viking' – follower of inlets)
thorpe – farm
stoke – holy place
by – village

What do the names of towns and cities tell you about them, in terms of their history, location, geographical features, population, main industries and so on? What differences would there be in the naming of Britain if our history were different? Try out these, or your own, scenarios:

1 Nazi Germany successfully invaded Britain in 1941 and began to rename every British city, town and village to restore the ancestral 'Anglo-Saxon' racial language to the landscape.

2 The Victorian Industrial Revolution created many more new towns alongside its rail and canal industrial centres, and steam-powered computers were perfected and built near where you live.

3 The Normans never invaded England and there was subsequently no French influence on the language.

4 A system of human-body defence was developed by the Romans so that castles and forts were never invented.

5 The Celtic-speaking Britons successfully repelled both the Romans and the Germanic tribes, so that everywhere retains Celtic names. Or, conversely, the Celtic people were wiped out completely even from Ireland, Scotland, Wales and Cornwall. Try to rename the towns in these regions on sound principles.

Update and modernise the place-names of the British Isles: so that you would visit *Oldcastle-upon-Tyne*, exchange *Blackpool* for *Dublin*, send for your driving licence to *Pigtown*, and so on. What modern features of the places near where you live could be used to rename them: *chemicalworktown, motorwaycrossing, hillside, southriverbank* and so on?

The Danish settlement (and the succession of Danish kings of England from Cnut in 1014) had a great effect on English. The pronunciation of /sk/ rather than /ʃ/ in words such as *sky, skin, skirt* rather than *scip, flesc, shirt* shows the former group's Danish origins. In Danish-influenced areas, such as Northumbria, the final -*s* inflection for third-person singular present tense (*he runs*) entered English and began to replace the Anglo-Saxon -*eþ* form (*he runneth*). The present participle ending -*ing* similarly replaced -*and*. Both of these innovations spread south over the next six centuries. Many words were borrowed. The agricultural, trading, commercial and 'day-to-day' domain of many of these words indicates a relatively peaceful integration of Danes and English.

In spite of the popular image of Viking invasions, the linguistic evidence is testimony to Danish integration into England at all but the political level. Anglo-Saxon king Alfred's success or (eventual actual) failure in permanently repelling the Danes would probably have made no difference to the ordinary rural accommodations being made by the people, who shared much of the law, customs, Christian religion and aspects of Germanic language anyway.

Of much greater linguistic importance was the period which began with the Norman-French invasion of England after 1066.

3.3 Middle English

It is difficult to convey the absolute disaster that the Norman Conquest was for English culture. Following it, the country was linguistically split for two centuries; official or valued literature written in English disappeared; the English court produced a wealth of literary, religious and administrative documents in Latin and French; and English was regarded as a sign of the speaker's social inferiority.

3.3.1 The effect of Norman settlement

Before the Norman Conquest there had been some borrowing of French words into the law and administration, because of the close contact between the English and French ruling classes. However, in the years after the invasion, it was the English earls who led rebellions against William, and who were subsequently killed or exiled. Within a very short period, the nobility of the country was replaced by native Norman-French speakers. This applied to all the high positions in the Church as well. English remained the peasants' language, and by the twelfth century England had become a nation of two languages (**diglossic**), stratified by social class. Celtic languages were still spoken in Scotland, Wales and Cumbria, and a heavily Danish-influenced English in the North of England. The social stratification of English and Norman-French can be seen in the domains of words borrowed from French into English in this period. Most of our modern words of government, parliament, administration, law, ecclesiastical organisation, military structure and strategy, architecture and medicine were borrowed from French.

3.3.2 The re-establishment of English

Although English took on an enormous French influence, the fact that it was English rather than French that dominated and established itself as the national language through the thirteenth century has a number of explanations. First, the Norman-French rulers – although socially powerful – were in a numerical minority, and the influence of French speakers gradually diminished as the rising middle class gained in economic power. Also, in 1204, King John lost his lands in Normandy to France, and the English aristocracy had to decide to which king they would declare allegiance. Worsening relations with France, culminating in the Hundred Years' War (1337–1453), further consolidated the position of English in the ruling class.

At the same time, the English-speaking community became economically more powerful. Not only did the merchant classes govern England's growing towns, but the peasants became more socially important; ironically, as a result of the Black Death (from 1348) which made labour a scarce resource. Estimates put the death rate at its height at 30% of the population, and – as with all contagious diseases – the burden fell more heavily on the poor. The lower clergy, preaching in English, came to speak Latin and English, rather than the increasingly unnecessary French. By the thirteenth century, manuals for learning French began to appear, indicating that widespread French usage was becoming unusual. By the end of the fourteenth century, with even parliament, the law courts and the king using English, it can be said that French had disappeared as a native language in general use in England.

3.3.3 Middle English grammar

By the time English re-emerged as the national language used for all linguistic contexts, it looked very different from the Old English of the eleventh century. The major difference was that there were no longer so many different inflectional endings, to the extent that the case system had effectively been abandoned. The tendency of Germanic languages such as English to stress initial syllables in words meant that final syllables were often lost or reduced in distinctiveness ('swallowed'). Norman-French misunderstanding of English inflections (especially amongst their manuscript writers) confused the inflectional system in the south. And Danish speakers' different inflections also led to a loss in the north. All of these factors encouraged inflectional endings towards an indistinct /ə/, usually written as '-e' on the ends of words. (By the fourteenth century, even this was disappearing in the north. Chaucer, in the south, only uses final -e, irregularly, to make the metre scan.) The grammatical information held by inflections came to be conveyed by word-order, contrastive intonation and a greater use of prepositions.

The variety of Old English plural endings (-as, -an, -e, -ena, -um and so on) became much reduced. Both in Northumbrian dialect and from French, -s came to be the commonest plural ending form. The old -en ending (*men, women, children, oxen*), the so-called mutated plural (*feet, teeth*) and the zero-inflection (*deer, salmon, sheep*) became frozen in these examples and tended not to be applied to new words.

ACTIVITY 43
Middle English texts

---

1   *The Lord's Prayer*

    Oure fadir that art in heuenys,
    halewid be thy name.
    Thy kyngdom come to,
    be thy wille don as in heuene an in erthe.
    Give to us this day oure breed ouer other substaunse,
    And forgiue to us oure dettes
    as and we forgiuen to oure dettouris,
    and leede us not into temptacioun,
    but delyuere us from yuel.
       Amen.

This is fourteenth-century English, but the language of the King James Authorised Bible was already archaic when it was published in 1611, and this version is fairly close to the familiar one still in use today. Compare this with the Old English version in Activity 41. What are the differences between them, and also between this version and the modern version?

---

2   From *Sir Gawain and the Green Knight*

    Bi a mounte on the morne meryly he rydes
    Into a forest ful dep, that ferly was wylde,
    Highe hilles on uche a halve, and holtwodes under
    Of hore okes ful hoge a hundreth togeder.
    The hasel and the hawthorne were harled al samen,
    With roghe raged mosse rayled aywhere,
    With mony bryddes unblythe upon bare twyges,
    That pitosly ther piped for pyne of the colde.
    The gome upon Gryngolet glydes hem under
    Thurgh mony misy and myre, mon al hym one,
    Carande for his costes, lest he ne kever schulde
    To se the servyse of that syre, that on that self nyght
    Of a burde was borne, oure baret to quelle.
    And therfore sykyng he sayde: 'I beseche the, Lorde,
    And Mary, that is myldest moder so dere,
    Of sum herber ther heghly I myght here masse
    Ande thy matynes to-morne, mekely I ask,
    And therto prestly I pray my pater and ave and crede.'
      He rode in his prayere,
      And cryed for his mysdede;
      He sayned hym in sythes sere
      And sayd: 'Cros Kryst me spede!'

(Glossary: *mounte* – hill, *harled* – tangled, *bryddes* – birds, *unblythe* – unhappy, *gome* – man, *misy* – bog, *carande* – uneasy, *costes* – religious duty, *burde* – maiden, *baret* – sorrow, *herber* – haven, *heghly* – devoutly, *prestly* – promptly, *sayned* – made sign of the cross, *spede* – help.)

This is a ripping yarn of King Arthur's court, written in the fourteenth century by an unknown poet somewhere in the north-west. In this passage, Sir

Gawain is searching for the green knight and probable death; it is Christmas Eve. The Anglo-Saxon alliterative style is followed, perhaps as an index of the archaic setting. You can tell by the regular rhythm how many of the words were pronounced. English spelling at this stage was closer to the pronunciation than it is today. Notice words which have since been abandoned, are rarely used nowadays or have changed their spelling. Make a list of these and use the complete *Oxford English Dictionary* or a good etymological dictionary to find out what happened to these words.

---

3 *Caxton's Prose*

Caxton's preface to his translation of Virgil's *Aeneid* into English, as *Eneydos*, contains his thoughts on the changing language and dialectal variation in 1490:

After dyverse werkes made, translated, and achieved, havyng noo werke in hande, I, sittyng in my studye where as laye many dyverse paunflettis and bookys, happened that to my hande came a lytyl booke in frenshe, whiche late was translated oute of latyn by some noble clerke of fraunce, whiche booke is named Eneydos... And whan I had advysed me in this sayd boke, I delybered and concluded to translate it into englysshe, and forthwyth toke a penne & ynke, and wrote a leef or tweyne, whyche I oversawe agayn to corecte it. And whan I sawe the fayr & straunge termes therin I doubted that it sholde not please some gentylmen whiche late blamed me, sayeing that in my translacyons I had over curyous termes whiche coude not be understande of comyn peple, and desired me to use olde and homely termes in my translacyons. And fayn wolde I satysfye every man, and so to doo, toke an olde boke and redde therin; and certaynly the englysshe was so rude and brood that I coude not wele understande it. And also my lord abbot of westmynster ded do shewe to me late, certayn evydences wryton in olde englysshe, for to reduce it in-to our englysshe now usid. And certaynly it was wreton in suche wyse that it was more lyke to dutche than englysshe; I coude not reduce ne brynge it to be understonden. And certaynly our langage now used varyeth ferre from that whiche was used and spoken whan I was borne. For we englysshe men ben borne under the domynacyon of the mone, whiche is never stedfaste, but ever waverynge, wexynge one season, and waneth & dyscreaseth another season. And that comyn englysshe that is spoken in one shyre varyeth from a nother.

What is Caxton saying here? How does the language he is using to express himself differ from Modern English? Identify differences under various systematic headings: syntax, idioms, spellings, for example.

3.3.4 Middle English dialects

Dialectal diversity continued along the regional lines of the Anglo-Saxon dialects. Northumbrian developed into Scots and Northern English north of a line from the Humber to the Lake District. The Mercian dialect of Old English became the West Midland and East Midland dialects, the latter with more Danish loan-words. Below the Thames and the Severn, the Southern dialect was spoken, while Kentish remained in the far south-east.

The commercialisation of the country in this period entailed a greater movement of people, and dialectal difference came to the consciousness of writers more prominently than before. Caxton, for example, in the prologue to his translation of the *Aeneid* (*Eneydos*) into English, commented on the differences in pronunciation between north and south (see text 3 of Activity 43 above). He printed in the East Midlands dialect. This was the area containing the universities of Oxford and Cambridge, and the London Inns of Court, and it was also the home area of most of those migrating towards London. Later, this dialect became the modern Standard English dialect, and this is why we are more likely to read Chaucer, writing in London, than Henryson or Dunbar (Scots) or the unknown poet of *Sir Gawain and the Green Knight*, writing in Cheshire. The rise of the prestigious image of Standard English can be dated from the policy of the Tudors in deliberately encouraging a unified national identity.

3.4 Modern English

The year 1500 usually marks the boundary of Modern English. At that time, Early Modern English looked very like our late version. The establishment of printing was leading to a standardisation of spelling forms, although letters were still added or omitted to help 'justify' the text (that is, fill the line with no gaps at each end, as can be done using a modern word-processor). The rapid growth of London and the increasing centralisation of power and commerce around the court encouraged the beginnings of the attitude that the 'best' English was this variety of English. By the end of the eighteenth century, this idea had hardened into notions of 'correct' and 'low' spoken English.

3.4.1 Lexical change in the Renaissance

The two most noticeable features of change in the Renaissance period (around the sixteenth century) were the introduction of many foreign loan words (mainly from Latin and Greek) and a large-scale alteration in the way many words were pronounced (since called the **Great Vowel Shift**, see below). The emphasis placed on classical learning spread across Europe from the Italian states, and was illustrated in England by the establishment of many 'grammar' schools. The grammar taught was Latin and Greek, not English, and so Latin and Greek terms came to be heavily borrowed into English. The so-called *aureate* writers who encouraged this borrowing regarded themselves explicitly as augmenting the language. However, there were many *purists* who resisted the use of words such as *maturity, consideration, invigilate, relinquish, lunatic, illecebrous, expede, ingent, obtestate* and *denunciate*, and ridiculed the users of these **inkhorn** terms or *Chaucerisms*. However, as you will realise, some of these words have survived and some have been discarded.

At the same time, the borrowing habit spread to include loans from Italian (*cameo, violin, design*), Spanish (*galleon, pistol*) and again from French (*bigot, probability, volunteer*). An estimated 10 000 new words thus introduced from over 50 other languages were used under the influence of 'aureate' writers such as Sir Thomas More, Sir Thomas Elyot and William Shakespeare. In the seventeenth century, the process was so far advanced that the earliest dictionaries began to appear, containing meanings for difficult words.

ACTIVITY 44

Sixteenth-century text

The Renaissance period was a very creative time for innovations in the language. The use of nouns as verbs, the appearance of *do* as a present-tense auxiliary, the disappearance of the *thou/you* distinction, the introduction of *tis* and *its*, the gradual, uneven modernisation of verb endings from *-th* to *-s*, and the universal use of *'s* for genitives all appeared at this time. Shakespeare was in the forefront of adopting such innovations, and was criticised for it by the language purists. In the following passage from the end of *King Richard II* (written in 1596), try to identify any words, idioms and word-order that are different from Modern English. You should be able to say something about every sentence that characterises this as Renaissance English. Notice, though, how much more similar to our English it is compared with Caxton's English of only a century previously:

> *I have been studying how I may compare*
> *This prison where I live unto the world:*
> *And, for because the world is populous,*
> *And here is not a creature but myself,*
> *I cannot do it; – yet I'll hammer't out.*
> *My brain I'll prove the female to my soul,*
> *My soul the father: and these two beget*
> *A generation of still-breeding thoughts,*
> *And these same thoughts people this little world,*
> *In humours like the people of this world,*
> *For no thought is contented. The better sort, –*
> *As thoughts of things divine, – are intermix'd*
> *With scruples, and do set the word itself*
> *Against the word:*
> *As thus, – 'Come, little ones,' and then again, –*
> *'It is as hard to come as for a camel*
> *To thread the postern of a needle's eye.'*
> *Thoughts tending to ambition, they do plot*
> *Unlikely wonders: how these vain weak nails*
> *May tear a passage through the flinty ribs*
> *Of this hard world, my ragged prison walls;*
> *And, for they cannot, die in their own pride.*
> *Thoughts tending to content flatter themselves*
> *That they are not the first of fortune's slaves,*
> *Nor shall not be the last; like silly beggars,*
> *Who, sitting in the stocks, refuge their shame,*
> *That many have, and others must sit there;*
> *And in this thought they find a kind of ease,*
> *Bearing their own misfortune on the back*
> *Of such as have before endured the like.*
> *Thus play I, in one person, many people,*
> *And none contented: sometimes am I king;*
> *Then treason makes me wish myself a beggar,*
> *And so I am: then crushing penury*
> *Persuades me I was better when a king;*

Then am I king'd again: and by and by
Think that I am unking'd by Bolingbroke,
And straight am nothing: – but whate'er I am,
Nor I, nor any man that but man is,
With nothing shall be pleas'd till he be eas'd
With being nothing. – Music do I hear?
Ha, ha! keep time: – how sour sweet music is
When time is broke and no proportion kept!
So is it in the music of men's lives,
And here have I the daintiness of ear
To check time broke in a disorder'd string;
But, for the concord of my state and time,
Had not an ear to hear my true time broke.
I wasted time and now doth time waste me...
...This music mads me; let it sound no more,
For though it have holp madmen to their wits,
In me it seems it will make wise men mad.
Yet blessing on his heart that gives it me!
For 'tis a sign of love; and love to Richard
Is a strange brooch in this all-hating world.

3.4.2 Pronunciation change in the Renaissance

Between 1400 and 1700, the pronunciation of vowels shifted to produce sounds
that we would more or less recognise today. Generally, vowel quality was 'raised'
on the tongue, so that Chaucer's pronunciation of, for example, *name* (/na:me/ to
rhyme with our modern *father*), became Shakespeare's /ne:m/. This is like
modern Northern English. RP has /neim/. Similarly, *sweete* was raised from
/sweitə/ (as modern *breaker*) to /swi:t/, as modern pronunciation. Almost every
word was affected by the Great Vowel Shift, which was first noticed and
commented on in the early fifteenth century, but had gradually spread across the
country by the eighteenth.

Many explanations have been suggested for this large phonological change.
One of the most persuasive is the sociological reasoning that focuses on speakers'
sense of their own language prestige. At a time of the urbanisation of London and
the rise of the modern class system, sensitivity to accents which betrayed your
origins must have been growing. People from rural East Anglia and the Midlands
moving towards London would not want to sound like hicks from the
countryside, and so would alter their accent. As always, when people consciously
aim to adjust their pronunciation to emulate their best guess at others' speech,
they would overdo (**hypercorrect**) the pronunciation, and get it wrong. However,
this hypercorrected accent gradually became the indicator of the rising wealthy
merchants, and would itself be copied by others. Thus the accidental innovation
would become prestigious and spread.

Many of the oddities of English spelling are ascribable to changes in
pronunciation at this time, since printing had begun to fossilise spellings before
the pronunciation of words changed. Many of our modern spellings retain
Middle English pronunciation, and many modern words now considered as slang
or non-standard are older variants that precede the Great Vowel Shift and

associated modifications in pronunciation. Thus, some older Irish speakers still pronounce *tea* and *quay* to rhyme with *bay*. Some Scottish speakers refer to a *house* to rhyme with *moose*, and *down* to rhyme with *moon*. Northern and Midland English speakers never adopted the lengthening of vowels in *staff*, *bath* and *glass* that characterises Southern accents. And some Scottish and Irish speakers retain Chaucer's /ɔ/ (as in *saw*) in *pot*. This was lengthened in England to /ɔ:/ in *lost*, *often*, *off* and *soft*, but more recently these words have taken on a spelling pronunciation and /lɔ.st/ is now rarely heard outside old 1940s British films.

3.4.3 The standardisation of written English

The eighteenth century is usually characterised by a greater emphasis on standardisation and prescriptivism. Elements of accent, word-choice and grammar that were previously merely prestigious acquired connotations of **correctness**. Influential writers set themselves up as arbiters of correct usage, and prescribed on matters of grammar, spelling and acceptable new words. Shortened forms of *mobile*, *reputation*, *fanatic* and *extraordinary* as *mob*, *rep*, *fan* and *extra* were condemned by people such as Jonathan Swift. John Dryden advocated the creation of an English Academy (like the academy in France) to decide on correct usage and fix the language once and for all.

Samuel Johnson's dictionary was a symptom of this desire to settle linguistic matters precisely and by the 'best' usage, and numerous other dictionaries appeared during the eighteenth century. Bishop Robert Lowth's grammar of English (1762) became a bestseller: he determined that *would rather* was better than *had rather*, infinitives (*to boldly go*) ought not to be split, things should be *different from* not *different than/to*, you should say *between you and me* not *I*, double negatives could not be used for emphasis, *you was* was not permissible, and so on. In spite of the fact that these usages had been regarded as good English for centuries, the influence of the eighteenth-century grammarians is still felt in modern prescriptive attitudes to the so-called Standard English dialect.

3.4.4 Explanations for prescriptivism

The basis of such decisions was often on an appeal to **logic**: mathematical criteria condemned the useful multiple negative. **Etymology** was often invoked to argue for certain forms, regardless of the fact that this was such a speculative science. **Analogy** with other similar words was argued: by this reasoning *coude* falsely acquired an *l*, because *wolde* had one prior to becoming *would*. Finally, **Latin** and **Greek** principles were applied to English (to eventually and bizarrely prevent split infinitives) since they were seen as 'pure' (although dead) languages that English should aspire to. Ending sentences with prepositions (as in the previous sentence) was also outlawed on this basis.

It is perhaps a corresponding part of the explanation for this desire to codify and standardise that the period of the nineteenth and twentieth centuries have seen wide-ranging influences from a variety of sources. The British Empire spread the language around the world, and more efficient communications brought many loan words back into British English. Australian English, South African English and American English are all national varieties of English with their own traditions of good usage. Indian English has more native speakers in the subcontinent than the population of the British Isles. New technology, foods, furnishings, architecture and ideas have introduced new words into the language, and the influences of different cultures – mainly through film and television, migration and easy international travel – have meant that English has borrowed from and lent words to most of the major languages of the world.

The English language can no longer be said to belong to any one group or nation; it is a shared resource, and it has as many good varieties as there are speech communities who share it.

ACTIVITY 45

Eighteenth-century text

Extracts from Jonathan Swift's *Proposal for Correcting, Improving and Ascertaining the English Tongue* (1712) are reproduced below. The conservative 'Golden Ageism' expressed here is often seen as characteristic of the eighteenth century, but every period (including our own) has seen writers pining nostalgically for the undegenerate linguistic past. The argument is usually allied to a moral and aesthetic framework. However, the evidence of language change that Swift cites, as well as the obvious differences between this passage and Modern English, show that this attitude is a delusion. Read the passage and identify examples of these points:

The Period wherein the English *Tongue received most Improvement, I take to commence with the beginning of Queen* Elizabeth's *Reign, and to conclude with the Great Rebellion in Forty Two. 'Tis true, there was a very ill Taste both of Style and Wit, which prevailed under King* James *the First, but that seems to have been corrected in the first Years of his Successor, who among many other Qualifications of an excellent Prince, was a great Patron of Learning. From the Civil War to this present Time, I am apt to doubt whether the Corruptions in our Language have not at least equalled the Refinements of it; and these Corruptions very few of the best Authors in our Age have wholly escaped. During the Usurpation, such an Infusion of Enthusiastick Jargon prevailed in every Writing, as was not shook off in many Years after. To this succeeded that Licentiousness which entered with the* Restoration, *and from infecting our Religion and Morals, fell to corrupt our Language; which last was not like to be much improved by those who at that Time made up the Court of King* Charles *the Second; either such who had followed Him in His Banishment, or who had been altogether conversant in the Dialect of those* Fanatick *Times; or young Men, who had been educated in the same Company; so that the* Court, *which used to be the Standard of Propriety and Correctness of Speech, was then, and, I think, hath ever since continued the worst School in* England...

...There is another Sett of Men who have contributed very much to the spoiling of the English *Tongue; I mean the Poets, from the Time of the Restoration. These Gentlemen, although they could not be insensible how much our Language was already overstocked with Monosyllables; yet, to save Time and Pains, introduced that barbarous Custom of abbreviating Words, to fit them to the Measure of their Verses; and this they have frequently done, so very injudiciously, as to form such harsh unharmonious Sounds, that none but a* Northern *Ear could endure...*

...In order to reform our Language, I conceive... that a free judicious Choice should be made of such Persons, as are generally allowed to be best qualified for such a Work, without any regard to Quality, Party, or Profession. These, to a certain Number at least, should assemble at some appointed Time and Place, and fix on Rules by which they design to proceed...

...The Persons who are to undertake this Work, will have the Example of the French *before them, to imitate where these have proceeded right, and to avoid their Mistakes. Beside the Grammar-part, wherein we are allowed to be very defective, they will observe many gross Improprieties, which however authorised by Practice, and grown familiar, ought to be discarded...*

...But what I have most at Heart is, that some Method should be thought on for ascertaining and fixing our Language for ever, after such Alterations are made in it as shall be thought requisite.

In the letters pages of newspapers, articles regularly appear that express similar modern attitudes to the 'decay' of language. These are written both by ordinary people and by influential politicians, writers and celebrities. Using your knowledge of the history of the English language, try to discriminate the valid points from the misunderstandings of linguistics contained in these opinions.

3.5 Types of language change

Throughout this necessarily brief review of how English has changed in the 1500 years of its history, particular sorts of change occur over and over again. In some respects, the language has become simplified. The complex case system of inflectional endings of Old English has left barely a remnant in Modern English. Within Britain, accents and dialects are far more convergent and mutually intelligible than they were, say, a couple of centuries ago, largely because of national newspapers, broadcasting, railways and the motorway network. In other respects, English has become more complex. There are a host of national varieties of English, with their own internal dialectal differences, artificial Englishes such as Air-Traffic Control English or Seaspeak, and transnational varieties of English such as, to an extent, Black English Vernacular, none of which existed five centuries ago (see Chapter 5 for more on these). Even within the English of Britain, there are more words in the vocabulary of the language than there have ever been.

   People throughout history, but especially in the past three centuries, have sought to attach moral values to the changes in language. However, English is neither improving nor degenerating; it has always simply changed as required by the different social conditions of those who speak it. The fact that English is not stable across history is because it is still a living language, and change is a necessary aspect of this. The next section considers in more detail the different grammatical and lexical ways in which English has changed.

3.5.1 Grammatical change

Many of the changes in the section above show how grammatical change has been a feature of the development of English. In Anglo-Saxon, the usual method of forming the past participle was to put the *ge-* prefix (pronounced /je/) onto the word (*gelufod* = loved). By Middle English, this was written *y-* (*yronne* = run), but this system had disappeared entirely by Modern English.

   Like German, French and Latin, Anglo-Saxon had a singular and plural form of the second-person pronoun; *þū* and *gē*, respectively. In Middle English, these came to be spelt *thou* and *you*, with slightly altered pronunciation. By this time, *thou* came to denote not simply singularity but also intimacy. It would be used by friends and family, while *you* was used politely to strangers. This developed into a marker of respect and social rank, *thou* additionally being used to servants and inferiors, and *you* to lords and masters. Shakespeare signals many social relationships by the use of this form (see especially the terms of address in *King Richard II*). However, by the seventeenth century, the distinction was already disappearing. Today, we only use *thou* in fossilised texts (old plays, prayers and so on), and we use 'you' indiscriminately. Some modern dialects do preserve a plural pronoun, though, in *youse* or *you-all*.

   In the twentieth century, the use of the subjunctive form has been disappearing from most people's speech. Where doubt, desire or hypothesis was intended, the subjunctive verb form was used: *If I were rich, ...* or *He wished he were there*. Today, it is likely that *If I was rich, ...* or *He wished he was there* will be used by all except middle-aged educated speakers. The fine gradation of meaning offered by the subjunctive is no longer required.

   Of course, the disappearance of a grammatical form rarely means that a notion becomes inexpressible. Word-order and prepositions took over the job of identifying noun-function when the case system was lost. The gradations of politeness which were carried by the *thou/you* distinction can now be conveyed by a whole set of other politeness strategies, including the name we use for people, the formality of the words we choose, the hedging and politeness markers we deploy, and so on (see Section 6.1.3). Often, gaps left by the loss of a grammatical form can be filled by lexical means: in Standard English, we can specify the plural second person lexically as *you two* or *you lot*, for example.

3.5.2 Lexical change

Changes in the bank of words available to English speakers are the most noticeable form of language difference over time. Some words have simply died, abandoned either because they were no longer needed or because they were replaced. The modern English speaker does not need dozens of words for a sword, nor for several different types of ship, or warrior. Some such old words hang around in frozen forms, but few people recognise their earlier meanings. In Anglo-Saxon, *wergild* (= man-gold) was the price to be paid in compensation if a man was killed. Perhaps the only remnant of the first element here is in *werewolf*.

Borrowing

English has exhibited a variety of means of creating new words over its history. Various foreign influences have resulted in words often being **borrowed** from other languages, on permanent loan, of course. Such words eventually lose their foreign connotations. Only a Latin-educated pedant, for example, would insist on using *dilapidated* to refer exclusively to stone (*lapis*) buildings, or insist only on breaking bread (*panis*) with *companions*, or consult the planets (*sideris*) when *considering* something. And it is now not only the possessors of testicles who are able to give *testimony*.

Affixing

Latin and Greek have also provided a bank of **prefixes** and **suffixes** (see Section 2.2.3) that allow a simple noun to multiply into many new words: *inter-*, *trans-*, *super-, sub-, ultra-, phil-, poly-, hydro-* and so on. Words from different languages are often mixed to give new English words. Greek *tele* (far) and Latin *communicare* give us *telecommunication,* and dozens of other *tele-* prefixed words: *telegram, telephone, telex, telethon* and *telescope,* as well as science-fictional items such as *telepathy, telekinesis* and *teleportation* that are as yet speculative.

Since Anglo-Saxon times, English has acquired many suffixes, such as *-less, -ness, -full, -ish, -ism* and so on, to attach to words such as *hope, kind, meaning, book* and *commune* respectively. These morphemes can even be combined, as in *hopelessness,* and can be used innovatively to create new references such as the approximate time – *fourish* – or the attitude of *ageism.* Affixes such as *-wise, mega-* and *hyper-* have become increasingly used with the hyperbole of advertising copy.

Compounding

Prefixing and suffixing are some of the oldest methods of creating new words, very common in expanding the vocabulary. Old English also inherited the Germanic pattern of **compounding** words together (into **kennings**) to create **neologisms**. Modern English uses this system as well: *head waiter, ozone friendly, crash test dummy* (see also Section 2.2.4).

Back-forming

English also uses the opposite process of **back-formation** to create new words. Morphemes that look like affixes are removed (often mistakenly) to create a word: thus *editor* and *burglar* have produced the verbs *edit* and *burgle,* along the same lines as the joke-words *ept* and *couth* as the apparent opposites of *inept* and *uncouth.*

Shortening

Furthermore, the sort of **abbreviation** that was condemned in the eighteenth century has since become a very common means of word-formation in *pram, bus, zoo, phone, fax* and so on. **Acronyms** are the extreme form of this, an especially productive process in the domains of modern government bureaucracy, computer-speak and the military: *radar, laser, AIDS, BASIC, CD-ROM, quango, INSET* and so on.

An illustration

The principles behind many of these processes of neologising (to coin a word) are often irregular and unpredictable. For example, a *veggieburger* is a round slab of non-meat product in a bun. The various observable spellings of this indicate the relative newness of the word. It is formed by the **blending** of *vegetarian* and *hamburger,* first abbreviated to *veggie* and *burger.* Hamburgers were originally simply items/people from the German town of Hamburg. *Ham,* in this context, has nothing to do with food (it is related to the later English word *home*), but in an American English context the etymology was wrongly guessed to be associated with pig meat (although, in fact, hamburgers were usually made with beef). Thus, *burger* was coined by abbreviation as the word for the meat-in-a-bun, and this is now even expanded into the compound *beefburger.* Numerous alternative affixes produce *cheeseburgers, chilliburgers, chickenburgers, fishburgers* and so on. This is an example of how words are introduced based on etymological misunderstanding, but only a pedant would argue against the 'correctness' of *beefburger.*

3.5.3 Semantic change

Where the shape of the word itself has remained fairly constant, it is common that the *meaning* of the word has substantially changed over time. The many influences on English from various foreign languages have meant that at times in our history two or more words for the same thing have existed side by side. Where these **synonyms** have both survived, they have usually become specialised in meaning, or taken on slightly different connotations. Thus the French word for *lamb* became *mutton* and was specialised to refer to the meat of the animal that kept its original English name. Words borrowed from foreign languages have often altered their meanings in the process: a *juggernaut* is not a Hindu ceremonial cart but an articulated lorry; there is a world of difference between a Persian *bazaar* and a jumble-sale in a British church hall; our *barbecues* are not like those of the Arawak Indians; and we have Anglicised the Arabic for *The king is dead* in the game of chess into the English-sounding *checkmate*.

Directions of semantic change

Words have changed their meanings within English in a variety of ways. **Narrowing**, or specialisation, has happened to *deer* and *meat*, which once meant all livestock and all food respectively. In contrast, **broadening**, or generalisation, has happened to *bird* and *dog*, which once meant a nestling and a specific breed respectively. **Metaphor** has provided innovations which have passed into common, literal usage. *Bitter* is a dead metaphor with no current general echo of biting; and something can be *harrowing* with no connotations of ploughing. **Metonymy** provides semantic shift by virtue of closeness of meaning: *jaw* originally meant the cheek. **Synecdoche** exchanges the whole for part of the meaning: a *stove* was a heated room; a *town* was a fence around a habitation. **Hyperbole** exaggerates *astound* (to strike with thunder and lightning) while **litotes** understates *kill*, originally meaning to torment. Words take on degenerating overtones (*knave*, meaning a boy, became an insult) or elevating connotations (*knight*, also meaning a boy, became an honour).

  Such meaning change can present a problem when the past impinges on the present, as in reading old literature or hearing proverbs and fossilised sayings. In the 1920s, *gay* men were simply joyful. *Manufactured* items no longer have to be hand-made. The word *nice* has changed meaning numerous times, from *silly*, to *fastidious*, to *precise*, to *blandly pleasant*. Many misunderstandings can arise on this account. *Proof* had the original sense of *successfully test*, as in *waterproof*, so that *It's the exception that proves the rule* is nonsensical in Modern English but coherent in its former meaning.

3.5.4 Pronunciation change

The effects of the Great Vowel Shift on the pronunciation of many English words have already been outlined, but pronunciation change has been a feature of the language throughout its history. The movement of English speakers around the world has meant that such change has spread unevenly, and this accounts for pronunciation variants in American, British and Australian English. The Australian accent recalls the London and East Anglian pronunciation of the original white settlers, although there has, of course, been two centuries of domestic development to produce the modern version.

The prestige/stigma of rhotic accents

At the time of the British settlement of North America, the rhotic accent (/r/-pronouncing in words such as *farm* and *car*) was prestigious. It is still prestigious across the USA, but in eighteenth-century England it became fashionable to have a non-rhotic accent. Today, Irish, Scottish and rural West Country, East Anglian and Lancashire English accents are the only rhotic accents in Britain. In the USA, the New England area followed Britain in dropping rhoticity, and today Boston speakers can be identified by this accent characteristic.

Pronunciation change is today sensitive to the standardisation offered by the broadcast media and recordings. However, there is also a local force in regional language loyalty working in the opposite direction. An Irish or Scottish speaker might accentuate their characteristic pronunciation in ethnic areas of London, or might modify or adapt to a southern accent in order to 'fit in'.

Accent change in progress

One of the most debated accent changes currently in process is the spread of **Estuary English** across the South-East of England. Whereas RP used to be the educated, middle-class prestigious accent, a form of pronunciation that is closer to East London/Essex speech is emerging and being popularised by numerous (mainly young) broadcasters and politicians. This is spreading as far north as the Wash and west to Hampshire. Estuary English is widely written about as a new accent, but it seems it is part of a wider phonological movement at the end of the twentieth century, away from RP. This accent is becoming more casual and relaxed, perhaps as the national institutions and workplaces are also becoming increasingly casualised. However, RP is casualised in each region towards the nearest urban centre. In the South-East, Estuary English is the casualised form of RP in the direction of eastern London. But equally, the prestigious accents heard on regional television are forms of RP casualised towards Geordie, or Scouse, or Mancunian or Brummagem, and so on. These pronunciation changes have been less well documented.

Spelling pronunciations

Finally, a major change in pronunciation has come from the unifying and standardising effects of mass literacy. The notion of a 'correct' pronunciation is carried over by (false) analogy from the standardised writing system, so that **Spoken Standard English** is even sometimes referred to. Over history, there have also been changes in pronunciation that follow the spelling of a word. Recently, the spelling of *forehead* seems to have almost everywhere changed the pronunciation from /forid/ to /fo:hed/, for example.

3.5.5 Reasons for language change

Language does not change of its own accord, but it is the dynamic instrument of those millions of people who have spoken English for fifty generations. Linguistic models and 'rules' of sound changes, of the sort outlined for ease of explanation in this chapter, are the patterned effects of this enormous potential for divergence. Sometimes linguistic textbooks have presented these rules as if they happen by themselves. This is not true.

Linguistic change determined by social change

Deliberate attempts to change the course of the language have almost always failed. English has continued to change in spite of efforts to fix and standardise it, and the language continues to evolve to best suit the contemporary needs of its speakers. This is not to say that speakers' attitudes to their language are unimportant; often, changes will spread more rapidly depending on the prestige or stigma attached to particular forms. The language has changed most fundamentally where there have been deep social changes to lead the innovation. New forms might be introduced by invading and settling people, by a desire for social distance, by borrowing from another language or dialect, or occasionally by the fortuitous creativity of an influential individual. But few such innovations survive unless there is a widespread social need for them. Change in English is not simply, then, a matter of creation, but also of the forces needed to maintain and reinforce the new form and allow it to spread.

The unpredictability of language change

Central to an understanding of the history of English is the idea that most change is unpredictable and chaotic because it has been either accidental or coincidental with other social movements. Our view of the linguistic past can never be objective, because each age applies its own standards of scientific enquiry to the 'facts' of the past, and we are of course still inside the history of the language, although as it comes near us we call it *sociolinguistics*.

Without the Great Plague or King John's foreign policy failures, we might all now be speaking a version of French. If William of Normandy had not felt so vulnerable and insisted on fortifying London, our capital might now still be Winchester, or maybe Birmingham, and our Standard English a modern descendant of the Mercian dialect. Chaucer might be regarded as an obscure and verbose dialect poet. If the 'Golden Age' of Northumbria had been unaffected by Danish invasions, and the Northumbrian dialect had eventually dominated English through to the Renaissance, then perhaps the Scottish kings would have been acceptable in the south somewhat earlier. Perhaps we would now still have a Catholic Stuart monarchy and we would speak a modern version of Scots, with a case system still intact. We might have many Latin, Greek and Spanish terms, but little French. There would be no African or Indian words, because there would have been no British Empire and no Commonwealth. Australia would be Dutch- or Portuguese-speaking, and the USA would have a special relationship with Spain.

You can play this game endlessly, but the moral is the same. Language change reflects and follows social change, and the complexity of this defies the easy philological rules that see predictability as an option in linguistics. Accidental change means that the whole basis of how we perceive the history of our language, and the methods we use to reconstruct our linguistic past, are perhaps ready to be fundamentally revised.

Further reading

On the general development of English, and with a good section on American English, the classic textbook with a wealth of detail is Baugh and Cable (1978). McCrum, Cran and MacNeil's (1986) *The Story of English* is excellent on later English and it accompanies the BBC TV series, also useful as a resource. Pyles

(1971), Wakelin (1988) and Strang (1972), which progresses backwards through history, are very detailed and more technical. Blake (1992) is a comprehensive overview in several volumes. Leith (1983) is a good introduction to a social view of English language history, and deals with the imposition of English on Celtic speakers in the British Isles.

The development of the writing system is covered by the readable Jackson (1987), and Scragg (1974) is good specifically on the history of spelling. On pronunciation change, Harris (1985) is very detailed and somewhat technical. Syntactic change is covered comprehensively by Traugott (1972). Advanced discussions of the whole enterprise of historical linguistics are contained in Rissanen *et al.* (1992) and Jones (1993).

For Old English, Quirk and Wrenn (1960) is a clear grammar of the language, and Bosworth and Toller (1898 etc.) is the standard dictionary. Fowler (1973) is an annotated collection of Old English prose and verse, and Hamer (1970) contains parallel verse translations of the best Old English poetry. Whitelock (1965) is a fascinating read of Anglo-Saxon social history.

On Middle English, Kurath and Kuhn (1953 etc.) is a dictionary, and McIntosh, Samuels and Benskin (1986) plots the geographical origins of dialect forms. Chaucer and Malory are good places to start with Middle English poetry and prose. 'Sir Gawain and the Green Knight' is edited in a collection by Cawley and Anderson (1976), and Scots poetry is enjoyably represented by Henryson's 'Poems and Fables', edited by Wood (1978).

The complete *Oxford English Dictionary* is indispensible in historical linguistics, but the *Concise Oxford Dictionary of English Etymology* (1986) and the *Concise Oxford Dictionary of English Place-names* (1960) are also very useful. Cameron and Gelling (1976) contains information on early place-names. There are numerous local histories that deal with your own part of the country.

The question of attitudes to linguistic decay and prescriptivism is addressed very readably by Aitchison (1992). Milroy and Milroy (1991) is an elegant and scholarly view of the notion of authority in language and linguistics. Crowley (1991) is a collection of original essays and extracts on English from the seventeenth century to the present, which makes fascinating reading.

Suggested projects

The language of the world around bears the imprint of its historical development. A good etymological dictionary (that is, one which gives the first recorded appearance of a word and its changing form and meaning over time) is an essential tool for the student of historical linguistics.

The history of the language is most accessible in old documents still in print. These will tend to be valued texts such as literature, and you can find examples of language from *Beowulf* to Dickens. Old dictionaries and grammars, essays, sermons and political writing also survive. The most difficult thing in studying the history of the language is being able to narrow down to examine an area small enough to be manageable. Don't, for example, try to write about the entire history of American English, or the whole grammar of Old English.

There are, in general, two ways of approaching the historical study of language. The first is to focus on a moment in time and examine a feature of language in its contemporary setting. Essentially this is historical sociolinguistics, and is like examining a 'snapshot'. The second approach is to follow a language feature through its development across time, tracing changes and differences in usage by different generations.

1 An example of the first approach would be to discuss dialect variation in Old English. Activity 41 gives a pair of texts in different dialects. You could take similar pairs and identify dialect features. You could trace the subsequent history of some of the words to see how many from each text survived into Middle and Modern English, and thus determine which dialect became more prestigious.

2 Another example of the first approach would be to plot the origins of place-names or family names. For example, you could take a random sample of, say, a hundred names from your local telephone directory. Organise them into categories such as *occupation, family trait, place of origin, ethnic background* and so on. Based on the pattern of distribution, you could then speculate on the migration patterns of your local area. You could look up the origins of the component words of surnames to see how they have changed and when they appeared.

3 An example of the second approach would be to investigate the language change contained in any short modern text. Use an etymological dictionary (such as the *Oxford English Dictionary*) to trace the history of each word back to its first recorded appearance. You would find out what the original sense of the word was, and whether it had gone through a series of changes in meaning over the years. Interesting texts to choose would be those written by Indian English or Caribbean English speakers, or texts using some sort of non-standard dialects.

4 One way of investigating language change is to talk to the oldest speakers in your area. Old people will have learnt to speak 70, 80 or even 90 years ago, and their vocabulary and grammar might be quite different from that of young people. They might also know local landmarks by different names. Record a conversation with an old person, trying to get them involved in the story while you are taking note of their language.

5 You might argue a particular case with supporting linguistic evidence. For example, you might take the point that Scots ought to be considered a separate language from English, on the basis that it developed from the Northumbrian dialect of Old English rather than the West Saxon, as did Modern Standard English. As evidence, you might use examples of literature written in Scots from the Middle Ages to modern writers trying to reclaim their vernacular language.

The Activities in this chapter can be developed into areas for study. You can either use the texts provided or find similar examples from the period.

Answers to Activity 40
1 *Sēo cwen clippeþ þone cyning.*
2 *Đaet gode bearn lufaþ þā ealdan cwene.*
3 *Đaet cyninges bearn wæs gode.*
4 *Sēo cwen brohte þone cyning þǣm bearnum*
(or) *þone cyning þǣm bearnum sēo cwen brohte*, for example.

Language acquisition

4.0 Introduction

We saw in Chapter 2 just how wonderfully complex the system of a language (for example, English) is. One of the remarkable things about us as human beings is how in a relatively short time – four to five years – we acquire our language. Or, if we are brought up to speak two languages, as bilinguals, we acquire two language systems simultaneously. This chapter looks at some of the main features of the language acquisition process.

4.1 Acquiring language

By the time children start school between the ages of four and five: they are able to articulate most of the sounds of English speech; they are able to produce appropriately structured sentences, having acquired the essentials of the grammatical system; they are able to operate as turn-takers in a spoken discourse; and they can use their language knowledge for a diverse range of purposes – to express their feelings, to get things done, to find out about the world, to make personal contact, and so on. And they understand far more language than they can themselves use.

In this chapter, we shall be concentrating on the early, pre-school, years; although we will also say a little (in Section 4.6) about learning to read and write.

4.2 Growth of language structures

In this section we will look in turn at the development of the acquisition of sounds, inflections, grammatical structures and vocabulary.

4.2.1 Sounds

The first evidence for parents that their child is beginning to acquire language is when the child begins to make sounds that can be identified with the phonemes of the parents' language and which they can associate with some meaning. Before that happens, from around the age of three months, the child goes through a process of playing with sounds, in which they appear to be trying out their articulatory organs. During this time, known as the **babbling period**, the sounds that the child produces appear to have no intended meaning; they are made purely for the pleasure of it.

By the age of one year, children seem to be able to recognise some of what adults are saying to them. But their own production lags some way behind. It is not entirely clear in what order children acquire sounds. The first phonemic contrast appears to be that between oral (for example, /b/) and nasal (for example, /m/). Just before the appearance of the first recognisable words at around this age, certain phonemes – plosives /b d g/ and nasals /m n/ – begin to establish themselves as predominant in the child's speech. At the same time children seem to begin intentionally to vary the pitch and rhythm of their voices, sometimes copying the pitch patterns of adult speech.

Children seem to acquire the vowel system (by age three) before they have completed the acquisition of all the consonants, which may not happen until the age of five or six. One of the frictionless continuant phonemes – usually /l/ – is acquired at an early stage; but the phonemic distinctions among plosives and nasals are likely to be established before the first fricative consonant appears. The last consonants to be acquired are the dental fricatives /θ ð/, although in some accents (for example, East London/Essex) these are never acquired, such speakers using the labio-dental fricatives /f v/ instead.

We could have said 'continuing to use the labio-dental fricatives', since it is /f v/ that children usually use instead of /θ ð/ until they have acquired the latter. This brings us to the general point that, until children have acquired the full system of consonants, certain substitutions and other adjustments take place which distinguish their pronunciation of a word from the adult model. Crystal (1987, p. 240) notes the following tendencies:

> replacement of fricatives by stops (that is, plosives); for example, *saw* is pronounced /to:/
>
> replacement of velar consonants by alveolars; for example, *gone* is pronounced /don/
>
> simplification of consonant clusters; for example, *snow* becomes /nou/, *please* becomes /pi:z/
>
> consonants at the end of words are omitted; for example, *mat* becomes /ma/
>
> unstressed syllables may be omitted; for example, *banana* becomes /na:na/
>
> as words become longer, consonants and vowels may 'harmonise'; for example, if *dog* is pronounced /gog/ or /dod/, *window* is pronounced /wouwou/
>
> /w/ and /j/ are preferred over /l/ and /r/; for example, *leg* becomes /jeg/

We may also notice the tendency to swap the positions of sounds (called 'metathesis'); for example, /wops/ for *wasp*, /pa:ka:k/ for *car park*.

ACTIVITY 46

Record the speech of a child aged between two and four.

Note down the ways in which the child's pronunciation of words differs from your own, adult, pronunciation.

Can you detect any regularly occurring adjustments?

4.2.2 Inflections

As we saw in Section 2.2.2, English words have relatively few inflections: possessive and plural on nouns; third-person singular present tense, past tense, present and past participles on verbs; comparative and superlative on adjectives. The acquisition load is not great by comparison with other languages.

The first inflections to be acquired are the present participle (*-ing*) form of verbs, which has no variant forms; then the plural of nouns, which has a small number of irregular variants, besides the three phonologically determined regular forms /s, z, iz/ (*bits*, *bobs*, *pieces*); then the possessive of nouns, with the same regular forms as the plural and no irregular variants. These inflections are often present during early syntactic development, from around the age of eighteen months. The past tense inflection and the third-person singular present tense follow on later.

Three stages have been identified in the acquisition of inflections (Cruttenden 1979, p. 59). In the first stage, a word that would be inflected in adult language may occur variably either with or without the inflection. In the second stage, the appropriate inflection is always used, but not necessarily the correct variant, if that is relevant to the case. In the third stage the adult target has been achieved. The transition from the second to the third stage may take several months. Where a word has an irregular inflection, a child in the second stage of acquisition will usually substitute the regular variants, as in *mouses* for *mice*, *foots* for *feet*, *seed* for *saw*, *breaked* for *broke*. Gradually the exceptional, irregular forms are acquired, but there is usually a long period during which both regularised and irregular forms may occur variably for the same word. In some dialects, some of the regularised forms are the norm in any case; for example, *buyed* (*bought*), *seed* (*saw*), *spitted* (*spat*).

4.2.3 Grammatical structures

We can begin to speak of structures, and so the beginning of syntax, once children start to form utterances of two words. This usually happens from around the age of eighteen months. Incidentally, any such indications of age should be treated with caution, because children develop linguistically in different ways and at different rates, and there is a fair variation in what is regarded as normal language development.

Attempts have been made to provide coherent analyses of children's two-word utterances, but they are not always amenable to such analyses. From a semantic perspective, a limited number of structures can be identified (Cruttenden 1979, p. 37): possession (*Daddy sock*), attribution (*red bus*), nomination (*that man*), recurrence (*more drink*), location (*Nanny home*), negation (*allgone drink*), exclamation/greeting (*byebye Susan*) and action, which is subdivided into agent-action (*Mummy push*), agent-goal (*Susan [eat] tea*) and action-goal (*fill cup*). From a syntactic perspective, the words occurring in such utterances have been divided into a small class of 'pivot' words (for example, *more, allgone, that*) and a larger class of 'open' words, with structures typically consisting of one pivot and one open word.

Alternatively, the syntax of such utterances can be described in terms of subject, verb, object and so on. At the two-word stage, combinations such as the following occur:

> subject + verb (*Mummy go*)
> verb + object (*love Susan*)
> subject + complement (*teddy happy*),
> subject + object (*Mummy [make] cake*)
> adverbial + other (*Mummy kitchen, go home, where car?*)

It is at the three-word stage that full syntactic structures begin to appear:

> subject + verb + complement (*Mummy looks sad*)
> subject + verb + object (*Susan played tig*)
> subject + verb + adverbial (*Jimmy goed shops*)

but also structures such as:

> verb + object + object (*gave him ball*)
> verb + object + adverbial (*sent her shops*)

From around the age of two, children begin to produce three- and four-word utterances, with more variation of grammatical structure and also the appropriate inclusion of inflections. Questions and commands begin to be used, in addition to statements; for example, *Where Mummy gone? Go there now!* What is striking about early grammatical structures, by comparison with adult language, is the omission of many function words (determiners, prepositions, auxiliary verbs), which has led some to characterise especially the two-word stage as 'telegraphese'. Towards the age of three, these items (such as *the, is*) are beginning to be regularly used.

From about the age of three, sentences with more than one clause begin to be produced; for example, infinitive clauses as syntactic objects of verbs such as *like* or *want*, as in *want to go to bed*. There is also the occasional occurrence of adverbial clauses with *because* (*cos*) or *if*, and the coordination of clauses with *and* or *but*. Later on, children will produce embedded *that*-clauses, *wh*-clauses and relative clauses (see Section 2.3.5). During this time, children have also acquired how to form various kinds of question, with appropriate syntax and intonation, and how to make sentences negative, proceeding from structures such as *No smack me* to *I don't want no/any tea*.

Asking a question in English involves not only the use of the appropriate intonation, but also syntactic manipulation of the sentence and the use of auxiliary verbs, specifically the inversion of the subject and the first auxiliary verb (compare *They have come home* with *Have they come home?*). Crystal (1987, p. 243) notes three stages in children's acquisition of questions. In the first stage, during the two-word utterance period, children just use intonation: a high rising tone indicates that a question is being asked (*Mummy come?*). In the second stage, during their second year, children begin using question words, first of all *what* and *where*, then *why, how* and *who* appearing later. The questions retain the statement form: *Where teddy gone? Why you laughing?* In the third stage, the acquisition of auxiliary verbs (*be*, *have*, *do*) means that the child can begin the appropriate syntactic manipulation: *Is Susan crying? Has the postman come?* However, with questions containing a question word (*where*, *what*, *why* and so on), where the question word is already a marker of the interrogative, there is a longer transition to the adult syntactic form. So, *Why Mummy is laughing?* gradually develops into *Why is Mummy laughing?*

ACTIVITY 17

We have been able to indicate only some of the main developments in grammar. Specialist textbooks and your own observation can teach you more.

Try to record the speech of a two-year-old child and also that of a child aged between four and five. Make a transcript of part of each recording and compare the grammatical structures and inflections used.

Compare notes with fellow students.

4.2.4 Vocabulary

The growth in a child's vocabulary is perhaps the most difficult aspect of language acquisition to ascertain and yet one of the most remarkable and one of the most obvious. It has been estimated that a child's vocabulary grows from around 100–200 words at age eighteen months to around 500 words at age two, and then by the age of five a child is probably using around 2000 words, a figure that doubles by the age of seven. Notice that we are talking here about a child's 'active' vocabulary, the words that they can be observed using. It is certain that a child's 'passive' vocabulary – the words that they understand – is far greater. When we talk about the words that a child knows or uses, we must bear in mind the discussion (in Section 2.2.1) of what we mean by a 'word'. Incidentally, it has been estimated that an educated adult 'knows' at least 50 000 words and may know as many as 250 000: there is still a lot of vocabulary learning to be done after the age of seven. Indeed, this is one aspect of language acquisition that carries on throughout life.

Children's words do not necessarily mean the same as the equivalent items in adult language. A child's limited vocabulary means that they sometimes overgeneralise or overextend the meaning of a word, applying it to a range of things that they perceive as having some feature in common. For example, the word *car* may be applied to all vehicles, the word *cat* to all animals, and so on. As a child's vocabulary grows, new words are acquired to fill the lexical gaps, so that the meaning of the first-acquired word in the field of meaning narrows to conform to the adult norm.

The opposite tendency also occurs in early child vocabulary: children undergeneralise or underextend the meaning of a word, so that it has a narrower meaning than in adult language. The word *cat* or *pussy* may be applied only to the family's cat, as a kind of proper name, and not generalised to all cats.

At a later stage (age five to seven) children, having learned to make the appropriate differentiations between words in an area of meaning, are then able to group things together on the basis of common features and so understand and use 'abstract' words. For example, using an abstract noun such as *furniture* requires both knowledge of the words included in its meaning (*chair*, *table*, *stool*, *sofa*, *bed* and so on) and perception of some common feature (items that equip a house).

Aitchison (1987) identifies three tasks facing a child acquiring the vocabulary of a language, which she calls **labelling**, **packaging** and **network building**. Labelling involves using sequences of sound as names for things, associating a pronunciation with an object in the environment. This is a task that children begin sometime after the age of one, and it is quite a sophisticated skill. Initially, the child is likely to underextend and use a word for an object only in a particular situation, gradually generalising to the occurrence of the object in other contexts. Packaging involves discovering what the range of reference of a word is – what objects can be packaged under that label. Both underextension and overextension may occur, until the adult norm of packaging has been achieved. Even then, as adults, we may argue over whether a particular plant should be called a *shrub* or a *bush*. Network building is about making connections between words: working out which words are included in others (for example, that *robin* is a kind of *bird*), which words are synonyms and antonyms of each other (see Section 2.2.6); discovering the – often subtle – differences between semantically related words (for example, *say* and *tell*); and finding out which words collocate (see Section 2.2.7). This is a slow and laborious task that continues into adult life.

ACTIVITY 48

From the recordings that you made for the previous two Activites, make a list of one child's vocabulary, arranging the list into areas of meaning (called 'semantic fields'); for example, food, clothing, animals and body parts (see Crystal 1987, p. 244).

What does your listing tell you about the size of the child's vocabulary and the range of meaning that it covers? It is, of course, difficult to make estimates of overall size of vocabulary on the basis of a small sample.

4.3 Development of language functions

Children do not acquire language to no purpose. They acquire language because it serves various social and personal functions. It is, for example, a more sophisticated way of making needs and wants known than crying, moaning, grunting or pointing. You can be more specific about what you want, and perhaps more insistent too.

A study undertaken by the linguist Michael Halliday in the 1970s (Halliday 1975) identified seven types of function that language serves for children in the early years, as they attempt to find out about their environment, control it, interact with other human beings, and comment on their environment and their experience.

The first such function identified by Halliday is the **instrumental**. This is the 'I want' function, where a child makes known their desires and needs (*Gimme sweetie*). The second is the **regulatory** or 'Do as I tell you' function, where a child is exercising control of people in their environment, telling them what to do (*Wash hands*). The third is the **interactional** or 'Me and you' function, where a child uses language to establish personal contact and enter into social relationships (*Love Mummy*). The fourth is the **personal** or 'Here I come' function, where the child uses language to assert their individuality and to express their identity and feelings (*Jimmy good boy*).

In these first four functions, language is used to enable a child to satisfy their physical, emotional and social needs. The next two functions concern the use of language by the child in relation to their environment. The fifth function is the **heuristic** or 'Tell me why' function, where the child uses language to explore their environment, to find out about the reality that they inhabit (*Why the bus stop here?*). The sixth is the **imaginative** or 'Let's pretend' function, where a child uses language to create their own imaginary environment or where they simply use language playfully (for example, in rhymes or riddles).

The last function identified by Halliday, and probably the last acquired by children, is the one most readily associated with adult language: the **representational** or 'I've got something to tell you' function, where language is used as a means of communicating information or expressing propositions. It is a later development for a child to realise that others (adults, including parents) do not know something and need to be told it, or for a child to discern and so communicate what is 'newsworthy'. These are judgments that adults routinely make in their linguistic interactions.

ACTIVITY 49

Listen again to your recordings of child language, or look again at your transcripts of the recordings, and attempt to identify the function that each child utterance has, according to Halliday's scheme outlined above.

Do one or two functions predominate in the child's language? Is this related to the context in which you made your recording and the activity that the child was engaged in at the time? Or is it related in part to the age of the child and therefore the limited functions that language is called upon to perform?

4.4 Language in thinking and conceptualising

Does the acquisition of language precede that of thought? Is thought dependent on language? These are questions that have troubled philosophers, psychologists and linguists for centuries. They have a bearing on our view of how children acquire language. Do children have to develop cognitively to some extent in order to acquire language? Or do children have to acquire language in order to develop cognitively? Or are the two types of development quite unrelated?

Psychologists and linguists who subscribe to 'behaviourist' theories believe that thought is 'internalised speech', simply speech that is not spoken out loud. They also believe that all learning takes place through interaction with the environment. According to this theory, no thought occurs without language. Thinking is enirely dependent on language, and so cognitive development is subservient to linguistic development. This view is particularly associated with the psychologist B. F. Skinner and the linguist Leonard Bloomfield.

There are several reasons why such a view is unlikely to be the case. First, as we have seen, children understand far more than they can articulate, which could not be the case if thought depended entirely on language. Second, there is evidence that people who are unable to speak, for whatever reason, can still understand language spoken to them and can often communicate in other ways (for example, by signing or finger spelling). And, third, we have all had the experience of talking about one thing and thinking about something quite different!

Another view among psychologists and linguists is that the development of language is separate from and parallel to other kinds of development. Human beings are uniquely and innately programmed to acquire language. Part of a child's mental equipment that they are born with is a **language acquisition device** (LAD), which provides the parameters and controls for the acquisition of language. According to this view, language can be seen as the expression of thought, but the development of one is not dependent on the development of the other. This view is particularly associated with the linguist Noam Chomsky, who presented a trenchant critique of the behaviourist position.

Part of the problem in determining the answer to this question is that much of our evidence for the development of cognition is derived from language – from what children say and are observed to understand. Independent evidence derives from work undertaken by the Swiss psychologist Jean Piaget. To test children's cognitive development, Piaget set them certain types of task to undertake. One of the most famous is the 'conservation' task, which requires a child to judge whether water tipped from a short, wide container into a tall, narrow container has the same volume. Piaget sees the first eighteen months of life as the development of a child's 'sensori-motor intelligence'. Towards the end of this period, a child begins to be able to talk about their actions before they perform them. Language, then, is a means by which a child can think about reality, but it depends on the child's prior conceptualisation of that reality. This implies that the development of language is, at least to some extent, dependent on general cognitive development.

This question is by no means completely resolved as yet. On present evidence, however, it would appear reasonable to accept that the development of thought, or general cognitive development, is independent of the acquisition of language. The acquisition of language, though, does presuppose other, general, physical and mental developments. There may also be some specific innate characteristics that constrain the form that any language may take; in terms, for example, of its phonology and grammar. Language develops to serve as a tool for expressing thoughts, for representing constructions of reality, and for engaging in social interaction. Some linguists would argue that a social perspective on language (as in Section 4.3) is a more productive way of investigating language than a pyschological or cognitive one.

4.5 Language and the development of communication

If we adopt the social perspective and see language primarily as a means of establishing and maintaining social relationships and of interacting with our fellow human beings, then it is an interesting study to trace the development of communication skills on the part of children. This is now referred to as pragmatic development (see Sections 1.3.8 and 6.1).

From the moment of a baby's birth, parents – and especially mothers – treat the child as a person with whom they must interact. For example, in attending to the child's needs, parents talk to the child and act as if they are having a conversation, even to the extent of leaving pauses for the baby to reply. Gradually, as the baby becomes more responsive, parents impute turns to the baby and construct a conversation with their child, often with extended contributions of their own. In due course babies begin to attend to adult conversations going on around them, directing their attention to the person currently speaking: 'By the time their first words appear, babies have learned a great deal, both from observation and from practice, about what a conversation is and how to participate within it.' (Crystal 1987, p. 239).

It is well known that parents adapt their speech when talking to very young children. The term **motherese** has been coined to refer to this phenomenon, although __parentese__ might be more appropriate these days. They use a smaller vocabulary, simplify grammatical structures, talk more slowly and repeat the child's utterances with expansion. All of this contributes to a child's general acquisition of language. Parents also ask their child a lot of questions, in order to engage the child in conversation and encourage them to speak. It becomes clear to the child that using language involves interaction and that there are 'rules' of conversation. How to engage in conversation needs to be learned and refined, just as pronunciation, grammar and vocabulary do.

Between the ages of two and four, a child's conversational skills develop considerably. Before that, it has been the parents who have ensured that a conversation keeps going and who have provided the major input to verbal interaction with the child. Now, children become full participants: they learn to initiate interaction and introduce topics of conversation; they become skilful in turn taking; and they respond appropriately to questions and requests that are put to them.

As children approach school age, they become aware of various social factors affecting communication, such as the age and status of the person you are talking to, which may require you to use language that reflects your deference or may need you to attempt to be polite, by contrast with interaction with your peers. There is still more to learn: how to interact in the context of school, in the larger groups of peers in the playground; and then later on in more formal discussions, meetings and debates.

ACTIVITY 50

Compare the communication skills of a child illustrated in the two extracts below, taken from Fletcher (1985). In the first, the child is aged two years and four months. In the second, she is three years and eleven months. She is interacting with her mother (M = mother; C = child):

1
        M: what's what lovey
        C: me want that
        M: what is it
        C: [si:n]
        M: Plasticine
        C: mm

M: *what's it for*
  what are you going to make
C: *see Jack. Amy see me. see me. not Jack*
M: *mm*
C: *not Jack. only me*
M: *only you*
C: *you take a bissy*
M: *cos I was hungry*
C: *me want a bissy*
M: *there you are. you have a bissy too*

---

2   M: *no you didn't disturb me. did you have a nice time though*
C: *mm*
M: *good. what did you do*
C: *horrible things*
M: *I don't believe you. you always say that*
C: *I ... did*
M: *did you*
C: *I had to look after Qunity. to get him inside*
M: *why*
C: *just did*
M: *what, when you were playing outside*
C: *mm. I took ... I had to get him inside*
M: *did you manage*
C: *he'll go a different way than me*
M: *oh dear, did you manage in the end*
C: *yes*
M: *is he a naughty boy*
C: *no he wasn't. he got in the end with me*
M: *oh, good*
C: *when that... mummy here's another dog coming along, a smaller dog, one, two, let's see that nose*

4.6 School years: reading and writing

General language acquisition does not stop when a child begins school. The phonological system may be more or less in place, although many children still have some refinements to acquire, as well as learning to exploit rhythm and pitch in the course of spoken interaction. The grammatical system is largely acquired as far as the essential elements are concerned, but there is still more to learn, both in refining what has already been acquired (for example, irregular inflections) and in acquiring more complex grammatical structures (for example, embedded clauses). Vocabulary continues to develop, as it will do throughout the school experience, as a child is introduced to new areas of knowledge and becomes a reader of books. Children's communication skills will also continue to develop, as they interact in an increasingly diverse range of contexts and with a greater variety of people, beyond family and the immediate peer group.

The process of acquisition continues, then, especially through infant and into junior school. However, school brings a further aspect of language learning: reading and writing. As educated people, we take reading and writing for granted; but they are not 'naturally' acquired. Left to ourselves, we would not acquire the skills of reading and writing. We have to be taught them. In that sense, learning to read and write is different from acquiring the skills of listening and speaking. Children do not have to be taught how to speak: given the stimulus of spoken language around them, they cannot but help acquire language through speech. They are greatly helped by the input of parents, who do correct and improve on the child's language. But their 'teaching' is not of the same kind as is needed for reading and writing.

Writing is an alternative medium of language to speech. It has developed its own conventions, and to some extent its own grammar and vocabulary, in the sense that there are some of the more complex grammatical structures that we would rarely use in speech and some (for example, technical) words that we almost only ever encounter in the written form of the language. The written language is, however, at the centre of education, and learning to read is a necessity for participating in education. Equally, education utilises the ability to listen and to speak: information is transmitted both by the spoken and the written medium, and criticism, debate and reflection occur in both modes. Schools, therefore, have the task both of developing children's skills in listening and speaking and of teaching children how to read and write. All four skills are attended to in the National Curriculum for English.

What is involved in learning to read and write? Reading involves making sense of quite small marks on (usually) paper and relating these to language that is usually already known through speech. It involves, as far as English is concerned, the recognition that writing proceeds from left to right on a line, and from top to bottom on a page. It involves relating visual shapes (of words) with patterns of sound, and may also involve relating individual letters or pairs of letters with individual sounds. For English, as we have seen (in Section 2.1.5), there is no one-to-one match between letter and sound. Reading means being able to make an interpretation of the language on the page, to assign an intonation to what is read, so that it makes sense. Reading uses a complex of skills, if what is read is to be meaningful to the reader.

In learning to write, a child has to acquire the skill of using an instrument – pencil or pen – to make letter shapes, and then to combine these letter shapes according to the spelling conventions of English, to produce the written equivalent of words that are familiar from speech. The child also has to learn other conventions of writing: spaces between words, the notion of a sentence, capital letters, full stops and other punctuation marks, and eventually paragraphing. Initially, it is a matter of translating speech into the new medium; later, the specific characteristics of writing and the construction of texts (see Section 2.4) need to be learned, including being able to make a text cohesive and coherent, by providing appropriate connections between sentences and paragraphs. Learning the conventions of writing is almost like learning another language.

Learning to read and write requires a certain awareness of language on the part of children: the distinction and relationship between sounds and letters and between the spoken and written shape of words; the notion of a word and of a sentence; the difference between statements and questions; the function of punctuation to structure language; and so on. Learning to read and write makes some knowledge about language explicit in a way that the acquisition of the spoken language does not. Reading and writing make a greater demand on cognitive and motor skills than do listening and speaking. Writing inevitably requires you to think about what you want to communicate, as you construct sentences and texts, and make corrections and amendments, before you send your communication to the receiver.

We have not said anything about approaches to the teaching of reading and writing here. That is really beyond the scope of this book. We have focused in this section on the nature of reading and writing, and especially on the learning task that a child faces when entering school, learning that goes beyond the acquisition of the spoken language. In Section 6.2 we go on to consider the social importance of literacy.

ACTIVITY 51

With a small group of fellow students, continue the discussion of what is involved in learning to read and write, drawing on your own experience and on that of young children who you know and who are in the early stages of literacy. Make a list of the skills that are needed, and of the kinds of knowledge that need to be taught, so that someone can become a successful reader and writer.

One way of making the skills more obvious is to try to read something presented in an unfamiliar way; for example, by holding a text up to the mirror. Or try reading the following sentences and reflect on what you have to do to make sense of them:

s'tI semitemos thguoht taht eht hsilgnE levon tnew otni a enilced retfa eht dnoces dlrow raw. gnidroccA ot emos snairotsih, ti saw neht taht hsilgnE sretirw decnuoner noitibma, ssengib dna noitatnemirepxe ni ruovaf fo a laicnivorp, gnikool-drawkcab aiglatson.

4.7 Finding out about language acquisition

In the first two Activities of this chapter, you were asked to make a recording of child language, in order to obtain a small amount of data to analyse. As you will have found, this is not an easy task: you have to find your subject, set up your recording equipment, hope that the child produces enough data; then you have to listen to the tape, probably several times, and attempt to make a transcript, which may include varying degrees of detail. All this is very time-consuming and laborious. What you have done is to collect what is called a 'naturalistic sample'.

If you wanted to trace a child's language development over time, you would need to make a series of such recordings at regular intervals, in order to map the progress made. As the child grew older, you would want to record them in contexts that involved interaction; not just with their parents or siblings, but with their peers, perhaps without any adult present. Gordon Wells, at the Bristol Language Project (Wells 1985), did this by strapping radio microphones to children while they were at school, playing out with friends, and so on.

The size of the samples that you take (half an hour of recording, say) will depend on the purpose of the sampling. If it is to investigate a child's phonological acquisition, the sample can be fairly small, because a small sample is likely to contain most, if not all, of the phenomena that you would want to find. For a grammatical investigation, the sample would need to be somewhat larger, and for a lexical investigation larger still.

An alternative, or a complement, to naturalistic sampling is **elicitation** by experiment. The investigator sets up an experiment, either by initiating a controlled dialogue, or by getting a child to undertake a series of tasks or to respond to pictures; or, if they are old enough, to read a list of words or a text. Such experiments will be geared to elicit certain types of response from the child, so that particular features of the child's language can be investigated; for example, specific phoneme contrasts, grammatical structures and discourse strategies.

Elicitation experiments are valuable if the area of investigation is specific and circumscribed. They also enable data to be collected from a range of subjects, so that it can then be tested statistically for validity. A number of standardised tests – which are readily available and routinely used by psychologists and speech and language therapists – have been developed to elicit information on a variety of language areas. One such test is the British Picture Vocabulary Scale, which requires children to point to pictures in response to a verbal stimulus and is used to position children on a standard scale of passive vocabulary acquisition. However, experiments require an intrusive experimenter, and they usually take place in an unnatural environment and with experimental props, all of which may have effects on the responses of the subjects. It is often possible, however, to take account of these effects in assessing the results. The next step is to make sense of the data that you have collected. You need to have some question in mind that you are trying to answer; for example, 'What stage has this child reached in acquiring the verb inflections of English?', 'Does this child have a vocabulary within the range for their age?', 'How far has this child progressed in the acquisition of English consonants?' The question that you have formulated may lead you to choose one of the standardised tests, and the interpretation of the score is made against the standard scale provided by the test. If you have made up your own elicitation test – for example, to find out about a child's acquisition of consonants – you can chart the consonants that you have found and note the substitutions that have been made. If you have collected naturalistic data – for example, to investigate acquisition of grammatical structures – a form of profiling may be appropriate, such as the Language Assessment, Remediation and Screening Procedure (LARSP), used by speech and language therapists (see Crystal 1987, p. 233; Fletcher 1985, pp. 52–6).

ACTIVITY 52

Construct an experiment to test the acquisition of fricative consonants in English in a child aged between four and five. You can assume that the child will be able to read simple words from a list. Make sure that your list of words includes each fricative in at least initial and final position in the word.

For example, 'ship' and 'rush' would attempt to elicit the voiceless palatal fricative.

Your list should also include so-called **distractors**, words that contain none of the targeted consonants, so that the child doesn't realise which sounds you are concentrating on.

You need to balance the desirability of attempting to elicit each sound at least twice against the risk of tiring the child by presenting too long a list, with consequent flagging concentration.

4.8 Acquiring a second language: bilingualism

A minority of children in the UK acquire two (or perhaps even three) languages in the course of their childhood. You may be one of these fortunate few. For most of us, access to a second language – becoming **bilingual** – only takes place at school, and usually not until secondary school, when it then involves a conscious learning effort and a rather less than perfect grasp of the language.

A child may acquire two languages in one of two ways. In a small number of families, the parents may speak different languages, and they may choose to speak to their children, from birth, in their preferred language. For example, one parent may be an English speaker, and the other a Polish, Ukrainian or Greek speaker. Thus the children are exposed to two languages from the start, and they develop **simultaneous** or 'infant' bilingualism.

Alternatively, and more commonly, the language of the home, spoken by both parents, may be different from the language of the community at large. In this case, the children acquire the home language for the first four years or so of life, and then, when they enter the education system – at nursery or infant school – they are exposed to the dominant language and begin to acquire this alongside their home language. For example, the language of the home may be Punjabi, Bengali or Cantonese – to pick only three of the more than 100 minority languages spoken in the UK – while the language of the community at large is English. Such children are exposed to two languages during childhood, but with one language substantially acquired before they are exposed to the second; they then develop **consecutive** or 'child' bilingualism.

There has been much debate about the effects on children of acquiring two languages; which is, incidentally, the common experience of the majority of the world's children. Until the 1960s, the common opinion was that children who were exposed to more than one language were at a disadvantage in terms of their linguistic and general intellectual development. More recent studies support the view that there are certain distinct advantages to being brought up bilingually. Such advantages include developing a greater awareness of language, being able to think more creatively and divergently, being able to conceptualise more easily, and having a greater social sensitivity. See Saunders (1982, Chapter 1), for more detailed discussion of this point.

Initially, the impression may be given that a child brought up bilingually is linguistically confused. Crystal (1987, p. 363) notes the following stages through which such a child may pass (Crystal appears to be referring to simultaneous bilinguals, but this applies to some extent to consecutive bilinguals as well):

> In the first stage, a child's vocabulary consists of words from both languages, and the words are not usually translation equivalents.

> In the second stage, as the child moves into two-word utterances, words from both languages may be used within the same utterance, but the rate of mixing declines rapidly during the third year.

> In the third stage, translation equivalents begin to develop, as the vocabularies of the two languages grow, but the development of separate

grammatical systems takes a little longer. By this stage, in the fourth year of life, children become aware that they are speaking two different languages.

One of the advantages of acquiring a language during childhood is that you will have a native pronunciation, something that is very hard to achieve if a language is learned later (from teenage years on). Knowledge of two languages gives access to two cultures. As a child grows up, it is likely that one of the languages will become dominant for them, and they may develop a greater facility in this one. From the beginning, the languages may be used for different purposes or in different contexts; for example, home as against school. Consequently, the vocabulary acquired in the two languages will be different, reflecting the purposes and contexts in which each language functions.

ACTIVITY 53

Attempt to find someone who acquired two languages during childhood. Ask them about their memories of doing so, and find out what their present experience is of using the two languages. In what contexts do they use each language; for what purposes and for communicating with whom?

Write up your findings in a report. Compare your findings with those of your colleagues who have talked to different infant/child bilinguals.

Further reading

This chapter has depended especially on Cruttenden (1979) and Crystal (1987), with support from Fletcher (1985), Halliday (1975), Steinberg (1993) and Aitchison (1987).

The literature on language acquisition is now quite extensive. Introductory psycholinguistics textbooks will contain a chapter or more on the topic. See also Baker (1995), Goodluck (1991), Ingram (1991), Saunders (1982/1988) and Wells (1985).

Suggested projects

A number of choices present themselves, and the options that you select will determine how you undertake a project in the area of child language acquisition. Clearly, you need to have access to one or more children of the appropriate age. Here are the decisions that you need to make:

1   Will you investigate the language of a single child or will you make a comparison between children of, say, different ages?

2   Will you investigate some quite specific area, such as the acquisition of consonants, or will you look more generally at the stage reached in the acquisition of language?

3   Will you construct an experiment to elicit the features of language that you intend to investigate, or will you collect a naturalistic sample by making tape-recordings?

Your answer to each of these has implications for the others. For example, if – in answer to 1 – you decide to study a single child, you would probably want to investigate – in answer to 2 – at a more general level, say, the sound system, the grammatical system or the vocabulary; and this would probably involve you in naturalistic sampling – in answer to 3. On the other hand, if you decide to investigate a specific language feature, you may prefer to construct an appropriate experiment and have a number of children participate in it, perhaps at different ages, so that you could trace a development over time.

Within these parameters, there is a large number of projects that you could devise. Here are three suggestions:

1   Compare the acquisition of consonants by a small group of two-year-olds with that of a matched group of four- or five-year-olds. You will need to construct an appropriate experiment, remembering that you cannot assume reading skills: the elicitation will need to be oral.

2   Ascertain the grammatical competence of a three-year-old child by recording naturalistic samples and profiling the structures used, noting the frequency of their occurrence. If you use the LARSP profile, you can see how the child compares with a standardised measure.

3   Ascertain the vocabulary of a five-year-old child. You may do this either by using one of the standardised vocabulary tests, if one is available to you, or by taking naturalistic samples. Make a list of the semantic fields represented by the vocabulary, and note the distribution of words among the fields.

Language and society

5.0 Introduction

In Chapter 3, we looked at how the language has changed as society has changed over time, and in the previous chapter, we followed through how individuals acquire language from their environment in the first place. The rest of this book will look at language in its social setting. In the final chapter, we discuss the many varieties of language and how the forms of English relate to meanings and usage. In this chapter, we examine how language operates in society. The chapter outlines the main factors which affect the form and function of language, and it discusses reasons for the variations.

5.1 Sociolinguistics

The branch of linguistics to which this chapter belongs is **sociolinguistics**. It is concerned with relating variations in language usage to social factors that explain the variation. Examples of such factors are the social class of the speakers, their age, gender, where they live, who they generally communicate with, and what the content of their talk is. All of these factors are discussed in this chapter.

However, people also often have strong ideas about the status of their own and others' language usage, and the sociolinguist must take these attitudes into account as part of the description of the language. The reason for this is that – as discussed in Chapter 3 – people's attitudes to aspects of language can have an effect in changing the forms and usage of the language. Some people can express their sense of group-solidarity by language loyalty, or they can disparage the language of others to whom they may be opposed culturally or politically. These attitudes, of course, ought not to be held by the sociolinguist, but the fact is that they exist, they are a major explanation for the way language is, and they ought therefore to be examined as part of sociolinguistics.

5.2 Accent and dialect

Within the English language, the most obvious variations across speakers in society are the differences in how people pronounce words, how their intonation and pitch varies, and how different words, phrases and constructions might be used in their everyday speech. It is usual in linguistics to distinguish between **accent** and **dialect**. *Accent* refers to the sounds that speakers produce: the vowels and consonants in the words they use will be placed in particular patterned ways; the speed of their talk, their intonation to express statements, questions, scandal, surprise, annoyance and so on, and where they characteristically pitch their voices will all contribute to a recognisable pattern.

Dialect refers to the structural content of speakers' language: the particular words used, characteristic syntactic constructions, certain ways of expressing negatives, plurals, tense and so on. Dialects must not be so different from one another that they are considered to be mutually unintelligible; in that case, they are separate languages.

It is important to remember that it is the pattern of features that constitutes the dialect, rather than any single feature marking the variation. For example, the Tyneside dialect shares some features with Scottish English, such as *divven* as the assimilated negative form for *do not*. But it does not have the syntactic form for the continuous present: Scottish English has *this needs washed* for the Tyneside English *this needs washing*.

Of course, all dialects share most features of English in common; this is why they are classed as dialects rather than separate languages. Certain differences from **Standard English** (SE, which is discussed further below) recur in a variety of non-standard dialects. Among the most common are the following:

> Multiple negation (or, negative concord) for emphasis: *I don't want none* for the SE *I don't want any*.

> Variation in negative marker: *Did you do it? No, I never* for SE *Did you do it? No, I didn't*.

> Non-standard adverbial usage: *He ran in slow* for SE *He ran in slowly*.

> Non-standard plural of demonstrative article: *Next to them people* for SE *Next to those people*.

> Non-standard past forms: *We was only playing. It weren't my fault. It was him as done it* for SE *We were only playing. It wasn't my fault. It was him who did it*.

Although the distinction between accent and dialect looks clear enough, in practice it is not so easy. For example, some speakers of what has been called **Black English Vernacular** in the USA regularly and systematically do not pronounce /d/, /s/ and /z/ on the ends of words such as *old*, *cold*, *glasses*, *dog's legs* and *he runs*. Is this simply a difference in their accent, or do they have a different dialectal means of expressing certain words, possession, plurality and the third-person verb ending? Furthermore, some communities will deny being able to understand another group, purely on the basis of a desire to distance themselves from that group. Thus Germans and Dutch along the border will deny that their respective dialects are observably very similar to each other. Early

British cinema audiences claimed not to be able to understand American voices in the first 'talkies', because they had never been exposed to them before. Language loyalty and custom is clearly a factor here.

5.2.1 Regional geography

Because Britain was invaded and settled so many times, because of a long-standing village structure, and because of a relatively non-centralised state, there is a great deal of linguistic variation across the islands. Regional dialects in Britain are usually associated with particular regional accents. For example, it would seem odd, although not impossible, to hear the Tyneside dialect spoken in a Cornish accent. In the past two centuries or so, however, one dialect – now called Standard English – has come to be regarded as neutral with respect to regional origin. This is the dialect that emerged among the educated speakers of the southern East Midlands, and was codified in grammar books and dictionaries. It is promoted by the government as the national variety of English.

Standard English (SE) is regularly spoken with a regional accent. It is the distinction between accent and dialect that allows SE to be a useful means of communication across regions of the country. It should be emphasised that everyone speaks with an accent; it is as impossible to speak without an accent as to speak without making sounds. When people deny they have an accent, this is a statement of social prejudice and not linguistics.

There is a prestige form of pronunciation in Britain known as **Received Pronunciation** (RP). This is the accent which is aspired to in elocution lessons, on the World Service and in London-based BBC News (although regional accents are increasingly being heard here). Many people regard this prestige accent as 'properly spoken' English, or 'Queen's English', although in fact only about 3% (and falling) of the British population speaks with an RP accent, and the Queen speaks in a particularly 'advanced' form of upper-class RP.

As with perceptions of SE users, speakers of RP tend to be regarded as highly educated, honest and trustworthy. In tests of accent-preferences, RP, Scottish and Welsh accents are highly regarded, whereas 'Brummy', Scouse and particularly Cockney accents are disliked. The latter two accents are often taken, quite irrationally, to signify speakers who are violent or dishonest.

Accents can be differentiated from one another most obviously in the different realisations of the sounds of words. For example, some accents (such as casual Cockney) omit the final /t/ in words such as *pot*, or pronounce /t/ medially in *butter* as a glottal stop. Vowel variations tend to mark out different accents even more obviously. The first vowel in *butter* is pronounced in three different ways if uttered by an RP speaker (/ʌ/), a Cockney speaker (/a/) and a Geordie speaker (/u/).

Intonation is also a strong regional marker across accents. A Geordie accent is easily recognised by the characteristic rising intonation in most utterances, whether questions or not. A Birmingham accent is recognisable in the narrower range of the intonation pattern across utterances. It has only been in the past few decades, thanks to easily portable recording equipment, that linguists have been able to study accent in its natural social setting.

ACTIVITY 54
Descriptive linguistics applied
Try to give a linguistic account of your own accent and dialect. You should be as objective and neutrally descriptive as possible; that is, you should avoid any evaluative words or impressions such as *flat, rough, sing-song, good*. For accent description, it is often very illuminating to tape-record yourself and examine the vowels, consonants, intonation, pitch and stress separately. Do you alter certain sounds in rapid speech, or change in formal or casual situations? Similarly, describe your dialect under the headings of **lexical variation** (for example, non-standard words such as Yorkshire *neb* for *nose*) and **syntactic variation** (for example, East Lancashire *I'll be here while ten o'clock* for SE *I'll be here until ten o'clock*). It might be helpful to contrast your variety with RP and SE, unless you naturally speak these yourself. Are there any features in your own accent and dialect that might be confusing to non-speakers of the variety?

5.2.2 The linguistic variable

In order to investigate differences between accents, linguists have used the notion of the **linguistic variable** as a marker of accents. One sound is selected, and used as the *dependent* variable while other factors (such as social class, age, gender, region, ethnic group and so on) are varied, with a view to discovering correlations between the occurrence of the sound and these factors.

For example, one very noticeable linguistic variable in accents of the English language is **rhoticity**. This refers to the pronunciation (or not) of /r/ when it does not occur before a vowel (as in *car, cart, burn*). In the British Isles, rhoticity differentiates Scottish, Irish, Cornish, rural East Anglian and Northumbrian accents from most Midland and southern accents. In Britain, rhoticity is regarded as a low-prestige feature, associated with rural, 'backward' areas. The fact that this is a local prejudice is illustrated by the fact that the opposite holds in most of the USA, where rhoticity is prestigious and its absence is stigmatised.

The linguistic variable has been the basis of much of modern sociolinguistics. Any feature of language can be set against a social factor: a particular intonation, syntactic pattern, use of a particular word and so on. However, there are problems in collecting data such as this for study. It is difficult to set up a natural situation in which many people will say a particular word several times, or use a particular syntactic construction, without them realising that they are being observed. The fact that people change the way they speak when they are aware of being watched is known as the **observer's paradox**, and data collected in such circumstances must be regarded as suspect.

For this reason, many sociolinguistic studies have used variations in single sounds as the linguistic variable. People are less aware of individual sounds, there is a high chance of hearing the feature several times in a variety of words, and the sound can occur when the content of the talk is formal or casual, friendly, hostile, careful or everyday, and so on. Groups of speakers will often share the feature, making its study genuinely social, rather than simply part of the individual's speech style, which is known as their **idiolect**. Two studies which use this approach are described below.

5.2.3 Age and language loyalty

One of the most famous sociolinguistic studies was conducted by William Labov on the Massachusetts island of Martha's Vineyard. There are 6000 native inhabitants, but every year 42 000 tourists descend upon the island; the locals refer to them as the 'summer people'. They have bought property and land in the east of the island, and a seasonal tourist trade has become dependent on them. This area, incidentally, was used as the setting for the film *Jaws*. The west of the island – around Chilmark – is still rural, and the remains of the declining fishing industry operate there.

As a linguistic variable, Labov selected the way people pronounced the diphthongs [au] and [ai] in words such as *house* and *night* respectively. It had been observed that islanders tended to pronounce these sounds more centrally on the tongue (as [əu] and [əi]), although a previous study had found that, thirty years beforehand, this centralisation had been dying out. Labov interviewed about sixty people from all over the island. Surprisingly, he found that the use of a centralised diphthong was actually on the increase, and was especially noticeable in the speech of fishermen aged 31–45 living in Chilmark.

Labov's explanation for this is that those islanders who were committed to island life wanted to mark themselves as being real islanders, separate from the 'summer people'. Their centralised diphthong was the means of conveying this, and had been exaggerated by some of the islanders. Labov produces results that indicate a correlation between centralisation and whether informants had a positive or negative attitude to island life. Those people who centralised the most tended to be those who liked Martha's Vineyard, while those who centralised least were those who had a negative view of the island.

Furthermore, this **language loyalty** was more apparent in certain age groups than in others. When the use of the centralised pronunciation was set against age bands, a definite generational pattern emerged. Middle-aged men presented the feature most often, closely followed by those young people who had been away to study on the mainland but had made a conscious decision to return to the island. This generational 'snapshot' allowed Labov to discuss how the use of the feature was changing over time.

The Martha's Vineyard study indicates several important areas in which sociolinguistic methods can provide insight. Labov was able to observe language change by analysing its effects. He was able to link language use with subjective attitudes, and illustrate that this correlation was not random but principled. And language use was seen to be patterned according to age, attitude and social situation in ways that can be quantified.

5.2.4 Social class

Another social factor available for study is **class stratification**, the perception of a social hierarchy based on wealth, family status, attitude and occupation. Peter Trudgill, in a study in Norwich, set a variety of linguistic variables in pronunciation against both the social class and the gender of the speaker. Using local council wards as the unit from which informants were derived, he categorised people's social class on the basis of income, house and the occupation of the father of the family. He had the informants speak in a casual, relaxed situation, followed by a more formal, interview-style setting. He then got them to read a passage that contained many of the sounds that he was interested in. Finally, he had them read lists of words, many of them in pairs that contrasted with each other. By this method, he was able to gain examples of the linguistic variable from a continuum of casualness and formality. He also ensured that informants first spoke without being aware of which parts of their speech were being analysed, and then gradually became acutely self-conscious.

The table below (after Trudgill 1983, p. 94) contains a large range of information. The social class bands are shown, from middle middle class (MMC), through lower middle class (LMC), upper working class (UWC) and middle working class (MWC) to lower working class (LWC). These bands are further subdivided according to gender. The informants were then recorded for their use of the variable /ŋ/. For example, in a word such as *singing*, the final sound may be pronounced as either /ŋ/ or /n/. Such words were placed into various styles – word list style (WLS), reading passage style (RPS), formal style (FS) and casual style (CS) – in order to vary the awareness of the speaker regarding his/her own language use. The table shows the percentage of people in each group who used the /n/ pronunciation.

The /n/ variable in Norwich:					
Social class	Sex	WLS	RPS	FS	CS
MMC	M	000	000	004	031
	F	000	000	000	000
LMC	M	000	020	027	017
	F	000	000	003	067
UWC	M	000	018	081	095
	F	011	013	068	077
MWC	M	024	043	091	097
	F	020	046	081	088
LWC	M	066	100	100	100
	F	017	054	097	100

This table clearly shows that the low-status pronunciation of /n/ generally increases in frequency the lower down the social scale the speaker is. So, the MMC almost always use /ŋ/, whereas the LWC almost always use /n/ as the final sound of words like *singing*. It also shows that people are aware of the prestige value attached to these forms, since generally they tend to move towards the higher-status form when they are more aware of their own language use.

5.2.5 Gender

More interesting than these general trends, though, are the different results for men and women of the same social class. Women tend more towards the higher-prestige form than do men. Conversely, men seem to incline towards the lower-prestige pronunciation. Aiming for high prestige (and sometimes over-judging the matter) is known as **hypercorrection** (already referred to in Section 3.4.2 as a factor in language change). Aiming for low prestige is called **covert prestige** by

Trudgill. Notice in the table how LMC men use the lower-status feature more when they become aware of it (in formal style, FS) than in their everyday, *vernacular* speech (casual style, CS). Along with other sociolinguists, Trudgill suggests that women tend to be socially aspirational since they are often prejudicially assessed on the basis of their accents, and that therefore they are linguistically insecure. Men, on the other hand, desire to be thought of as 'tough' and 'down-to-earth', and so aim for the lower class speech patterns, even if they are themselves middle class.

In support of this, Trudgill also observes that, when asked subjectively about their accents, women tend to claim that they have a higher-prestige accent than in fact they use. Equally, men claim to use more lower-prestige forms than they are actually observed using.

There has been a great deal of interest in the issue of whether men and women use language differently. In the 1970s and 1980s, prescribed changes to the language were advocated by many feminists in order to make the language system itself less sexist. Examples include using *Ms* in preference to *Miss* or *Mrs*; dropping the gender qualification in *lady doctor*, *female executive*, *career woman* and also *male nurse*; and using neutral terms such as *personpower* (for *manpower*), *chair/person* (for *chairman*), *herstory* (for *history*), *himmicane* (for *hurricane*), *wimmin/womyn* (for *women*) and *mistress copy* (for *master copy*). The argument was that language is sexist because it is *man*-made, and men determine meanings because they are largely in control in society.

Such prescriptive recommendations have had limited success, in large part precisely *because* they are prescribed. There are, in any case, two serious flaws in this position. The first derives from the assumption that language is controlled and fixed by a dominant group (men), and that only they can exercise this power. Therefore, any feminist prescriptive intervention is futile, since women – it is claimed – do not have the same sociopolitical power. This particular feminist position is based on the idea that linguistic expression strongly determines patterns of thought. But if this *was* the case, then deterministic feminists would not even be able to discuss the issue in English, since they would, on their own argument, be unable to think about it.

A second counter-argument is that the position is based on ignorance of linguistics, particularly of etymology and language change. For example, the initial morphemes in *history* and *hurricane* have nothing, historically, to do with gender pronouns. *Woman* is not (as has been claimed) the *woe of man*, but a derivation of *wifman*, where *man* was simply Old English for *person*. Males were similarly distinguished by prefixes – *werman* or *wæpman*. In fact, in Anglo-Saxon society, women were allowed property rights, which were subsequently not regained until 1922!

It was through the medieval period that *wif* narrowed its meaning to its current sense, and later prescriptive 'authorities' decided that *man* should be both male-specific and also generic (a position actually embodied by a nineteenth-century Act of Parliament). This produces oddities such as the following:

> *Early man developed a large skull which caused him problems in giving birth and thus shortened his gestation period.*

Clearly, whatever the shortcomings of the prescriptive approach, there is something bizarre to be accounted for here.

A more recent, less deterministic position claims that differences are the products of the different uses that men and women make of language, rather than language being itself inherently sexist. Language simply reflects social discrepancies, and men and women have their own **genderlects**. From this viewpoint, language is only one part of an individual's social experience, and men cannot fix meanings because meanings cannot be fixed. Language, therefore, can express the needs and experience of women just as well, and linguists must consider the social and political uses of language.

For illustration, it has been shown that many words which are supposed to have common gender (that is, are gender-neutral) are in fact used in ways which exclude women:

> Readers *choose resorts by asking their wives where they would like to go.*

Consider also the connotations of the following pairs of words and associated phrases. A *waiter* works in a high-class restaurant, a *waitress* in a lower-class cafe. Compare *head waiter* and *?head waitress* (the question mark indicates doubt over the validity of the phrase). A *master* is in control, but a *mistress* is kept for sex. Compare *old master* and *?old mistress*. A *bachelor* is an approving term, but a *spinster* is a sad thing to be. Compare *bachelor pad* and *?spinster pad*. A *patron* is a business client, but a *matron* is an old nurse. If a man has a client, he is a businessman; if a woman has a client, she is a prostitute. If a man is a pro, he is competent; if a woman is a pro, she is a prostitute. If a man is a tramp, he is a homeless scruff; if a woman, a prostitute.

It has often been noted that, in mixed groups, men and women use different sets of politeness strategies, intonation markers, and turn-taking supports and challenges in conversation. Studies on school-children illustrate that boys' monopolisation of classroom resources and playground space also extends to their domination of linguistic space. This early socialisation is carried on into later life. Generally speaking, there is evidence to show that men in mixed groups speak more than women. When men speak to men, topics tend to be competition, teasing, sports, aggression and doing things, whereas women tend to talk about self, feelings, relationships and ideas.

In mixed groups, men have been found to initiate exchanges more, and women to support and reply. However, there is some accommodation and convergence for the other gender in each case: men speak less of 'their' topics and women less of 'theirs'. This also seems to be culture-specific: in the USA, women shift their topics more towards the men; in Britain, it is the men who tend to converge more towards the women's topics.

Generally, though, women tend to apologise more, men explain things to women, men interrupt and women give way. In simultaneous talk, men persist longer and so more often win the floor. Women ask more questions and make more supporting sounds and comments. Men tend to use assertive forms, while women use the more suggestive constructions of interrogatives and supposition.

It has been suggested that these differences arise because men and women are socialised into different understandings of the rules and functions of language. For example, when women talk of domestic matters and men of business matters, they all may be applying the same rule, *talking about work*. However, traditionally, men's work has been external to the home while women's work has been internal, and so the topics of talk seem to vary. Alternatively, with interrogatives, women may perceive the function of questions to be the maintenance of conversation, while men perceive the function as the elicitation of information, and act accordingly. Women may regard forcefulness as hostile personal aggression, while men regard it as part of normal conversational organisation.

Of course, the fact that cultural differences exist, and that usage has changed over time, suggests that there is nothing inherently male or female in any of the above patterns of use. An overriding consideration is the balance of power between participants in discourse. The so-called 'female' genderlects have been found in the stylistic choices of powerless men, and many women in positions of power tend to use the language of power as well. That power has in the past been associated very much with men goes a long way to explain why these particular patterns of language use have been seen as 'male'. However, the pace of social change over the past thirty years has already rendered many of the classic linguistic studies dated and obsolete, and *genderlects* perhaps need to be re-evaluated as linguistic choices to express and manage power.

ACTIVITY 55
Gender and ideology in language
Examine the flyer on page 126 for a restaurant. Consider the ideology (that is, the set of ideas and general assumptions) that is encoded by the different sections of the advertisement. Discuss who is the narrator of the text, and to whom the different parts are addressed. What sort of reader does the text construct or imply? Is it possible to reverse or equalise the gender-positions suggested by the text, while retaining the basic message of the advert? Or is there something inherently sexist in the actual message that is ideologically loaded below the level of language and regardless of the form of expression?

THE
- COACH HOUSE -

THE ONLY RESTAURANT ON THE FYLDE COAST TO SATISFY YOUR EVERY NEED!

- - - - LADIES - - - -

Finish that busy shopping trip with lunch in Chasers Bar
(We won't break the bank after all that spending)

* * *

Treat the family to our super Sunday lunch
12 noon to 5.30 o.m. — £6.95
(We do the washing up)

* * *

Had a hard Day?
Come and enjoy our Early Evening Snack 5.30 p.m. - 7.30 p.m.
Tuesday - Saturday from £1.55

* * *

Family Birthday ? Anniversary ? Wedding ? Christening ?
See our Special Party Menu Brochure :—

- - - - GENTLEMEN - - - -

Business lunch in the privacy of one of our upstairs rooms
(Just the thing to clinch that deal)

* * *

Romantic dinner for 2 in the cuddly nook
(Who knows where it might lead)

* * *

Want to eat early ?
Our excellent 5 course Table D'Horte Menu £8.95
from 5.30 p.m. to 7.30 p.m. Tuesday - Sunday.

5.3 English as a world language

Because of British colonialism and, more recently, the prominence of American culture globally, the English language is now the most widely spoken across the world. Perhaps more importantly, it is the world's most frequent second language. English is the language most likely to be used as a lingua franca (a common means of communication) when two different language speakers first meet.

However, English is not the same across the world. There are as many varieties of English as there are needs for different forms of the language. English no longer 'belongs' to the British, or even to the Americans, but is a resource for speakers who have developed their own proper varieties for their own circumstances. Every English speaker's language is perfectly adequate for their requirements; as new needs arise, so the language changes to accommodate and express them.

The job of the linguist is not to prescribe a model form of English (although there is a debate around which variety of English ought to be taught to foreign learners); it is to describe world-wide usage as it exists in its local forms, and to theorise about origins and effects.

The appearance of varieties of English around the world is almost entirely a result of trade, backed up by British military and naval power. In the cases of North America and Australia, native English speakers formed the majority of the established settlers. In the cases of Africa and India, English became associated with positions of government and power. Furthermore, many nations, upon their independence from Britain, kept English as a main language to avoid privileging the language of any one tribe or regional group. English thus stayed on as a useful neutral compromise, as well as an international language used in trade.

5.3.1 American English

American English now dominates the world. It is often Standard American English which is taught to foreign learners wherever the influence of the USA is strong, and so it is not unusual to find people from the Pacific, the Far East and also Germany speaking English with an American accent and using American idioms. Since the Second World War, American English has consolidated its position through its dominance of the entertainment industry.

The main feature of American English in contrast with Standard (British) English is in lexical variation. Many words have been borrowed from the languages of non-English speaking immigrants, as well as from the indigenous peoples; so *moccasin*, *jazz*, *zucchini*, *burger*, *bagel* and *kosher* can all now be heard in Britain. Some recognisably British words have developed variant meanings such as *mad* (= angry), *are you through?* (= are you finished?) and *bad/wicked* (= good). American technological innovation has also given us *program* (spelt this way in computing), *telephone* and *typewriter*, as well as *lynch*, *blizzard*, *joy-ride* and *prairie*, to express a culture and environment different from the British.

So, if you take a train journey in Britain, your railway train has a driver, a guard and perhaps a guard's van. You have luggage and your train may pass goods trains, level crossings and points. If you were in America, your railroad train would have an engineer, a conductor and a baggage car. You would pass freight trains, grade crossings and switches. In your automobile you fill up with gas, wipe your windshield, check your hood and trunk are shut, and drive down the freeway, expressway or divided highway, overtaking trucks. At home, you take the elevator to your apartment, read your mail, change the baby's diaper, and put in a trunk call to your foreign friends, making the call collect if you are mean. Finally, you drink a root beer that you've seen in a commercial while watching TV.

Of course, there is variation within the USA as well. Most domestic dialectal variation is based not so much on region as on divisions between urban and rural areas, and between ethnic groups. Some regional variations include the Boston *tonic* (soft drink). A *square* in Philadelphia is a *block* in New York. In Los Angeles people *park* cars, in Trenton they *rank* them, and in Delaware cars are *filed*.

However, there are also grammatical differences in word-formation and syntax that seem to be spreading. The suffix *-ise* is very useful for making verbs out of nouns, although there are plenty of British newspaper letter writers who complain about English fraternising with and being terrorised by words such as *hospitalised*, *prioritised* and especially *burglarised*. However (apart from the last example), British English can only express these concepts in a more roundabout way.

Syntactic variation tends to reveal the linguistic ignorance of such purist letter writers, since many American variants are actually older British forms which have not changed in America. Verbal auxiliaries such as *gotten* and *done* are acceptable in ways that would be regarded as ungrammatical in Britain. And many variants – such as *dove* (dived) and *hung* (hanged) – are American regularisations of British English oddities.

ACTIVITY 56

Cultural invasion?
List as many American words, phrases and constructions as you can that differ from Standard (British) English. Are there any areas of confusion or misunderstanding? Is American English a dialect, a language or some other kind of variety of English (is it, for example, legitimate to talk of *national* varieties of English, each with their own standard)? How many *Americanisms* have now passed into British English and are acceptable in the UK?

5.3.2 Artificial varieties of English

There are some varieties of English that are designed specifically for particular uses, and **English for Special Purposes** (**ESP**) is the area that studies and promotes these as codified and conventional lingua francas. For example, **Maritime English** (or **Seaspeak**) has been developed specifically to enable ships' navigators to communicate with each other regardless of their respective nationalities. Similarly, a reduced form of English is used by air-traffic controllers across the world to ensure precise and clear communication. The pilot of an Italian jet landing at Milan airport would nevertheless speak to the Italian controller in English. **Business English** is another example of an artificial variety to be used in international trade.

Such artificial varieties, often sponsored and commissioned by regulating bodies, serve such a narrow function that they can exist in highly simplified forms. This not only makes them easier to learn, but it also reduces the potential for ambiguity. Technical words are prominent, with specific jargon for particular industries forming *dialects* within Business English.

Of course, for the purposes of accuracy and safety, and because artificial varieties have no native speakers, they exist in a frozen form. Innovation tends to be introduced only by some sort of statute, rather than by individual creativity.

5.3.3 Pidgins and creoles

Where several languages come together – often in trading ports, refugee camps and slave markets – and communication is essential, a hybrid language may develop to be used in a few specific contexts. Since its functions are limited, such a **pidgin** is usually a restricted language system. If it is derived from English, the pidgin English will often have simple clauses, few prepositions and a small range of vocabulary (which is often mainly drawn from the other, non-English language). However, pidgins are not simply telegrammatic 'broken English'; they have to be learnt just as any other language, and are incomprehensible to the monolingual English speaker. By definition, a pidgin has no native speakers.

If, however, a pidgin persists in a particular region, it may extend its social functions and become the first language of the new generation. At this point, the language becomes a **creole,** a fully fledged language in its own right. Development at this point is often rapid, with increases in complex clauses and in the phonetic range, and with extra lexical items, synonymous terms, a tense and aspect system, and other complex grammatical forms. Standardisation of pronunciation and spelling often follows, and codification in dictionaries, in grammar books and through education.

Not all lingua francas develop into pidgins, and not all pidgins develop into creoles. Nor do all pidgins and creoles derive from English. All of the languages of the old European imperial powers are represented in pidgin/creole languages, with only a quarter being based on English. Many pidgins and creoles exist side by side; such as in Sierra Leone, where West African pidgin and *Krio* are spoken regularly in everyday life.

One of the most well documented examples of a pidgin is *Tok Pisin* (= *pidgin talk*) in Papua New Guinea. This language (also called *New Guinea Pidgin, Melanesian Pidgin* and *Neo-Melanesian*) has existed since the end of the nineteenth century. At that time, German planters shipped workers into Samoa to pick coconut and cocoa. Although a quarter of them died, 6000 were eventually repatriated to New Guinea on English ships, where a lingua franca developed. Back in New Guinea, with its 700 languages, the lingua franca continued to be used and became Tok Pisin pidgin.

Some of the English origins of Tok Pisin can still be seen in some words: *pik* (pig), *dok* (dog), *het* (head), *lukim* (see/look), *spaida* (spider), *kol* (cold) and *sikis* (six). Many of these result from the simplified sound system, with only five basic vowels available. New words are often formed by metaphor or compounding. Thus, *gras bilong het* is hair, *haus bilong spaida* is a web, and *haus bilong pik* is a pigsty. A *plantihan* is a centipede (plenty hands), *haus sik* is a hospital and *haus pepa* (paper house) is an office. Intensification can be expressed by repetition; thus, *look* means *look*, but *looklook* means *stare*.

Tok Pisin has for the past twenty years been in the process of **creolisation**; that is, it has native speakers for whom it is a first language. This process is very rapid once begun, since children quickly innovate new words and structures to express every facet of their lives. The language comes to be used in all contexts, with a corresponding increase in available forms and potential functions.

Particularly important in the process is the **codification** of the language, helped by linguists who were originally concerned simply to provide a descriptive account of Tok Pisin. The linguistic account of the language, since it is written down, becomes the 'stable' form which can then be taught in schools as a national standard. This in turn confers authority on the language as having prestige, and so many more people are willing to learn it. This both encourages and is supported by literary activity in the language, with original fiction written in Tok Pisin, and the Bible being translated into the language. Tok Pisin is now regarded as a fully fledged language in its own right.

Some creoles (such as in Jamaica, with the creole known as *Patois*) are in a post-creole situation, with the pressure of English through the education system being felt very strongly. With much word-borrowing, occurring especially in highly influential areas such as law, government and advertising, several varieties of the language are emerging, spread out through society.

The full creole version (the **basilect** variety) tends to be spoken by those who have received very little formal education. Within the education system, a variety of Patois is spoken that is beginning to be influenced very strongly by English (this is known as the **acrolect**). Between these varieties are a variety of **mesolects** which share features of the creole and of English. For example, the acrolectal *I told him* is identical to Standard English, but the basilectal *mi tel am* obeys different rules. A whole range of mesolectal versions (*a tel im*, *mi tel i* and so on) lie in between.

For example, it is rare to hear acrolectal speakers of Tok Pisin using the full phrase *Taim bilong san i godoun* (the time of the sun going down). Instead, it is likely that you would hear simply *sikis klok* (6 o'clock). Similarly, words such as *sandwich*, *lunch* and *tea* have been imported from Australia. If the use of the acrolect becomes more widespread in the future, Tok Pisin or Patois may become completely **decreolised** and English may become dominant altogether. Against this, language loyalty could work to save the creole.

5.4 Multilingualism

The term **multilingualism** is generally used in two senses. First, an individual can be said to be bilingual or multilingual if they are able to speak two or more languages reasonably fluently. Second, the term *multilingual* is used of whole speech communities (or regions, areas or nations) in which two or more separate languages are used regularly by most of the population in everyday life.

At first glance these two uses of the term might seem to be inclusive of each other, and therefore the same. However, in multilingual speech communities, all individuals who are members of that community will be multilingual; whereas an individual may be multilingual within a monolingual community. It is also often the case that the monolingual community will generally view the multilingual individual in particular ways that may be prejudicial to that individual. It is therefore useful to keep the two senses of the term.

There is a popular conception in Western societies that the monolingual situation is reproduced throughout the world. It is a belief which the increasing numbers of Spanish speakers in the USA, and Asian language speakers in the UK are beginning to render false. In the monolingual outlook, the multilingual individual is often regarded with either suspicion or admiration, but in both cases as someone unusual. In fact, multilingualism is the norm rather than the exception throughout the world, and it is monolingual communities which occur less frequently.

One of the most obvious examples of multilingualism within Europe is in Switzerland. Swiss varieties of German, French and Italian are regularly encountered, with almost all speakers having native competence in two or more of these languages. All three variants are recognised by government and represented in official documents, road signs and on television. In practice, there are areas in which one of the languages tends to dominate in usage, but these areas often blur into each other across the country. To complicate the picture, languages and dialects other than these three 'official' languages are also used by minority groups throughout Switzerland.

Although linguists make a distinction between linguistic terms such as *speech community* and geographical/political terms such as *nation, ethnicity* and so on, in practice people often use language as a symbol for political views and cohesion. Historically, linguistic oppression (such as of Irish Gaelic and Welsh by the English) has been seen as an important part of territorial invasion. Resurgent nationalist movements have subsequently allied themselves with the native languages as a sign of resistance and identity. Thus Irish Gaelic, although spoken by only a tiny minority of the population, has been the Irish Republic's official language since the 1920s and is taught in schools. And in Wales, although there are virtually no monolingual Welsh speakers, Welsh is now 'officially' sanctioned in schools, on road signs, on television and in the courts, largely as a result of campaigns by the *Welsh Language Society* and *Plaid Cymru*, the nationalist party.

Even England itself, of course, has only been generally monolingual for the past 700 years, following long periods of English/French and Anglo-Saxon/Latin bilingualism.

5.4.1 Code-switching

Where two or more languages are widely used in everyday life, the choice of which language is spoken in any specific circumstance is usually a highly principled matter of social rules. For example, one language may be regarded as being more casual than another, or more appropriate to the written form, or more polite, or to be used on religious occasions, and so on. It can then happen that a speaker may move from one language to another fairly suddenly, sometimes even within an utterance. Any such rapid movement between one variety of speech and another is called **code-switching**.

This behaviour involves two factors: the language used and the context of utterance (the situation). Two types of code-switching can thus be described: in **situational** code-switching, the context determines a change in language (for example, entering a Catholic church fifty years ago would prescribe a switch from English to Latin); in **metaphorical** code-switching, a change in the topic of conversation, in the language itself, serves to redefine the social setting (for example, an official switching from a *polite* language to a *casual* one will thus signal an end to official business).

The social rules which govern code-switching can be very subtle and complex, to the extent that speakers are often unaware of what they are doing. For the linguist, it is fairly easy to observe switches between different languages by multilingual speakers. It is much more difficult in observing monolingual speakers who code-switch by means of dialect, register and accent variation. In these cases, though, the fundamental phenomenon of code-switching is the same as for the multilingual. People who adopt a 'telephone voice' that comprises the use of a more prestigious accent, more formal words and more polite grammar can be said to be code-switching.

The terms *multilingual* and *bilingual* are often used to refer to people who are equally competent in two or more languages. Such genuine multilingualism is rare in Britain; speakers tend to see themselves as having a particular language first (L1) and other languages second (L2). In many cases, particularly for those children who have recently arrived in the country, for whom English is very much an L2, the assumption of bilingual equal competence can be harmful and prejudicial. It is therefore useful to differentiate multilingual speakers from speakers of English as a second language (**ESL**) and speakers of English as a foreign language (**EFL**), which provides a gradation of competence in English relative to the other language spoken.

It has also recently been recognised that the problems encountered by ESL and EFL speakers are not always strictly linguistic ones. Individuals from Asia, Africa, South America and the Caribbean, as well as from Eastern Europe, often find that cultural differences that are encoded in language are so different that inferred or obscure meanings can easily elude them. Irony, idioms and jokes are particularly difficult. Clearly, other sorts of knowledge as well as grammar and vocabulary need to be mastered. Learning the culture seems to be a necessary complement to learning the language.

5.5 Language and disadvantage

It is within the field of education that sociolinguistic approaches to language study have been most strongly debated. Argument has often centred around the issue of how language skills affect students' performance across the curriculum. Complaints throughout this century about school-leavers' poor spelling, grammar and general communicative skills have led politicians and journalists to call for changes in the way language is taught in schools. The strongest form of this position is that poor linguistic expression is a sign (and even a cause) of low intelligence, racial inferiority and criminal tendencies.

There are two facts which are documented and widely accepted: first, the language of middle-class and working-class children is different; and, second, working-class children do less well at school than middle-class children. A theory of language and education would link these facts, but there are a variety of possible connections. It could be that the language of working-class children is not good enough to enable them to do well at school. This is a **deprivation** theory, claiming that language differences entail cognitive differences. Alternatively, a **difference** theory would argue that there is an intolerant attitude to working-class language so that it is implicitly discriminated against in schools. Or, working-class language could simply be one part of a culture that regards the middle-class education system as alien, and this also could cause those children not to engage in school-work.

A famous deprivation theory was put forward by Basil Bernstein in the 1960s. He claimed that there are two patterns of language used by children: **restricted** and **elaborated codes**. He said that middle-class children use both codes in different contexts, but lower working-class children only have access to the restricted code. This limits the latter's abilities of expression and ability to form concepts, and they are disadvantaged because 'schools are predicated upon elaborated code'.

Elaborated code typically features the following:

    accurate grammatical order and syntax
    complex sentences, with coordination and superordination
    frequent use of prepositions, showing logical structure
    impersonal pronouns
    passive constructions
    unusual adjectives and adverbs

It is thus *universalistic* and context-free (that is, it makes sense without the immediate reference to the context of utterance).

Restricted code is comprised of:

    unfinished and short sentences
    simple clauses
    commands and questions
    categoric statements
    repetition of conjunctions
    hesitancy
    rigid and limited use of adjectives and adverbs
    confusion of reasons and conclusions
    sympathetic circularity ('you *know*')

In relying on implicit meaning it is thus *particularistic*, and dependent on the context.

Bernstein emphasised that these codes are not the same as dialect; both can be expressed in SE. They do, however, appear to present a linguistic explanation of educational failure.

Various studies were produced to support the theory. Mothers reported how they talk to their children, and working-class mothers were observed to use only restricted code, whereas middle-class mothers used both codes. The former gave commands whereas the latter gave reasons for decisions. The working class were said to manipulate the environment physically, whereas the middle-class used language to alter their environment.

In a famous study (Bernstein 1973), 300 children were shown a picture sequence, and asked to tell the story verbally. From the results, two 'slightly exaggerated' versions were produced as typical of middle-class and working-class children respectively, as follows:

1   *Three boys are playing football and one boy kicks the ball and it goes through the window the ball breaks the window and the boys are looking at it and a man comes out and shouts at them because they've broken the window so they run away and then that lady looks out of her window and she tells the boys off.*

2   *They're playing football and he kicks it and it goes through there it breaks the window and they're looking at it and he comes out and shouts at them because they've broken it so they run away and then she looks out and she tells them off.*

The first version, with thirteen nouns and only six pronouns, is context-free and explicit, whereas the second, with only two nouns but fourteen pronouns, is context-bound and needs the pictures to 'decode' the meaning. It is argued that these 'considerable differences' 'may well have important *cognitive* consequences'. This is based on the fact that the second version has limited scope for descriptive adjectives (pronouns cannot be modified). Such understanding of differences would naturally lead to advocating some form of compensatory education scheme. Indeed, Bernstein's work has been used to argue both for and against comprehensive education, grammar versus creative writing teaching, and the National Curriculum through the 1970s, 1980s and 1990s!

There has been much debate and criticism of such research. First, there has been little practical proof of the assertions. Experimental results are indirect (based on mothers' reports rather than their actual observed behaviour) or invented (which seems suspicious, given that 300 real stories were collected!).

Methodological procedure is also highly unsystematic. In the 'picture' experiment reported above, the restricted code users are condemned because they act as if the listener can see the pictures. But, of course, this is precisely the case, and it can thus easily be argued that in fact it is the restricted code users who act with language appropriate to the situation. The elaborated code version is largely redundant in terms of information conveyed. Moreover, the interview setting is inappropriate to test the natural language of five-year-olds.

Finally, many of the linguistic assumptions made are highly contentious. The direct link between linguistic expression and cognitive capacity is far from proven, and ignores, for example, the possibility that restricted code users may know elaborated code (part of their *competence*) but simply choose not to use it in most circumstances (as part of their actual *performance*). There is also often a naivety in associating linguistic forms with their functions. For example, it has been claimed that the middle class use more complex sentences of the *if..., then...* type, as a means of rational argument: *If you eat that now, you won't want your dinner*. However, a non-reasoned threat has the same structure: *If you do that again, I'll hit you.*

In response to criticisms, Bernstein's theory has become more abstract. He moved to regarding codes as high-level **symbolic orders** which children use to organise experience, and withdrew from equating linguistic form with cognitive capacity. So, later versions of the theory present codes as abstract frameworks at a psychological level of verbal planning. Bernstein also became interested, not simply in the rough working/middle class distinction, but in the types of family from which children came. At this point it becomes more of a social theory and entirely non-linguistic.

However, there are clearly political and educational consequences to this debate. We believe that it is important that teachers (especially English teachers) have a knowledge of linguistics. However, such a view risks being discredited if Bernstein's analysis is teachers' prime example of linguistics. There is also an anxiety that the emphasis placed on Standard English as 'correct' English, backed by the authority conferred by government and the National Curriculum requirements, is heavily influenced by the assumed direct link between linguistic performance and cognitive capacity and achievement.

5.6 Attitudes and correctness

Any language or dialect is perfectly adequate for the needs of its speakers. There is no such thing as a language or dialect that is inherently better than any other. However, as we have seen already, social attitudes vary towards different dialects. In modern-day Britain, many people still have a perception of a SE speaker as someone who is educated, trustworthy, honest and civilised. SE can be said to be a **prestige** dialect, and is even seen by some as the only 'good' and 'proper' variety of English. The word *standard* here is understood to mean a level to aspire to, an ideal model. By contrast, linguists use the word to mean simply the variety of English in which most books and newspapers are written.

Certain other dialects in Britain have very low prestige. The dialect of the London inner city, Black English, Merseyside English and West Midlands English, for example, are often received as being 'poor' or 'bad' varieties, betraying low social class and low education. This is especially true when these dialects are spoken in the accents which characteristically accompany them (Cockney, Jamaican-British, Scouse, 'Brummy').

From a descriptive linguistic point of view, such judgements are part of the system of prejudice and stereotyping in society. Linguists prefer to talk not of good and bad English, but of *appropriate* English; that is, a variety of English which fits the circumstances of its use. So, for example, in a formal job interview, it is probable that SE would be the most appropriate form of English to use. This would also be the case in various other formal contexts: textbooks, after-dinner speeches, business letters, newspaper stories and most written contexts. However, SE would probably be inappropriate on the football terraces, in a pub, when telling a joke, in casual conversation, in private letters and so on. In these contexts, the non-standard dialect of the speaker/writer is much more likely to be used, and is entirely appropriate.

The pressure towards a standard tends to take two forms. First, there is pressure from **usage**. Historically, increased social and geographical mobility, mass transport and media have encouraged the standardisation of dialects as a matter of communicative convenience. Second, there is often pressure towards standardisation by **directive**, from authority figures such as bishops (see Chapter 3), from journalists and writers, or from government.

Most people have an instinctive feeling for what is 'good' English. This feeling tends to be conservative, in that people like to look back at a version of English that they learnt by relatively clear and fixed rules. However, descriptions of this variety of English tend to be expressed in terms of what is not allowed: double negatives, ending sentences with prepositions, split infinitives, and incorrect subject–verb agreement are all among the most frequently mentioned sins. Spelling words to a standard dictionary form is also highly important socially today (such uniformity is a relatively modern obsession). Although, as we have seen from Chapter 3, these features all have historical explanations, the fact that attitudes against them are so widespread means that a speaker/writer will be stigmatised for using them, however well-educated and intelligent they are. It is a fact that linguists must recognise, especially when concerned with teaching English as a foreign language, that these cultural attitudes are as much a part of mastering the language system as learning to say the 'right' words in the 'correct' order in a 'good' accent.

ACTIVITY 57

Prestige and stigma of language varieties
The sociolinguist Roger Bell (1976) has provided seven criteria which can be used to describe the prestige of a language variety, whether an accent, a dialect or an entire language. These are as follows:

Vitality – whether there is a living community of speakers; for example, British English.

Historicity – whether the speech community has been historically defined by their language use; for example, the French, but not Gaelic-speaking Irish, who live today alongside monolingual English-speaking Irish people.

Autonomy – the sense that speakers have of their own linguistic independence; for example, Afrikaans speakers' perception of Dutch, to which it is closely related.

Reduction – the sense speakers have that their speech pattern is limited to certain functions, and that other dialects exist to be used in different contexts; for example, speakers of pidgin languages.

Mixture – the speakers' sense of the purity of their own variety, or whether they think it has low status; for example, the perception of 'pure' Cockney.

De facto norms – whether there is an unofficial, non-codified, non-dictionary sense of proper usage; for example, speakers point to an old speaker who is seen to use a more 'pure' variety.

Standardisation – the adoption of one variety as standard, which is then codified in dictionaries, grammar books, and the education system; for example, the south-east Midland dialect which became Standard English.

Take examples of a local dialect close to where you live, or a language that you speak, and test its prestige value by discussing the variety in terms of Bell's factors above. You should decide which features are descriptive and which depend on the attitude of the speakers and listeners of the variety.

Further reading

There are several very good introductions to sociolinguistics which contain many useful passages and examples from around the world. Wardhaugh (1992) and Holmes (1992) provide the most detailed introductions, while Trudgill (1983) is easier and contains his Norwich study. Montgomery (1986) is also a good starting-point. Bell (1976) and Hudson (1980) are more advanced texts. All of these deal with accent and dialect, but more detail can be found in Trudgill's (1990) survey of England and Trudgill and Chambers' (1991) collection of essays. Milroy (1981) includes variation from the whole of the British Isles. Dialect maps (such as Orton, Sanderson and Widdowson 1978) are interesting to compare with your own experience. Accent is comprehensively covered by Wells (1982). Much seminal work in sociolinguistics is contained in Labov (1972), although this can be very technical for the beginner.

The sociolinguistics of gender has recently been well supported by writing. Cameron (1990), Coates and Cameron (1988), Tannen (1992), Graddol and Swann (1989), Lakoff (1990) and Poynton (1989) are all essential reading. Cameron (1992) and Coates (1993) are probably the best places to start, since they survey developments in the field as well as providing an intelligent and provocative discussion themselves.

English around the world is described and surveyed by Trudgill and Hannah (1984), and detailed discussion is provided by Platt, Weber and Ho (1984), Kachru (1982, 1985) and L. E. Smith (1983). Chapman (1987) outlines the influence of American slang. Many classic case-studies from around the world are contained in Pride and Holmes (1972), Fishman (1971–2) and Gumperz and Hymes (1972). Pidgins and creoles are described in detail by Romaine (1988) and Holm (1988–9), although these are advanced. A simple treatment and examples from Tok Pisin are in the very readable Aitchison (1987).

Bernstein's work is intelligently described and evaluated by Stubbs (1983a). Cummins and Swain (1986) discuss bilingualism and education. The classic treatments of Black English in Britain are Edwards (1986) and Sutcliffe (1982). Language use in the education system is discussed by Stubbs (1986), and excellent materials can be found in Carter (1991). The Standard English debate is well discussed by Wilkinson (1993) and Milroy and Milroy (1993), and the whole issue of prescriptivism in language study is also covered by Milroy and Milroy (1991).

Suggested projects

The sociolinguistic study of language involves collecting real, natural examples of linguistic data and analysing them in terms of one of the frameworks mentioned in this chapter. The most efficient way of ensuring that you gain good examples of language use is to set up a situation that encourages people to say the sorts of things that you want them to say. In other words, think of a linguistic variable to investigate, and a social factor (ethnicity, gender, region and so on) to set against it, and find people who fit the description. Then, either by interviewing them, or getting them to discuss an issue, record what they say.

The easiest linguistic variable to use is a phonological one, since it is quite difficult to set up situations in which you can guarantee that people will unself-consciously use a particular word or pattern of grammar. You will begin the study with expectations (an hypothesis) as to what you think people are likely to do, and your experiment will confirm or reject these.

1   Gender differences can be at the phonological level (as Trudgill found), but many of the most interesting features form what have been called genderlects. Do women really support others in conversation? Are men really more aggressive in dominating the floor? You could record real examples of single-sex talk and mixed-group talk to see if the patterns or content of the conversation is different along gender lines.

2   Instead of going out into the world and collecting fieldwork data, you could be an armchair sociolinguist by collecting data from the television or radio. Recorded music by British, American and African bands can also provide sociolinguistic data. You could examine regional or class accents by comparing local radio with Radio 1, or with Radios 3 and 4. You could look at the influence of Black English on the lyrics of jazz, soul, blues or rap music, or how even British-born white rock singers adopt American accents. Do they even hypercorrect?

3   Creolisation is a term usually applied to recently emerged languages originating in the contact with the speech of the colonial powers. As such, you might argue that it is ideologically loaded. Could you make a case, with evidence, that English itself is a creole language, based on Germanic but with a vocabulary collected from French, Latin and Danish?

4   Find someone you know who speaks more than one language. Do they ever code-switch? You could either secretly observe or record them to discover their actual linguistic behaviour, or you could interview them or use a questionnaire to find out what they think they do when they code-switch. You might do both to see if there is a discrepancy between what they actually do and what they think they do. Any difference is likely to be explainable with reference to language loyalty and language prestige.

The Activities in this chapter could form the basis for extended study.

Language in use

6.0 Introduction

So far in this book, we have looked at the structure of the English language and the rules under which it is arranged to be meaningful. We have followed its development through time and through the early stages of acquisition by the individual. In the last chapter, we examined how groups of people employ language to define themselves within society. In this final chapter, we consider the social uses to which language is put, and how those functions and contexts affect the form of expression of particular texts and discourses. In short, what we will be doing is focusing on the form of the language rather than its content. So we will discuss not only single utterances but the social force of what is said; how conversation structure can be as meaningful as the content of dialogue; how the assumptions and world-view of the speaker are encoded in discourse; and how all of this linguistic knowledge that you have gained can be applied to the stylistic study of any kind of text in context.

6.1 Pragmatics

Semantics is the branch of linguistics that is concerned with the meaning of words and sentences. However, often the meaning of particular utterances or whole exchanges between people depends as much on the context of the speech and the purpose of the speakers as on the literal meanings denoted by the sentences themselves. To account for such use of language in context, the discipline of **pragmatics** has developed.

6.1.1 Speech acts and conversational maxims

One of the central frameworks within pragmatics is the treatment of <u>speech acts</u>. This is the notion that utterances not only contain a message but have a social force in themselves. So, saying *I promise I'll be there* not only conveys information but itself constitutes the act of *promising*.

Whenever a speaker makes an utterance, they perform a **locutionary** act; that is, a sequence that conforms to the phonological and grammatical conventions of the language. Otherwise, the utterance will be regarded as nonsense (as if you said, *aarggh glopus fintin plurp,* which would not be **felicitous** to the rules of English). Locutionary acts are handled by semantics. Pragmatics is further interested in **illocutionary** acts; that is, the communicative purpose that is intended or achieved by the utterance. You might *promise, threaten, inform, question, greet* and so on. This distinction is useful because there is not always a one-to-one correspondence between syntactic forms and illocutionary acts. All of the following various forms, for example, can be intended or taken as questions:

> *what time is it, please* – interrogative form, direct

> *can you pass the salt* – interrogative, although apparently asking about ability rather than for the salt itself

> *you're the teacher* – declarative statement, which looks as if the speaker is informing

> *Wednesday* – incomplete sentence, intonation as a question

> *to be or not to be* – that *is* the question, although it has no main verb and so is incomplete, and, of course, is rhetorical in context

Obviously, hearers infer the likely intended purpose from contextual clues such as the previous utterance, facial expression and situation, as well as from the intonation of the speaker.

There is a special class of illocutionary acts called **performatives**. Like the *promising* example above, these contain a verb which enacts the social force of the utterance. *I baptise this child Mary, I sentence you to prison, You're sacked* and *I'm writing to you to complain about bad language on television* are all examples of performatives. All speech acts (and especially performatives) depend for their effectiveness on various **felicity conditions** being satisfied. In other words, the utterance must be said by the right person to the right person in the right place at the right time in the right manner and so on. The effect of inappropriacy is often simply funny: for example, a gardener cannot ordinarily baptise a baby with a hosepipe; you cannot send your dog to prison; a caretaker cannot fire a headteacher; and you cannot write a letter of complaint by standing on the top of a mountain painted blue with two semaphore flags.

The fact that humorous – even surreal – effects can be generated by being infelicitous illustrates an important point about pragmatic rules. This is that they operate as normal conventions which are often broken in everyday talk. The point is that it is rare that dialogue breaks down every time this happens; it is more likely that the listener will try hard to infer an intended message from an utterance that seems, on the surface, somehow odd. Labelling any of the above examples as intentional irony, humour or avant-garde art, for example, is a common way of preserving the assumption that the speaker meant something by what they said.

Underlying all this is what has been called the **cooperative principle**. The assumption in communication is that speakers intend to mean things and that hearers accept this in trying to work out intended meanings. This is essential when, as often happens, the inferred meaning of an utterance is indirect or apparently a long way from the literal meaning of the sentence. Such indirect inferences can be accounted for by imagining that there are conversational **maxims** that are assumed by interlocutors when they talk.

There are four such maxims that constitute the cooperative principle. The maxim of **quantity** dictates that you should not say too much or too little for the circumstances. The maxim of **quality** states that you should tell the truth. The maxim of **manner** insists that you must not be obscure, ambiguous or rambling. And the maxim of **relation** tells you to say things that are relevant to the conversation and context.

Clearly, people rarely keep to these maxims in normal conversation. However, the point of this framework is that these are norms that are supposed to be broken (that is why they are called *maxims* rather than *rules* or *laws*). When the maxims are broken, then the hearer understands that certain **implicatures** must be inferred from the utterance. Speakers can ostentatiously **flout** the maxims, to indicate to the hearer that an implicated message must be derived.

For example, if in response to a request as to the effectiveness of a cold remedy, the pharmacist simply tells you that it tastes nice, then the maxim of quantity has been flouted in order to generate the implicature that it is not medically much good. The nicknames *Little John* of a tall man, *Cary Grant* applied to an unsophisticated slob, *Curly* for a bald person, or *Flash* for a tortoise are such outrageous floutings of the maxim of quality that the hearer must implicate an intended irony, and so on.

6.1.2 The supermaxim of relevance

It has been proposed that all of these maxims can be subordinated to overriding maxims, such as *Be Polite* (about which more later, in Section 6.1.3). It has also been suggested that the maxim of relation (*Be Relevant*) is more important than the others in communication. Assuming that speakers are saying something relevant to the situation prods hearers into working hard to figure out what they meant by what they said.

In this framework, **relevance** has a very precise meaning. An utterance is relevant if it can have a contextual effect. Hearers assume that all utterances are relevant to the context (on the basis of the cooperative principle) and so even obscure utterances are interpreted as if they mean something. There is a trade-off here, of course, since very obscure or unclear utterances will require a great deal of brain effort in interpretation on the part of the hearer. The hearer is only likely to be bothered to expend this effort (on a principle of optimum efficiency rather than just laziness) if there is some reasonable expectation of a pay-off in terms of a relevant inference.

For an example of an exchange that requires little processing effort, consider the following genuine conversation, heard next to a ticket vending machine in a car park:

> Woman: *Excuse me, do you have two fifties for this pound coin?*
> Man: *I've got twenties.*

Strictly, the man's reply does not explicitly and directly answer the woman's question. The literal preferred response should either have been *yes* or *no*. However, people do not communicate in this robotic fashion. The man interpreted the relevance of the woman's utterance, first, as being a *question-type* speech act, requiring a response. Furthermore, it is not a question about the man's possessions simply out of curiosity, but the proximity of the ticket-machine determines that the woman's utterance is intended as a request that the man exchange any smaller coins he might have for her larger one, so that she can buy a ticket. His reply is literally irrelevant, but it is fairly easy for the woman to assume that he is being relevant at a slightly deeper level, and that his declaration of possession of twenty-pence pieces can be interpreted as an offer of these smaller coins to her. This can be confirmed by the fact that this verbal exchange was immediately followed by the exchange of coins.

An example of a resolution of relevance that is more effortful (and more bizarre when considered simply literally) is the following (genuine) exchange. The context is a sixteen-year-old trying, illegally, to buy four cans of beer in an off-licence:

> *Customer: Just these please.*
>
> *Shopkeeper: Are you eighteen?*
>
> *Customer: Oh, I'm from Middlesbrough.*
>
> *Shopkeeper: (very brief pause) OK (serves him the beer).*

The preferred response to the shopkeeper's question is either *yes* or (less likely) *no*, the former usually supported by some document of proof. However, the shopkeeper is assuming a cooperative principle in the exchange, and so struggles to resolve a relevant inference from the customer's bizarre response. It is impossible here to discover what satisfactory inference she eventually resolved from the reply: she cannot have thought that people from Middlesbrough were exempt from the licensing laws. However, the proof that she derived some inference or other is in the fact that she served the sixteen-year-old the beer. Perhaps the assumption of relevance is so strong that any reply is assumed to be relevant and therefore satisfactory. Clearly, there was some processing effort involved (perhaps causing the brief pause) on the part of the shopkeeper. However, there is no explanation for the sixteen-year-old's bizarre reply in the first place!

In order to understand the mechanism by which a resolving inference is arrived at under the principle of relevance, it is first necessary to discuss how an utterance 'carries' a set of **propositions**. A proposition is the meaning-content of an utterance or sentence. An utterance involves a set of propositions that might be **asserted**, **presupposed**, **entailed** or loosely **inferred** from the 'surface' meaning of the utterance. An assertion is the easiest to process since it is the proposition that is literally, explicitly and directly stated by the utterance. A **presupposition** is a proposition that is taken for granted in what is said. Here are examples of three different types:

1   *He realised that she had arrived by plane.*
    (presupposes *she arrived by plane*)

2   *The shopkeeper served him the beer.*
    (presupposes *the shopkeeper exists*)

3   *The boat which is black will be painted tomorrow.*
    (presupposes *the boat is black*)

The easy test for presupposition is that the presupposition persists even after negation of the main verb of the sentence. Thus, *He didn't realise that she had arrived by plane* still presupposes *she arrived by plane*, and similarly with the other examples. Presuppositions are very relevant in the set of propositions associated with an utterance, and require little brain effort to derive a resolution of meaning. They are likely to be the first resort of the effort to resolve meaning from a non-literal utterance.

Entailments are next in ease of providing a resolution of meaning. These are propositions that logically follow on from the utterance, and can usually be derived by turning parts of the sentence into more generalised factors. Thus *The shopkeeper served him the beer* entails:

> *The shopkeeper served someone beer,*
>
> *The shopkeeper served him something,*
>
> *Someone served him beer,*
>
> *Some beer was served,*
>
> *There was a shopkeeper,*
>
> *There was some beer,*
>
> *Something happened,*

and so on. Figuring out entailments requires a bit of processing work by the hearer.

Finally, and requiring the most effort, are **inferences**. These propositions typically rely on the application of cultural and contextual knowledge about the world for their derivation. Thus, one of the inferences of *The boat which is black will be painted tomorrow* is that *someone will paint the boat*. A hearer knowledgeable about boat maintenance might also infer that this means that the person likely to be the painter will be unavailable for other work tomorrow, and that the regular sailing will tomorrow be cancelled, and that the dry-dock will be occupied so that he cannot get his own boat in until later in the week.

In context, hearers are likely to 'try out' the easiest resolutions of utterance meaning first. Thus, if the plain assertion of the utterance resolves the search for relevance, then the hearer will accept that as the intended meaning. If not, then the hearer is likely to try out any presupposed, entailed or inferred propositions as the intended meaning. As an example, if a man says to his friend *I'm hungry*, this simply asserts a piece of information. But where is the relevance in providing this? The utterance presupposes that *I exist*, but this is hardly directly relevant and interesting either. The entailments of the utterance are barely more satisfying. However, an inference might be that the friend possesses food and that the utterance is a request to eat some of it. Thus resolved, the friend is likely to respond to the utterance *I'm hungry* by offering the speaker some food.

6.1.3 Politeness

All of the material discussed so far is about how people relate to each other and manage communication. It has been suggested that a principle of politeness governs all of this behaviour. The norms of politeness are culture-specific and differ between languages. In this section, we consider some of the aspects of politeness in English.

Names and addresses

Many languages distinguish between *you* when it is singular (*tu* in French) and plural (*vous* in French). Such languages are said to operate *T/V* systems of address. Latin (*tu/vos*), Russian (*ty/vy*), Italian (*tu/Lei*) and German (*du/Sie*) are examples of such languages. Even English, up until the Renaissance, once had a *thou/you* distinction, deriving from the Old English *ðū/gē* (see Chapter 3).

This distinction has a variety of functions. Originally, it served only to mark differences in **number**. Some British dialects retain a T/V differentiation to this effect (*you/youse, you/you-all*). Many languages have developed their T/V system into a marker of **politeness**, so that the T form is used to familiars and the V form is used to signify respect. This naturally developed into a marker of **social rank**, with V used to superiors and T to inferiors or those of equal status. Finally, the two forms can serve to indicate **solidarity** or intimacy. T is used within the social group to establish an affinity; V is used to non-group members or even to indicate outright hostility.

English went through most of these stages, so that by the Renaissance, *thou/you* signified *number*, *politeness* and *social rank*. The form is preserved in 'frozen' language such as the speech of Quakers, scripted prayers, wedding services and productions of Renaissance plays. For example, Shakespeare uses the T/V system to signify noble and peasant characters in *A Midsummer Night's Dream*, to show the development of the relationship between Romeo and Juliet, and to mark the fall of King Richard II by shifting from the respectful *you* to the inferior *thou*.

Since the English language lost the T/V distinction in general usage, speakers have developed other ways of signifying social relationships in their speech. One way is by the use of titles. Options available in English are as follows:

> T = Title (*Mrs*, *Professor*, *sir*)
>
> FN = First Name (*Peter*, *mate*, *pal*)
>
> LN = Last Name (*Stockwell*, *Jackson*)
>
> no name/avoidance of address form

These forms can of course be combined: *Professor Jackson* (TLN), *Peter Stockwell* (FNLN), *Father David* (TFN).

In our culture, asymmetric use between participants, with one using TLN and the other using FN, usually indicates inequality in power. Mutual TLN can indicate inequality and unfamiliarity, and is a safe, neutral option. Mutual FN usually indicates equality and familiarity. Switches in naming strategies are almost always initiated by the most powerful person, as in the following exchange:

> *A: Professor Jackson?*
>
> *B: Please, call me Howard.*

Of course, all these 'rules', like maxims, are normative, and other effects are generated when they are flouted. T alone tends to be reserved for professionals (*Doctor*, *Professor*, rather than *Mister* in Britain), but if it is over-used in an utterance, or receives heavy stress, it can be intended as hostile or sarcastic.

Similarly, TLN used in a pub or in an argument can indicate formality or hostility. FN in a job interview would probably be considered too forward. Asymmetrical FN is heavily marked for power: in many schools, teachers use FN and receive T (*Sir*) or TLN (*Miss Jones*) back. Female teachers invariably receive *Miss*, regardless of marital status.

In English, avoidance is allowable in many contexts (*Good morning*, *Thank-you*) whereas, for example, in French an address form (*Bonjour, Monsieur; Merci, Madame*) would be required. In many situations in which all of the other options seem awkward, avoidance is used almost by default. Thus, boyfriends and girlfriends often evade naming potential parents-in-law, since TLN may seem too formal but FN alone too forward.

Many other complexities arise in the naming of pets, for example, depending on factors such as what the pet is doing at the time, whether it is in trouble, whether you are being observed, and so on. Naming strategies here involve three-way values between the speaker and the third-party participant; with the animal, of course, being able to respond to forms of address often only by taking intonation cues. Such complexities, however, are probably at the edge of linguistic analysis!

Face and politeness strategies

Central to an understanding of politeness is the notion of **face**, which is the sense that a speaker has of their own linguistic image and role. Every speech act is potentially an imposition on somebody else's sense of *face* – their desire to be unimpeded in their life. Speakers must mitigate the force of these **Face Threatening Acts** (FTAs), and they have a variety of strategies at their disposal in English to accomplish this. They may use **positive politeness** in being complimentary about the addressee before asking them to do something ('buttering' them up). Alternatively, speakers may employ a variety of types of **negative politeness** strategies to mitigate the imposition:

> hedge – *Er, please could you, er, perhaps, close the window?*
>
> indicate pessimism – *I don't suppose you could close the window for me?*
>
> minimise the imposition – *Could you close the window just a tiny bit?*
>
> indicate deference – *Excuse me, sir, would you mind if I asked you to close the window?*
>
> apologise – *I'm terribly sorry but could you close the window please?*
>
> impersonalise – *The management requires all windows to be closed.*

Of course, the normative nature of these social rules requires particular strategies to be matched to the appropriate circumstances. The following two examples would probably be considered nervous and rude, respectively:

> *I'm sorry to trouble you, I know it's an awful imposition, but I don't suppose I could I possibly ask you, sir, if you could see your way to telling me more or less what time it is at the moment, please?*
>
> *Lend me your car.*

There is a negotiation that needs to be undertaken in these situations, depending on the magnitude of the imposition, and the social position of the speakers involved.

Phatic tokens

One of the most important factors that play a part in the decision of appropriateness is the relative power of the participants. This can be seen especially in the ways people greet each other or acknowledge each other's existence at the beginning of conversations. Such utterances, which have more social cohesion about them than explicit content, are called **phatic** tokens.

There are three possibilities for phatic openings in conversation. **Neutral** tokens refer to the context of the situation and are not personal to either participant. The classic example is British people talking about the weather. **Self-oriented** tokens are personal to the speaker (*My legs weren't made for these hills*). **Other-oriented** tokens are personal to the hearer (*Do you come here often?*).

The choice of token is determined by power. A superior uses an other-oriented token such as *That looks like hard work*. In the same situation, the inferior would use a self-oriented token such as *Hard work, this*. In all cases, tokens should be emotionally uncontroversial and require a positive response.

ACTIVITY 58

As an illustration of what would happen if these 'rules' were broken, consider the following (invented!) exchanges from behind the scenes at the Royal Command Performance:

> Queen: *That was a wonderful show!*
>
> Actor: *No it wasn't, we were awful, the songs were appalling and the audience was rubbish.*
>
> (further along the line...)
>
> Queen: *Do you know, I had a very uncomfortable seat for the whole performance!*
>
> (even further along the line...)
>
> Actor: *Hello, your Majesty, that's a terrible boil you've got on your neck.*

What, according to the pragmatic rules given above, has gone wrong in each of these cases?

Try to write your own brief scripts that each break a pragmatic rule. What effects are generated by these?

There are other factors, of course, in these delicate social negotiations. Generally, people moving into others' space intitiate exchanges. This is to mitigate the sense of spatial imposition in the same way as strategies are needed to mitigate verbal imposition, as discussed above. Although these decisions begin to be questions of psycholinguistics and psychology, they are all concerned with how English speakers use their language to negotiate social circumstances in ways that are necessarily more subtle and complex, given our loss of an explicit T/V system.

6.2 The analysis of discourse

Much of the work of the last section has developed in reaction to the old-fashioned view of language simply being a code which is transmitted and decoded without difficulty by the hearer. As linguistics has become more holistic in its interests and methods, so there has been a growing interest in whole text examination and the analysis of discourse. This section discusses some of the ways in which linguists have talked about these global levels of language use. Later, we will see how advances in artificial intelligence research have had implications for linguistics, and how dialogue and large-scale exchanges have been made available for linguistic study. But first we discuss the fundamental division of the whole of language into speech and writing.

6.2.1 Oracy and literacy

The linguistic study of **literacy** has been neglected until very recently. One of the reasons for this is that the term covers such a wide range of areas. It includes both reading and writing, which involve psycholinguistics and a study of the mechanical aspects of receiving and producing written texts. It covers the whole literary system, meaning not just texts which are valued as Art or are fictional, but all verbal documents and their reception, analysis and criticism.

The term also is not clearly defined, making it difficult to compare like with like in apparently similar communities across the world. Deciding on a definition involves all sorts of political and cultural factors as well as linguistic aspects; the notion of literacy is perceived by many as conferring power and prestige in various ways.

Two of the so-called 'three Rs' of a basic education, reading and writing, are encompassed by the term. However, beyond this it is not easy to formulate exactly what is meant by *literacy*. For a start, reading and writing are not symmetrically related, although many people's 'folk-theory' of linguistics sees the one merely as the reverse of the other. In fact, the two processes involve completely different motor skills (of the eyes and the hands, respectively), and also different mental procedures (concerned with reviewing, recapping, anticipation and guessing on the one hand, against composing, editing, redrafting and selection, on the other).

Literacy is itself a relative term, determined by the context in which it is used. To say that someone is *literate* can mean either that they are able to read reasonably well, or that they are well-read in valued texts, such as the classic prose fiction of the nineteenth century. It can also be used to imply that someone is cultivated, civilised, polite and intelligent. Literacy thus relates a language-user to their society, and marks a standard in that context. Sociolinguistic studies have shown that language is used in a variety of ways across the world, and so a blanket, absolute definition of literacy is impossible. In some cultures, a person can be sufficiently literate if they are able to fill out a census form and sign a name. In China, a person would need to learn some 3000 characters to be considered reasonably literate. They would not be considered fully literate until around 50 000 characters had been learned.

Clearly then, literacy depends on what use it is being put to in any specific circumstance. In 1956, UNESCO (the United Nations Educational, Scientific and Cultural Organisation) adopted a definition of **functional literacy** based on the degree of reading and writing skill required for an individual to function effectively in their own society.

Most people perceive written text merely as a means of recording and transcribing the spoken form. Of course, it is true that speech is chronologically prior to writing. Writing seems to have originated in Mesopotamia at some time around 3500 BC, and presumably speech goes back to the origins of the species. Speech is also prior to writing on an individual basis; unless they are deaf or have speaking problems, children speak long before they can write. It is therefore argued that the ability to speak is biologically based, since all human communities have speech but not all have a writing system. Mass literacy is a very recent occurrence; even in the developed West, by no means all people are functionally literate.

Because of all this evidence for the sequential priority of speech over writing, it is assumed that the writing system merely represents the sound system (and English spelling is often then criticised for not representing its sounds very well). Writing has enormous social prestige in its own right, and thus has a social priority today over speech. The writing system has even influenced patterns of pronunciation because of this. Examples include the 'rule' of not 'dropping your aitches' when the word is spelled with *h* initially, even though there is a long tradition in British accents for doing precisely that. Spelling has changed the pronunciation of words such as *often* (in which the /t/ was never pronounced) and *diphtheria* (in which the *ph* grapheme is changing from a /f/ pronunciation to a /p/).

There is a linguistic argument that neither speech nor writing represent the other. Rather, they realise, in different ways, the abstract system of language, and they do it for functionally different purposes. Indeed, we have seen so far in this chapter how the medium itself can encode social meaning. Speech tends (other than in unusual contexts such as radio or tape-recording) to occur face-to-face, spontaneously, and cannot be 'unsaid'. Writing, on the other hand, can be uncertain as to audience, can be displaced in time and can be edited. (Incidentally, it has often been noticed that Bernstein's distinction between *elaborated* and *restricted* codes (see Section 5.5) relates to the differences between the functions of writing and speaking.)

Literacy undoubtedly confers power and prestige in the world today. In the past, the Protestant movement, with its emphasis on personal reading of the Bible, led to higher literacy rates in Sweden, Scotland and Switzerland than in Catholic France and southern Italy. This, in turn, led to a perception of the people in these areas as backward and stupid. Until very recently, there was a literacy test to acquire voting rights in the southern USA, which served to disenfranchise many black people who had been deprived of the right to schooling.

The claim of a link between literate ability and intelligence often accompanies such situations. Many studies have attempted to discover whether there is any difference in performance on IQ tests by those who are able to read and those who are illiterate. Several studies show that readers perform better on such tests.

However, the relationship between literacy and IQ test success might not be directly causal. It could be argued that IQ puzzles test decoding ability rather than intelligence itself (the point that by learning to read it is possible to raise your IQ score is further evidence of the dubious validity of supposedly fixed and objective IQ tests as well). It is probably also the case that literate people tend to do better on such cognitive and reasoning tests, not because of their literacy but because of **schooling**. In other words, it is the practice of education that encourages the sort of abstract thought that is also coincidentally associated with literacy.

Why should this be the case? There is an argument that the practice of education, through a recordable form of language (writing), encourages people to perceive the world in ways that are different from those without schooling and literacy. In other words, knowledge itself is different because of literacy.

The philosopher Karl Popper developed the notion of different *worlds* of experience based on this distinction. **World One** is the objective world of physical objects and material things, which can be experienced directly by all sentient creatures. **World Two** is experienced only through the subjective medium of the mind, through consciousness. Worlds One and Two are thus accessible by all human communities. **World Three** experience, however, is comprised of 'objective knowledge' as held in books, libraries and now electronic databases and networks. It is realised in statements, theories and verbal models. In order to be objective it must be recorded in language and stored in a writing system. World Three knowledge thus exists externally to knowers, and can only be accessed by those able to read the system of storage (writing).

World Three knowledge, in the form of writing, eliminates inconsistency and fosters a critical attitude to statements and theories, since they can be perceived to exist objectively in their own right. In oracy, there is less emphasis on the differentiation between the speaker and that which is spoken. Oracy encourages the directness of the relationship between the word and the object that it refers to. There can be no appeal to dictionary definitions – only to concrete situations. This is not to say that people in oral communities are cognitively inferior, but merely that their view of the world is differently skewed than for those accustomed to literacy and schooling.

Oracy has many advantages over literacy. For example, memorised family and social histories can encode changing social relationships and norms by changing themselves. A famous example concerns the Gonja nation of Northern Ghana which formerly comprised seven tribes: an oral legend told of how the original founder, Jakpa, divided power among his seven sons. When British control was extended to the region, two of the tribes disappeared, and the legend was then told of Jakpa and his *five* sons. No memory or oral record was kept of the earlier version, since the story functioned not as an historical document but as a socially cohesive device.

As soon as myths and legends come to be written down, they become unchangeable. The stories and parables of the Old and New Testaments of the Bible, for example, still talk of donkeys, goats and sheep, camels, vineyard workers and sowing seeds, and are read today in industrialised societies that are very different from their original contexts. In this literate circumstance, relevance has to be made by allegorical reading and metaphorical adaptation, by glosses, sermons and exegesis. Notions of documentary truth and falsity become more important as a result of the frozen nature of the written text.

The standardisation of print also further fixes the spelling system, making it resistant to change in response to accent change. Thus, as in British English writing, spelling and pronunciation have diverged. Educational codification further reinforces prejudice against spelling innovation, so thut unfmilya forms liyk this wud probly arowz feelins uv discumfet in reeduz yoost te u more ceudifiyd form uv spellen az lurnt in skool frum an urly ayj. Our spelling system has changed little in the past 400 years, whereas pronunciation patterns have changed enormously. The innovative spelling used two sentences above corresponds to the accent of the writer of this chapter. Our antiquated and frozen spelling has the advantage of not privileging any one accent in the writing system.

Oral cultures, of course, do not even encounter the problem: the form of the story changes with the voice of the speaker. Whereas Western literature currently values word-play and self-reference, oral 'literature' (notice the culture-specific nature of the word for verbal art itself) values sound patterns and rhythm. In modern communities deprived of access to schooling, the everyday 'literature' more resembles oral patterns than the patterns of the surrounding, dominant, print-rich culture. The distinction between speech and writing for these cultures is an essential and self-defining one.

6.2.2 Conversation analysis

The relative status of speech and writing can be seen in the fact that we spend far more of our time speaking and listening than either reading or especially writing. And most of our language behaviour takes place in interaction with other people in the activity that we call conversation. Like any other part of language, the practice of conversation operates with rules and conventions and can be analysed. This is the basis of this section.

Taking turns

The most obvious structural feature of conversation is that it is based on individuals taking turns to speak, *holding the floor* while the other participants listen and await their turn. In formally structured situations, such as business meetings, televised discussions and parliamentary debates, turns are allocated by a chair and speakers are nominated or bid to speak. In everyday conversation, however, turn-taking is negotiated by speakers as the talk develops.

In English-speaking culture, there is an intolerance of silence in conversation. Turns are therefore often made up of **adjacency pairs**, where an initiation or request for information is followed immediately by an answer or response of some sort. This is optionally followed up by feedback from the first speaker to confirm that the response has been given satisfactorily:

> A: Can you give me a hand?
> B: Sure.
> A: Thanks.
> B: What do I do?
> A: If you could just push, I'll be able to jump-start it.
> B: OK.

In this example, two adjacency pairs are connected by feedback to acknowledge the answer. Of course, not all conversational exchanges are as straightforward as this, and in fact we missed out a part of the above example:

> A: Can you give me a hand?
> (Before B has a chance to answer, A shouts across the road to C)
>> BOB! Any chance of a hand here?
> C: Yeah, be there in a minute.
> B: Well, will it take long – it's just that I'm in a rush and...
> A: No, a couple of seconds. Can you?
> B: Sure. I've got to be at the station soon.
> A: Thanks...

and so on. The adjacency pairs are still there, but underlying other material, which has been inserted into the conversation. First, there is a **side-sequence**, as A 'breaks out' of the first adjacency pair to call across the road to Bob (C) and begin another adjacency pair. This is independent of the first pair, which is interrupted. Second, B starts an **insertion-sequence** by asking a question (*will it take long?*) which is answered (*a couple of seconds*). The answer of the surrounding adjacency pair is dependent on this internal pair. (The beer-buying youth in Section 6.1.2 was also involved in an insertion-sequence with the shopkeeper.) Finally, the passage has an example of **skip-connecting**, as B begins to explain that he is in a rush, and returns to this interrupted topic to complete his explanation a few turns later.

All of these features introduce potential for the conversation to break down because adjacency pairs are disrupted, which is a threat to coherence. In each case, the second half of the disruptions act as **repairs** to allow the conversation to continue.

Claiming and keeping a turn

Often, the gaps between speakers in a normal conversation, while no one is speaking at all, are very brief, usually fractions of a second. People are clearly skilled at anticipating the boundaries of turns in order to be ready to begin speaking as soon as the other person has apparently finished. To claim the floor, it is common to begin with an introductory phrase that picks up on an item from the previous speaker's subject-matter.

Sometimes, especially in rapid or heated conversation, speakers wish to start talking before the other person has finished. They might interrupt, which is usually done by picking up a phrase from the first speaker and incorporating it into their own speech. They will raise their voices slightly above the level of the first speaker. Very often, the first speaker will give way to this tactic and the second speaker will thus gain the floor.

However, sometimes the first speaker will simply keep on talking, perhaps making their speech louder and slower, and simultaneous talk goes on until one person gives in and stops talking. Such simultaneous talk is perceived as being rude if it goes on for more than two or three clauses. Longer than this, and very often a specific type of insertion sequence will begin whereby one speaker will step outside the topic of the conversation to comment on the tactic directly. For example: *I sing in smokey rooms every night and I can keep talking for far longer than you can, Teresa* (singer Billy Bragg's response to being interrupted by MP Teresa Gorman, on Channel 4's *After Dark*); *Stop hectoring me, Tom – let me finish what I'm saying* (interviewee to poet/critic Tom Paulin, on BBC2's *The Late Show*). Such commentary involves **metalanguage** in that speakers talk explicitly about their own language. This can seriously disrupt the flow of conversation and the activity is usually followed by lots of repair work to re-establish the topic.

People can anticipate the boundaries of turns in a variety of ways. Speakers might ask a direct question or nominate the next speaker by name. Dropping intonation often signals that the point has been made and ended. Pauses for breath at the end of a complete clause will often provide an entry point for other speakers to claim their turn. Open-hand gestures and catching another speaker's eye are often invitations to take a turn.

   People wanting to claim a turn can take advantage of these features to interrupt by pretending that a genuine mid-utterance pause for breath was actually a signal of ending. Skilful speakers can prevent others from taking the floor by blocking these features: they will avoid eye-contact; they will talk rapidly with few pauses; and when they do take a breath, it will be in the middle of a clause rather than at the end. This latter tactic uses an **utterance incompletor** to allow the speaker to hold the floor. Other examples would be to end each clause with a connective such as *and*, *therefore*, *and*, *so* or *but*, or to begin talking by saying *I want to make three points...* Often, pauses for thinking are filled in with noises (*um*, *er*, *well*) to keep the turn.

Maintaining and ending the conversation

The logical coherence of conversations helps to maintain a sense that a single **topic** is being discussed. Participants will often tolerate ambiguity or lack of clarity for several turns in the hope that all will eventually become clear, as long as they are confident that the topic is being maintained. Shifts of topic are usually consensual, and attempts by one speaker to force a change of topic prematurely will often be regarded by the others as rude or evasive. Most speakers' conversation structure is characterised by **recipient design**; that is, it tends to be organised in patterns and at a level that is understandable and appropriate to the hearer. Much talk consists of saying what other people want to hear, in the sort of language that they themselves use. Speakers 'tune in' to each others' preferred styles and expressions very rapidly.

   In normal conversation, hearers will support the maintenance of the conversation with direct **feedback** to the speaker. Comments such as *that's right*, *I heard that*, *me too*, *yeah*, count as feedback rather than attempts to interrupt or claim the floor. Also, speakers may make **backchannel noise** throughout the speaker's talk. This usually consists of agreement noises (conventionally written as *uh-huh*, *hmm*, *yeah*, *yeah*) accompanied by nodding, which tell the speaker that the hearer is interested and wants them to continue.

   Conversations come to an end in a variety of ways. These can be because the situation around the speakers changes; such as when, during a conversation on a train, one participant comes to their station, and the conversation is brought to a close usually with reference to the interrupting circumstance (such as, *well, this is my stop*). Speakers themselves can bring the talk to an end when they feel that topics have been exhausted. This can be cued by someone holding a silence for longer than usual, or picking up a newspaper, or looking out of the window, and so on.

   There are a variety of **pre-closing signals** that participants use to bring a conversation to an end satisfactorily. Metalanguage can be used to indicate that the topic has closed (*Well, that's sorted then*). *Well* is a common word used on its own to signal an end to the conversation. These signals are usually followed by various phatic tokens (*nice to meet you*, *we must do this again*, *see you later*) and farewells. Such intentional breaks in conversation can also be repaired, though, if one speaker decides to prolong the talk further (*Oh, I've just remembered, there was one other thing*). Such repairs, as in this example, tend to take the form of metalanguage.

ACTIVITY 59

Unless they have read a book on linguistics, for most people the features of pragmatics and conversation are below the level of consciousness. However, to prove that they are real and strong conventions, try to spend the rest of the week in situations with other people in which you do not keep to the rules. Try one or more of the following:

1 Answer the telephone without saying 'hello' or identifying yourself.

2 Let someone else talk without making any backchannel noises, giving feedback or nodding.

3 Don't use any phatic tokens when meeting someone, or reply to their phatic tokens by gently disagreeing with them.

4 Don't ever break any of the maxims of conversation. In other words, mean everything you say literally.

5 Don't use any strategies of negative politeness ever.

6 Use the full Title + Last Name for everyone you meet.

7 Every time you have a conversation, let the other person talk for four or five sentences, and then skip-connect back to the topic you last mentioned.

8 Break the maxim of relation by saying everything in a sarcastic tone of voice.

In the interests of linguistic research, you should be prepared to get into some fights, but the beauty of subconscious pragmatic rules is that you can deny you ever meant any offence, and that the other person has simply misinterpreted.

6.2.3 Coherence and framing

So far in this section, we have looked at how people use language to communicate with each other and talk about the world around them. But we have left many assumptions unexplained about the precise mechanisms involved in being able to do this. What is it, for example, in the words and sentences of conversations and written discourses that allows hearers and readers to build up a picture of the subject under discussion? How, specifically, are attitudes and views expressed in texts and how do readers make sense of them? In short, how does the cohesion of texts contribute to the sense of coherence in discourse?

We outlined how the sentences of a text are connected to each other in Section 2.4.2. This is known as textual **cohesion**. Sentences can be seen to relate to each other by co-reference, which can be realised as the repetition of words, synonyms, pronouns and so on. In this way, the same entity that is being referred to persists throughout the text. Cohesion helps to give a text its **texture**, in terms of the way in which the words and syntactic constructions relate to each other.

However, texture is a matter of the structure of the text, and what is at stake in discourse is the sense that a reader/hearer has of the process of reading/hearing. In other words, cohesion is a structural linguistic issue and **coherence** is its psychological counterpart – the perception that the world expressed in the text makes sense.

At this level of analysis, the study of language must become less structural and more procedural; that is, more concerned with the ongoing experience of reading and hearing. In the process of readers and hearers turning texts into discourse, a psychologically coherent 'world' is created. This mental model can be termed the **discourse world**, and readers/hearers use it to follow the way in which the text develops and progresses. Objects in the discourse world are created by **reference**, which is usually expressed textually by noun phrases. The relationships between these objects are expressed by verb phrases, which serve to alter the reader/hearer's discourse model in the course of reading/hearing.

Many of the frameworks for understanding the processes involved here were developed in the 1970s and 1980s as part of research into computer models of language and Artificial Intelligence. In particular, it is helpful to think of reading and hearing as involving two types of process which are used to check on each other while receiving discourse. By understanding the meanings of words and sentences, and accumulating this information through the discourse, people can use **bottom-up processing** to form a cumulative meaning for what has just been received. While this is ongoing, people can anticipate the meaning of what is to come by predicting possible likely meanings on the basis of their cultural knowledge of the world. This is called **top-down processing**.

The problem of how to account for the application of this knowledge of the world is handled by the notion of **frames**. A frame is a way of thinking about a memory structure, which consists of a set of slots arranged to compose a particular frequently encountered entity. Thus a *school* would consist of slots such as *desks, corridors, dining area, teachers, English rooms* and so on, with all the attributes that make up a school building and its staff and students. Frames represent knowledge not just of stereotypical entities, but can be created for newly encountered entities as well. In this way, people learn from experience and build up a larger repertoire of knowledge about the world.

The dynamic counterpart of a frame is a **script**. As it sounds, this is a memorised representation of a typical event. So, we use a *shopping* script to know how to go into a shop, pick up goods, take them to the till, have a conversation with the shopkeeper, pay for the goods, collect change and leave. We might have a *writing an essay* script that tells us how to organise the text, put together an argument, use evidence, and import other sub-scripts such as the content of the essay, what the teacher likes, and the method of handing it in.

Thinking of background knowledge as a systematic arrangement that we can call up when reading or hearing texts goes a long way towards explaining how inferences work, because we have the connections between propositions already in our heads. In the following examples, there is nothing literally in the texts that accounts for the normal inferencing that readers do in making them make sense. The coherence between **a** and **b** in each case depends upon the reader supplying the information in **c** from background knowledge:

a   *I spent most of the time on the beach.*
b   *The sea was really warm.*
c   *(Beaches are next to the sea).*

a   *The restaurant was great.*
b   *But the waiter was very rude.*
c   *(Restaurants have waiters).*

a   *Help yourself to the vegetable garden.*
b   *The radishes are lovely.*
c   *(Radishes are vegetables).*

a *The police were chasing a car.*
b *The Mercedes nearly crashed into a wall.*
c *(A Mercedes is a type of car).*

In each case, the use of the definite article (*the*) in **b** is a definite reference to the slot in the relevant script in the discourse world called up by **a**.

ACTIVITY 60

Try playing this game, for two or more players, to show you how good you are at interpretation and finding coherence. There are three versions to test your ingenuity and the adaptability of your script repertoire:

1 *The easy version.* Someone chooses a domain of play, which should be a word or event such as *On the beach*, *The football match*, *Fish*, *Music magazines* or anything else. Then, on slips of paper, everyone must write a short sentence that is associated with the domain. Slips are then paired and the challenge is to make the two sentences make sense by explaining the connection.

2 *The hard version.* Try the game completely at random, by not having a specific domain of play. Simply write sentences on slips of paper, and attempt to find coherence between pairs.

3 *The slinker.* Collect slips with sentences, and combine them in lines with any sentences that you can find written down around the room: look randomly in books and magazines, for logos on clothes, posters, sweets and drinks, for example. Write out your 'found poem' and explain it as if it were a published poem. You are allowed to give the poem a title.

6.3 Language and ideology

So far this chapter has been concerned largely with the organisation of texts and discourses, and how language users are able to resolve meaning from them. It would be easy to think of the form of expression as being separate from the content of the text. This view would regard the structure of texts as if it were mere 'decoration' for the meaning carried by the language. However, this would be a false perception. The study of pragmatics has shown that different forms of politeness, phatic token and speech act, for example, can generate different effects in the receiver. In other words, the content and the style of texts are in fact interdependent.

Another way of thinking about this aspect of discourse is to understand that all texts encode an underlying **ideology**. This means not just a political ideology, but an idea-system or set of assumptions on which the discourse is based. No text is neutral with respect to ideology. A useful analogy would be to think of texts as photographs: a picture must always be taken from a particular point of view. Very often, the ideological background of texts is implicit and can be revealed by linguistic analysis. Some of the features through which the ideological background of texts can be uncovered are presented in this section.

6.3.1 Lexical choice

A text is produced by **selection** and **combination**, which can be imagined as two axes which intersect. Words are combined into syntactically appropriate chains to form a sentence in English. Into each link in the chain, a word is selected from a whole bank of possible other words which might have gone in its place. The ideology of the text is reflected by which words are selected throughout the text. Thus, the **lexical choice** of the text gives an insight into the idea-system which underlies the discourse.

There are some obvious naming strategies which encode ideology, such as newspapers choosing to refer either to *terrorists* or *rebels*, and politicians talking about *weapons of mass destruction* or *nuclear missiles* or *weapons systems*. The forced displacement of people on the basis of culture is rendered less objectionable by calling it *ethnic cleansing*. In fact, refuse disposal and street-cleaning in major towns and cities is now routinely called *cleansing*, which gives it a far more professional and purifying image. The basis of this selection is **euphemism**. This involves the selection of a synonymous term which denotes almost the same thing but has very different connotations.

Usually, a text which is consistent and coherent will have words selected from the same ideological domain. A review, for example, would 'read' badly if it referred to *ageing musicians who are clearly past their sell-by dates* in the same text as *guitar-players matured and refined by experience*. The ideological set of lexical choices in published texts tends to be consistent because it usually expresses a particular world-view (or *mind-set*) of the author.

6.3.2 Agency

The combination of words often encodes the **agency** of events – basically, who does what to whom. The people or groups carrying out actions can be blamed or absolved of blame by the arrangement of the syntax of the sentence. For example, *Soldiers shoot demonstrators after riot* lays the blame clearly on the soldiers by making them the active agents of the shooting. A viewpoint sympathetic to the authorities would read *Demonstrators shot in riots*, deleting the agents of the verb altogether. Even a headline that added *by soldiers* after this last passive verb would not be as strong a statement as the first example. **Passivisation** is thus one way of deleting the agent of the action to express ideological viewpoint.

Another way of accomplishing a similar effect is to **nominalise** the action which was expressed by the verb. *Shooting in riot leaves demonstrators dead* deletes the soldiers again. *Demonstrators die in shooting* is similar, but almost blames the demonstrators by making them the syntactically active agents in the sentence, as well as nominalising the action of shooting. The psychological impact of the first element of an utterance (the **theme** of the sentence) is always stronger than the rest of the information in the sentence (the **rheme**).

A special case of nominalisation is **personification**, in which an action or state is given wilfulness and thus blame: *Death meets demonstrators after riot* or *Riot causes shooting of demonstrators* would encode this world-view. There is a difficulty even with the ideological basis of the terminology that we are using here, since to talk of events being *passivised* or *nominalised* or *personified* implies a neutral and objective state before the passivisation and so on. This is not the case. All possible lexical and syntactic selections and combinations are ideologically loaded one way or the other. Neutrality is simply not possible in language.

6.3.3 Modality

We have been discussing the world-view of texts, but readers routinely act as if this world-view is that of the author of the text. Usually, this is a reasonable assumption to make, although fictional texts, perhaps with an invented narrator, present special problems. The parts of texts that seem to encode the author's attitude to the content of the text are known as the **modality** of the text.

The most obvious examples of modality can be seen in explicitly evaluative adjectives and adverbials. Calling something *lovely*, *evil*, *enticing*, *tasteless* or *clueless* clearly conveys what the author thinks of it. Describing an action completed *quickly*, *with grace*, *in an efficient manner* or *with feeling* also encodes the perception of the author.

However, there are a whole variety of grammatical ways in which the modality of the author can be understood. The commitment of the author to the truth or reality of the event is part of the attitude encoded in the text. There is a big difference in commitment between categoric, generic sentences such as *All officials are corrupt* and sentences which use a range of modal auxiliaries to 'tone down' the commitment to the assertion: *You must agree that all officials are corrupt*, *You might say that all officials are corrupt*, *You could say that all officials are corrupt*, *It is possible that all officials are corrupt*, *I wish I could say that all officials are corrupt*, and so on. Verbs of knowledge, prediction and evaluation all encode authorial modality.

6.3.4 Point of view

All of this discussion is concerned with the **point of view** conveyed by the text. It is useful when considering this to distinguish between the author of the text and the narrator. Often, fictional texts imagine an invented narrator who tells the story in the first person, although the whole text has in reality been written by an author with a different personality from the imagined narrator. In non-fictional texts, such as instruction manuals or press agency reports, the authorial voice is likely to be indistinguishable from the narratorial voice. Such texts are usually in the second person (imperative and instructional) and third person (claiming objectivity) respectively. It is informative, when considering point of view, to ask the questions *Who speaks?* and *Who is addressed?* in the text.

There are essentially three possible options for point of view in texts. First, a **personal narration** presents a direct relationship between the first-person (*I*) narrator and the reader who is addressed. Such narratives are likely to have a highly direct and explicit modality to express personal perception and opinion. Evaluations, thoughts and feelings are typically presented in this style.

A second type of point of view is the **impersonal narration**, which typically appears in the third person (*he/she/it/they*). This appears less intrusive and is often accompanied by less personal modality. Sentences are likely to be more categorical and assertive.

The third type of point of view is the **authorial voice**, which again is usually in the third person. However, authors can pretend to be omniscient; that is, they can present the internal thoughts of all of the characters in a text. Alternatively, they can present the story simply as reportage, piecing together the facts impersonally without claiming special insight. With the authorial voice, it is sometimes illuminating to ask not only *Who speaks?* but also *Who sees?*, since omniscient authors can present even third-person narration through the eyes and perception of a fictional character. This is called **focalisation**, and an author can use it either consistently by following the narrative through a single focaliser, or can present a variety of perceptions by shifting focalisation throughout the text.

In Section 6.2.3, we outlined the importance for interpretation of the high-level, global decisions provided by receivers' scripts. The perception of the ideology of a discourse is also dependent on the sort of text that the receiver expects to process when they encounter a new piece of language. As experienced users of many different varieties of language, people build up expectations of the features of a range of different types of text (or **genres**). As with top-down and bottom-up processing, there is a two-way interpretative procedure at work here. Early features of the text being received help to cue up a particular text type that the text in question seems to belong to and, at the same time, the perception of that text type helps the receiver to make interpretative decisions about the text. The pragmatic circumstances also play a part in this.

Consider, for example, the following two sentences:

a   *The council refused the women a permit because they feared violence.*

b   *The council refused the women a permit because they were communists.*

Most British speakers of English would take *they* in **a** to refer to the council and *they* in **b** to refer to the women. However, there are ideological assumptions involved here. The interpretations of **a** and **b** here depend on a perception of official fear of disorder, and an understanding that councils issue permits for things such as demonstrations, which sometimes become violent. However, the interpretations become different if a different ideological background is assumed. Imagine that the council in **a** is strongly in favour of boxing matches and the women are pacifists. Or imagine that **b** is uttered not in Britain but in China. The sorts of narratives that these sentences might belong to change their character when such re-interpretation happens.

As a further example, try reading the following short text, first assuming the point of view of a land developer who wants to build a supermarket and then, second, that of a conservationist interested in a fieldwork study of the animals and birds on the site:

> *The area is situated close to a suburban railway station and is only half a mile from the main shopping centre and central housing. However, the trees at the periphery of the site are tall and dense and separate the area effectively from the residential zone. A disused quarry has left several large recesses which have filled with water, and small islands covered in bushes and small vegetation break these shallow lakes. Excess water drains into the nearby river over shale and a light topsoil. There is an electrical sub-station to the north of the site, by the access road left by the quarry workings. The road continues for a mile into the area, though most of it is overgrown. There are two paths through the site, one of which is a right of way used by children at the school in the town.*

It is likely not only that different interests determine which sentences are most and least relevant, but that the same sentences have different interpretations. For the land developer, the text functions as a report on the commercial viability of building on the land and the proximity of amenities. For the conservationist, it is a description of an area suitable for study over several days, comprising useful information on the sorts of flora and fauna likely to be found, and how much disturbance the researcher can expect.

ACTIVITY 61

It is fairly easy to analyse a newspaper report for the ideological position (in the political sense) of the proprietor or editor, using the features discussed in this section. However, all texts convey ideology in the sense of a set of ideas assumed by the text. Try to use the features discussed above to outline the ideological assumptions carried by non-political texts. What is assumed as background knowledge in a cookery recipe, or a flyer for a pizza delivery service, or a sports shoe advert, or a charity appeal, or a bus ticket, or the rules and regulations of an educational establishment, and so on? Look in particular at the inferences that the reader needs to make.

6.4 Stylistics

In this chapter, we have looked at the three main functions of texts and discourse. In discussing pragmatics and conversation analysis, we added to the discussions of Chapters 1 and 2 in giving features related to the **textual** function of language. This is to do with how texts are organised and have texture. We also explained meaning in terms of the **interpersonal** function of language, with discussions of how meanings are negotiated in real talk, to go with the sociolinguistic discussion of Chapter 5. Finally, we addressed the **ideational** function of language in discussing the ideological basis of all discourse.

A book such as this can only ever be the merest introduction to the study of language. However, we have covered a great deal of material and provided discussions from the range of frameworks and approaches available within the field of linguistics as it currently stands. One of the advantages of being a student of language is that you are already a native speaker of at least one language, and you can begin to find out new and interesting things about language as soon as you begin to analyse it. Although answers are provided for some of the Activities in this book to check your own progress, many Activities have no right or wrong answers. They are there simply to help you to think about language and its use. We hope that they will lead you to wonder further about language, and develop your own frameworks to discuss the issues you think are important.

Linguistic frameworks are tools developed by researchers to help us understand how language works. You can apply what you have learned from this book, and by following the further reading, to any of the enormous range of texts that have been written, spoken or are yet to be made in the world. Knowing about linguistics can help you to be a more reflective and efficient writer, and it can help you to negotiate your way around the world of meaning. The world can be seen as a series of interconnected discourses with language (broadly conceived) as the basis. Different types of text write the reality of different parts of life, and systematic knowledge of the analysis of texts and how humans communicate can thus be liberating and endlessly interesting.

The analysis of the language of texts and discourses is known as **stylistics**, and it can be applied to any artefact made of language. The rest of this section gives some examples of texts for you to see what systematic stylistic examination can do. The companion volume to this book, Urszula Clark's *Connecting Text and Grammar: An Introduction to Stylistic Text Analysis*, provides a more detailed introduction to stylistic text analysis.

6.4.1 Analysing types of text

To end the book, we will simply provide some examples of different types of text. You can find your own examples from the millions more out there in the world. For each, ask the questions that have been raised in this chapter, and apply your linguistic knowledge gained from previous chapters. Above all, you should be as systematic and descriptive as you can, and as an experienced user of language, trust yourself.

A scientific text

The following is an example of text written by a biologist. It is intended as popular science as well as a contribution to original knowledge. The author is concerned, therefore, to put an argument forward and be persuasive about it. How does he go about this? Can you construct an authorial voice from the text, by looking at the modality and point of view encoded here? What is the ideology involved? How is it expressed?

All organisms that have ever lived – every animal and plant, all bacteria and all fungi, every creeping thing and all readers of these words – can look back at their ancestors and make the following proud claim: Not a single one of our ancestors died in infancy. They all reached adulthood, and every single one successfully copulated. Not a single one of our ancestors was felled by an enemy, or by a virus, or by a misjudged footstep on a cliff edge, before bringing at least one child into the world. Thousands of our ancestors' contemporaries failed in all these respects, but not a single solitary one of our ancestors failed in any of them. these statements are blindingly obvious, yet from them much follows: much that is curious and unexpected, much that explains and much that astonishes.

Since all organisms inherit all their genes from their successful ancestors, all organisms tend to possess successful genes. They have what it takes to become ancestors – and that means to survive and reproduce. This is why organisms tend to inhereit genes with a propensity to build a well-designed machine – a body that actively works as if it is striving to become an ancestor. That is why birds are so good at flying, fish so good at swimming, monkeys so good at climbing, viruses so good at spreading. That is why we love life and love sex and love children. It is because we all, without a single exception, inherit all our genes from an unbroken line of successful ancestors. The world becomes full of organisms that have what it takes to become ancestors. That, in a sentence, is Darwinism.

Richard Dawkins, *River Out of Eden*, Weidenfeld & Nicolson, 1995

An engineering instructional text

The following is from the installation instructions for a lever control to operate forward and reverse on a boat. What sort of discourse world does it encode? What sort of script knowledge is needed and assumed here? What is it about the syntax of the text that tells you it is instructional? Look in particular at the cohesive features of the text that make it different from any other sort of text. What is the point of view and modality?

INSTALLING THE CONTROL

1.   *Place the control in position allowing clearance for full movement of the handle and free passage for the cables. Mark the fixing centres to suit No. 12 woodscrew.*

2.   *The operating unit is factory assembled for Starboard mounting but is quickly converted for Port mounting as follows:-*

    1.   *Ensure the throttle level and clutch pinion are in the IDLING and NEUTRAL position respectively.*

    2.   *Slacken the set screw securing the handle and withdraw the handle from the splines on the shaft.*
        Note that the embossed line on the exposed shaft is lined up with the run-up button for Neutral.

    3.   *Rotate the handle 180° and re-engage with the splines. At this position, when the operating unit is placed over the mounting holes, the handle should be vertical. Finally, retighten the set screw.*

3.   *Slacken the screws, rotate the trunnion retainers and withdraw the trunnions.*

4.   *Remove and discard jam nuts from remote control ends of throttle and shift cables. Screw the trunnions on to the threaded ends of the shift and throttle cables until the cable ends protrude 3/16 in.*

NOTE: Viewing the unit from the back, the inner levers are for clutch operation and the outer levers for throttle control.

5.   *Position the clutch trunnion assembly in the appropriate slot in the clutch pinion to provide the necessary stroke, rotate the trunnion retainer over the trunnion and tighten the screw to secure.*

6.   *Place the throttle trunnion in the appropriate opening in the throttle lever to provide a push or pull cable action, rotate the retainer over the trunnion and tighten screw.*

7.   *Route the cables through the openings in the body engaging the groove in the cable hub with the body. Fit the hub packers in the empty cable positions, and secure with the hub retainer and screw.*

8.   *Check that the assembled control operates correctly, obtaining full clutch selection and throttle movement.*

9.   *If operation is satisfactory place the operating unit over the mounting holes and secure with the screws, washers, shake-proof washers and nuts.*

from the installation instructions for the
A20 Single Lever Marine Control, Morse Controls Ltd

A cookery instructional text

The following is a recipe, not for the faint-hearted, for cooking a sheep's head. It is from the nineteenth century. Assuming that the reader is not actually cooking the item while reading, how does each word and sentence of the text effect a change in the ongoing discourse world of the reader? In other words, how does the text turn the ingredients into a dish? You might like to contrast the modality of this text which is presumably intended to be descriptive and 'neutral' with the perception of the modality brought by a vegetarian reader. Again, the cohesive features of the text are important. Without thinking about the content, can you tell the difference between the sort of text this is compared with the previous instructional text?

Ingredients
A sheep's head, bouquet garni, 10 peppercorns, salt and pepper, 2 tablesp. pearl barley or rice, 2 onions, 1 small turnip, 2 small carrots, 1 oz. butter or fat, 1 oz. flour, parsley.

If necessary, split the head and remove the brains. Wash the head several times, taking care to remove all splintered bones. Scrape the small bones from the nostrils and brush the teeth. Soak in salt water for 30 min. Cover with cold water and bring to the boil. Pour away the water and replace with fresh cold water and add the bouquet garni, peppercorns and salt. Boil up and skim well. Add the barley (blanched) or rice. Cook slowly for about 3 hr. Meanwhile prepare the vegetables and cut into dice; these should be added about 1 hr. before serving. Remove the skin and fibres from the brains with salt and wash in cold water. Tie the brains in muslin and cook with the head for about 15–20 min. Then chop coarsely. Heat the fat in a saucepan and add the flour. Stir over the heat and cook without browning for about 3 min., then add $\frac{3}{4}$ pt. of liquid in which the head is cooking. Stir until boiling, correct the seasoning and add the brains. Remove the head and take all the flesh from the bones. Skin and slice the tongue. Place the meat neatly on a hot dish. Pour the brain sauce over. If liked, garnish with some of the sliced tongue, vegetables and chopped parsley. Serve the broth separately.
3 helpings.

Mrs Beeton, *All About Cookery*

A political text

The following is from a speech by former leader of the Labour Party, Neil Kinnock. It was orally delivered as a monologue to a party conference. How is it effective in its language usage? How is the author presenting himself here? What sort of speech acts is Kinnock using, and how does he structure the dialogue with himself here?

Why am I the first Kinnock in a thousand generations to be able to get to university? Was it because all *our predecessors were thick? Did they lack talent – those people who could sing, and play, and recite poetry; those people who could make wonderful, beautiful things with their hands; those people who could dream dreams, see visions; those people who had such a sense of perception as to know in times so brutal, so oppressive, that they could win their way out of that by coming together? Were those people not university material? Couldn't they have knocked off their A-levels in an afternoon? But why didn't they get it? Was it because they were weak – those people who could work eight hours a day underground and then come up and play football? Weak? Those women who could survive eleven child-bearings, were they weak? Those people who could stand with their backs and legs straight and face the great – the people who had control over their lives, the ones that owned their workplaces and tried to own them – and tell them, 'No, I won't take your orders.' Were they weak? Does anybody really think that they didn't get what we had because they didn't have the talent, or the strength, or the endurance, or the commitment? Of course not. It was because there was no platform on which they could stand.*

A reporting text

The following is from the opening of the summary of a report prepared for the National Curriculum Council. Examine in particular the lexical choices that give this text its level of formality. What is the authorial voice here? What about modality and point of view (remembering that there is no such thing as 'neutrality' where these are concerned)?

SUMMARY, CONCLUSIONS AND RECOMMENDATIONS

Summary

Key Stage 1

The introduction of the National Curriculum English Order has resulted in more systematic, structured planning for the teaching of all aspects of the Order. Teachers commented on a greater sense of collaboration which was usually a feature of this planning. Details of explicit teaching strategies were located in the policy planning documents rather than the Schemes of Work. These were mainly in the form of learning objectives linked to specific Statements of Attainment.

Time spent hearing individual pupils aloud was specifically for the purpose of monitoring progress. Since the introduction of the National Curriculum this time has also included pupils talking about the content of their reading. This additional activity was seen by teachers to have been the greatest influence on their teaching of reading and they claimed there was not enough time for both activities. These teachers also reported a lack of time for teaching reading generally and they attributed this to the demands made by other subject Orders (see section 2, Manageability). They thought the requirements of the Statements for Level 2 Reading were too broad compared with those of Levels 1 and 3. Consequently they found it difficult to explain to parents why some pupils remained working within Level 2 for a relatively long time. Their concern was with the breadth of development required by Level 2, rather than its content.

Pupils spent their time on reading almost equally divided between activities that were designed to teach them to read and on reading as an activity itself. In learning to read, phonics activities were the ones which pupils experienced most often and for the longest time. Another common activity, used frequently by teachers to teach reading, was listening to pupils read. Also, they used this activity to monitor and assess reading as well as providing pupils with reading practice. However, hearing reading was perceived to be very time-consuming. To deal with this, teachers set their classes a variety of independent reading activities, such as phonic work, or repetition and practice activities, thereby releasing themselves to hear individual pupils read. Teachers also created other opportunities to hear reading, such as when other pupils were working in groups or as a class on a variety of activities not related to reading, or during the teacher's lunch break.

In teaching reading, teachers used a wide range of activities in the early stages. Their planning for teaching phonics was structured and followed a sequence of progression through checklists and published schemes. Teaching reading occurred most frequently in English, rather than as a cross-curricular activity.

The NSGs (NCC 1989, 1990) deal primarily with the classroom environment (e.g. the use of a particular area such as the reading corner), and use of time generally, rather than being specifically targeted towards meeting and identifying pupils' needs in learning to read. However, observations in classrooms showed that, despite limited guidance in this area, teachers were achieving this largely through management of resources and matching books and related activities to individual pupils.

from *Evaluation of the Implementation of English in the National Curriculum at Key Stages 1, 2 and 3 (1991–1993): Final Report,* HMSO/National Curriculum Council

An advertising text

The following is the complete text from a magazine advert:

You picked up the deliberate mistake, of course. ▶ But at the first reading? Probably not. ▶ A visual trick that demonstrates neatly Fuji's video magic: double coating technology. ▶ Just as one reading won't pick out all the details, so one layer of tape won't pick up all the detail. ▶ Enter then – into your camcorder or VCR – Fuji's double-coated tape. ▶ Two layers of magnetic particles, microns thick, cunningly sandwiched together to produce a tape of exceptional clarity and fidelity. ▶ An upper layer of ultra-fine particles to optimise the video signal. ▶ And a lower layer of larger particles to enhance response to the audio signal. ▶ Camcorder tape of such quality that Fuji's ME Position Hi8 has just picked up top prize in the recent European Imaging and Sound Association awards. ▶ And video tape of such reliability that no less than 80% of all BBC and C4 material is archived on Fuji. ▶ Given such a pedigree, do you really need to think twice about using Fuji's double-coating technology? ■

WHY FUDGE IT WHEN YOU CAN FUJI IT?

from the movie magazine *Empire* 66, December 1994

Who speaks and who is addressed here? How is this is a **metalinguistic** advertisement? Look at the lexical choices in the text. What domains of knowledge are being drawn upon here to get the message across? What sort of reader does the text imply?

A literary text

The following is the complete poem by e e cummings from which we took an extract in Section 2.5.3. Using your full repertoire of linguistic knowledge, give an account of the meaning, effect and relevance of the poem. You could apply frameworks from any level of linguistics to discuss this text. Do you think there might be a special *literary text* script that you could use to understand the poem? Try to work out how difficult the search for relevance is in attaching coherence to much of this text that in any other circumstances would be simply ungrammatical. Are literary texts different linguistically from other text types?

anyone lived in a pretty how town
(with up so floating many bells down)
spring summer autumn winter
he sang his didn't he dance his did.

Women and men (both little and small)
cared for anyone not at all
they sowed their isn't they reaped their same
sun moon stars rain

children guessed (but only a few
and down they forgot as up they grew
autumn winter spring summer)
that noone loved him more by more

when by now and tree by leaf
she laughed his joy she cried his grief
bird by snow and stir by still
anyone's any was all to her

someones married their everyones
laughed their cryings and did their dance
(sleep wake hope and then) they
said their nevers they slept their dream

stars rain sun moon
(and only the snow can begin to explain
how children are apt to forget to remember
with up so floating many bells down)

one day anyone died i guess
(and noons stooped to kiss his face)
busy folk buried them side by side
little by little and was by was

all by all and deep by deep
and more by more they dream their sleep
noone and anyone earth by april
wish be spirit and if by yes.

Women and men (both dong and ding)
summer autumn winter spring
reaped their sowing and went their came
sun moon stars rain

from e e cummings, *Complete Poems 1904–1962*,
W. W. Norton

Further reading
The two comprehensive treatments of pragmatics are Leech (1983) and Levinson (1983). The original work on speech acts was done by Austin (1962) and Searle (1969), both of which are readable. 'Gricean' maxims were discussed by the language philosopher H. P. Grice in 1957, but they are most accessible in print in Grice (1975).

Coulthard (1977) is an excellent introduction to the analysis of conversation, and Stubbs (1983b) furthers the discussion and provides many good practical examples and analyses of real conversations. The most comprehensive introduction to discourse analysis, with outlines of frames and coherence, is Brown and Yule (1983). This is essential reading in the area.

The classic text on politeness is Brown and Levinson's (1987) seminal work. Laver (1975) writes on phatic tokens. Relevance theory was first outlined in the carefully and clearly written book by Sperber and Wilson (1986). Naming and terms of address systems are detailed by Adler (1978) and Braun (1988). Much of this material comes under the heading of sociolinguistics and so it is outlined with good examples by Wardhaugh (1992).

Literacy is discussed in a collection of essays edited by Olson, Torrance and Hildyard (1985). A landmark in the study of orality and literacy is Ong and Jackson (1982), dealing with the philosophical consequences of writing and print technology. Oxenham (1980) writes clearly on literacy. The material on different orders of knowledge, highly relevant to the current electronic information revolution, is from Popper (1972). The mechanics of learning to read and the conceptual consequences are discussed by Scribner and Cole (1981) and F. Smith (1983).

The treatment of texts as global artefacts is the ground of text linguistics. De Beaugrande and Dressler (1981) is the standard introduction, and De Beaugrande (1980) is the longer work from which much of it is extracted, fascinating for those hardy souls willing to brave the welter of terminology. Language and ideology has most recently been studied by Gaitet (1991) and Fairclough (1989).

There are several excellent introductions and collections of stylistics, mostly concerned with literary texts primarily. Carter (1982) and Carter and Simpson (1989) are excellent collections of short articles by leading writers in the field. Toolan (1990) is also a good, clearly written source.

Urszula Clark's *Connecting Text and Grammar: An Introduction to Stylistic Text Analysis* is an introduction to stylistics, and is the companion volume to this book. It is an essential starting place for understanding and applying linguistic frameworks to real texts.

Suggested projects
The key to the study of language in use is keen observation. The most ordinary, everyday exchanges between people can contain the most sophisticated strategies of pragmatics, power or encoded ideology. Any text, whether spoken or written,

casual or planned, can be analysed in these terms. The field available for investigation is as large as there are texts to be analysed. However, here are some suggestions.

1   Be on the lookout today for short exchanges between people, in ordinary situations. Try to note down as many as you can. When you have examined all of them, try to account for any utterances that were either not intended or not accepted literally. In particular, look out for exchanges that were unsuccessful. Try to use pragmatic theory to explain what went wrong.

2   Take a longer exchange and record it or write it down from memory as accurately as you can. Break it down into single utterances and detail step-by-step what background knowledge is necessary to make sense of the exchange. You might collect this data from a scripted dialogue in film or television.

3   Record a debate, argument or heated conversation, either from a political programme on television or radio, or between people you know. Analyse the strategies adopted by each speaker to keep a turn and win points

4   Collect examples of children's writing from age seven upwards. Notice features which have developed and how the vocabulary and syntactic form change over the years. Consider also the writers' awareness of global levels of organisation such as genre and formality. Compare this early text-production with an adult text as produced by yourself.

5   Investigate how the ideology of a non-political text is constructed. Consider such texts as personal letters, train timetables, road signs, sweet wrappers, shop signs, advertising hoardings, CD sleeve-notes, toilet graffiti, radio jingles and so on. Think about authorship and target audience, fictionality and reality, the speech acts involved, point of view and modality.

As always, the Activities from this chapter can be expanded and developed into project areas.

Bibliography

Adler, M. K. (1978) *Naming and Addressing: A Sociolinguistic Study*. Helmut Buske.

Aitchison, J. (1987) *Words in the Mind*. Blackwell.

Aitchison, J. (1992) *Language Change: Progress or Decay?* (second edition). Fontana.

Ashby, P. (1995) *Speech Sounds* (Language Workbooks Series). Routledge.

Austin, J. L. (1962) *How To Do Things With Words*. Oxford University Press.

Baker, C. (1995) *A Parents' and Teachers' Guide to Bilingualism*. Multilingual Matters.

Baugh, A. C. and T. Cable (1978) *A History of the English Language* (third edition). Routledge & Kegan Paul.

Bell, R. T. (1976) *Sociolinguistics: Goals, Approaches and Problems*. Batsford.

Bernstein, B. (ed.) (1971/3/5) *Class Codes and Control, Volumes 1–3*. Routledge & Kegan Paul.

Blake, N. (ed.) (1992) *The Cambridge History of the English Language*. Cambridge University Press.

Bosworth, J. and T. N. Toller (1898 etc.) *An Anglo-Saxon Dictionary*. Oxford University Press.

Braun, F. (1988) *Terms of Address*. Mouton de Gruyter.

Brown, G. and G. Yule (1983) *Discourse Analysis*. Cambridge University Press.

Brown, P. and S. Levinson (1987) *Politeness: Some Universals of Language Use*. Cambridge University Press.

Cameron, D. (ed.) (1990) *The Feminist Critique of Language: A Reader*. Routledge.

Cameron, D. (1992) *Feminism and Linguistic Theory* (second edition). Macmillan.

Cameron, K. and M. Gelling (eds) (1976) *Place-Name Evidence for the Anglo-Saxon Invasion and Scandinavian Settlements*. English Place-Name Society.

Carter, R. A. (ed.) (1982) *Language and Literature: An Introductory Reader in Stylistics*. George Allen and Unwin.

Carter, R. A. (ed.) (1991) *Knowledge about Language and the Curriculum: The LINC Reader*. Hodder & Stoughton.

Carter, R. A. and P. Simpson (eds) (1989) *Language, Discourse and Literature: An Introductory Reader in Discourse Stylistics*. Unwin Hyman.

Cawley, A. C. and J. J. Anderson (eds) (1976) *Pearl, Cleanness, Patience, Sir Gawain and the Green Knight* (Everyman edition). Dent.

Chapman, R. L. (1987) *American Slang*. Harper & Row.

Clark, U. (1996) *Connecting Text and Grammar: An Introduction to Stylistic Text Analysis*. Stanley Thornes.

Coates, J. (1993) *Women, Men and Language* (second edition). Longman.

Coates, J. and Cameron, D. (eds) (1988) *Women in Their Speech Communities.* Longman.

COBUILD (1987) *Collins COBUILD English Language Dictionary.* Collins.

COBUILD (1990) *Collins COBUILD English Grammar.* Collins.

Coulthard, R. M. (1977) *An Introduction to Discourse Analysis.* Longman.

Crowley, T. (ed.) (1991) *Proper English?: Readings in Language, History and Cultural Identity.* Routledge.

Cruttenden, A. (1979) *Language in Infancy and Childhood.* Manchester University Press.

Cruttenden, A. (ed.) (1994) *Gimson's Pronunciation of English.* Edward Arnold.

Crystal, D. (1987) *The Cambridge Encyclopaedia of Language.* Cambridge University Press.

Crystal, D. (1988) *The English Language.* Penguin.

Crystal, D. (1992) *Introducing Linguistics.* Penguin.

Crystal, D. (1995) *The Cambridge Encyclopaedia of the English Language.* Cambridge University Press.

Cummins, J. and M. Swain (1986) *Bilingualism and Education.* Longman.

De Beaugrande, R. (1980) *Text, Discourse and Process.* Longman.

De Beaugrande, R. and W. U. Dressler (1981) *Introduction to Text Linguistics.* Longman.

Edwards, V. (1986) *Language in a Black Community.* Multilingual Matters.

Fabb, N. (1994) *Sentence Structure* (Language Workbooks Series). Routledge.

Fairclough, N. (1989) *Language and Power.* Longman.

Fishman, J. A. (1971–2) *Advances in the Sociology of Language* (two volumes). Mouton.

Fletcher, P. (1985) *A Child's Learning of English.* Blackwell.

Fowler, R. (ed.) (1973) *Old English Prose and Verse: An Annotated Selection* (revised edition). Routledge & Kegan Paul.

Gaitet, P. (1991) *Political Stylistics.* Routledge.

Goodluck, H. (1991) *Language Acquisition: A Linguistic Introduction.* Blackwell.

Graddol, D. and Swann, J. (1989) *Gender Voices.* Blackwell.

Graddol, D., J. Cheshire and J. Swann (1994) *Describing Language* (second edition). Open University Press.

Gramley, S. and K.-M. Pätzold (1992) *A Survey of Modern English.* Routledge.

Grice, H. P. (1975) Logic and conversation. In P. Cole and J. Morgan (eds) *Syntax and Semantics, Volume 3, Speech Acts.* Academic Press, pp. 41–58.

Gumperz, J. J. and D. H. Hymes (eds) (1972) *Directions in Sociolinguistics: The Ethnography of Communication.* Holt, Rinehart & Winston.

Halliday, M. A. K. (1975) *Learning How to Mean*. Edward Arnold.

Hamer, R. (1970) *A Choice of Anglo-Saxon Verse*. Faber and Faber.

Harris, J. (1985) *Phonological Variation and Change*. Cambridge University Press.

Hofmann, T. R. (1993) *Realms of Meaning* (Learning about Language Series). Longman.

Holmes, J. (1988–9) *Pidgins and Creoles* (two volumes). Cambridge University Press.

Holmes, J. (1992) *An Introduction to Sociolinguistics*. Longman.

Hudson, R. (1980) *Sociolinguistics*. Cambridge University Press.

Hudson, R. (1995) *Word Meaning* (Language Workbooks Series). Routledge.

Ingram, D. (1991) *First Language Acquisition*. Cambridge University Press.

Jackson, D. (1987) *The Story of Writing*. Barrie & Jenkins.

Jackson, H. (1988) *Words and Their Meaning* (Learning about Language Series). Longman.

Jackson, H. (1990) *Grammar and Meaning* (Learning about Language Series). Longman.

Jones, C. (ed.) (1993) *Historical Linguistics: Problems and Perspectives*. Longman.

Kachru, B. (ed.) (1982) *The Other Tongue*. Pergamon.

Kachru, B. (1985) *The Alchemy of English*. Pergamon.

Katamba, F. (1994) *English Words*. Routledge.

Knowles, G. (1987) *Patterns of Spoken English* (Learning about Language Series). Longman.

Kurath, H. and S. M. Kuhn (eds) (1953 etc.) *Middle English Dictionary*. University of Michigan Press.

Labov, W. (1972) *Sociolinguistic Patterns*. University of Philadelphia Press.

Lakoff, R. (1990) *Talking Power*. Basic Books.

Laver, J. (1975) Communicative functions of phatic communion. In A. Kendon, R. M. Harris and M. R. Key (eds) *Communication in Face To Face Interaction*. Mouton.

Leech, G. N. (1983) *Principles of Pragmatics*. Longman.

Leech, G. N. (1989) *An A–Z of English Grammar and Usage*. Edward Arnold.

Leech, G. N. (1992) *Introducing English Grammar*. Penguin.

Leith, D. (1983) *A Social History of English*. Routledge & Kegan Paul.

Levinson, S. (1983) *Pragmatics*. Cambridge University Press.

McArthur, T. (ed.) (1992) *The Oxford Companion to the English Language*. Oxford University Press.

McCrum, R., W. Cran and R. MacNeil (1986) *The Story of English*. Faber & Faber/BBC Books (revised edition published in 1992).

McIntosh, A., M. L. Samuels and M. Benskin (1986) *A Linguistic Atlas of Late Medieval English* (fourth edition). Aberdeen University Press.

Milroy, J. (1981) *Regional Accents of English*. Blackstaff Press.

Milroy, J. and L. Milroy (1991) *Authority in Language.* Routledge.

Milroy, J. and L. Milroy (1993) *Real English: The Grammar of English Dialects in the British Isles.* Longman.

Montgomery, M. (1986) *An Introduction to Language and Society.* Methuen.

Olson, D. R., N. Torrance and A. Hildyard (eds) (1985) *Literacy, Language and Learning: The Nature and Consequences of Reading and Writing.* Cambridge University Press.

Ong, W. and W. Jackson (1982) *Orality and Literacy: The Technologizing of the Word.* Methuen.

Orton, H., S. Sanderson and J. Widdowson (eds) (1978) *The Linguistic Atlas of England.* Croom Helm.

Oxenham, J. (1980) *Literacy.* Routledge & Kegan Paul.

Platt, J., H. Weber and M. L. Ho (1984) *The New Englishes.* Routledge & Kegan Paul.

Popper, K. (1972) *Objective Knowledge.* Clarendon Press.

Poynton, C. (1989) *Language and Gender: Making the Difference.* Oxford University Press.

Pride, J. B. and J. Holmes (eds) (1972) *Sociolinguistics: Selected Readings.* Penguin.

Pyles, T. (1971) *The Origins and Development of the English Language* (second edition). Harcourt Brace Jovanovich.

Quirk, R. and S. Greenbaum (1990) *A Student's Grammar of the English Language.* Longman.

Quirk, R. and C. L. Wrenn (1960) *An Old English Grammar* (second edition). Methuen.

Quirk, R., S. Greenbaum, G. N. Leech and J. Svartvik (1985) *A Comprehensive Grammar of the English Language.* Longman.

Rissanen, M. *et al.* (eds) (1992) *History of Englishes: New Methods and Interpretations in Historical Linguistics.* Mouton de Gruyter.

Roach, P. (1992) *Introducing Phonetics.* Penguin.

Romaine, S. (1988) *Pidgin and Creole Languages.* Longman.

Salkie, R. (1995) *Text and Discourse Analysis* (Language Workbooks Series). Routledge.

Saunders, G. (1982) *Bilingual Children: Guidance for the Family* (updated and republished in 1988 with the title *Bilingual Children: From Birth to Teens*). Multilingual Matters.

Scragg, D. G. (1974) *A History of English Spelling.* Manchester University Press.

Scribner, S. and M. Cole (1981) *The Psychology of Literacy.* Harvard University Press.

Searle, J. R. (1969) *Speech Acts: An Essay in the Philosophy of Language.* Cambridge University Press.

Smith, F. (1983) *Essays Into Literacy: Selected Papers and Some Afterthoughts.* Heinemann Educational.

Smith, L. E. (ed.) (1983) *Readings in English as an International Language*. Pergamon.

Sperber, D. and D. Wilson (1986) *Relevance: Communication and Cognition*. Blackwell.

Steinberg, D. (1993) *An Introduction to Psycholinguistics*. Longman.

Stenström, A.-B. (1994) *An Introduction to Spoken Interaction* (Learning about Language Series). Longman.

Strang, B. (1972) *A History of English*. Methuen.

Stubbs, M. (1983a) *Language, Schools and Classrooms* (revised edition). Methuen.

Stubbs, M. (1983b) *Discourse Analysis: The Sociolinguistic Analysis of Natural Language*. Blackwell.

Stubbs, M. (1986) *Educational Linguistics*. Blackwell.

Sutcliffe, D. (1982) *British Black English*. Blackwell.

Sweet, H. (1975) *An Anglo-Saxon Reader in Prose and Verse* (fifteenth edition, revised by D. Whitelock). Clarendon Press.

Sweet, H. (1978) *A Second Anglo-Saxon Reader, Archaic and Dialectal* (second edition, revised by T. F. Hoad). Clarendon Press.

Tannen, D. (1992) *You Just Don't Understand: Women and Men in Conversation*. Virago.

Toolan, M. (1990) *The Stylistics of Fiction*. Routledge.

Traugott, E. C. (1972) *A History of English Syntax*. Reinhart & Winston.

Trudgill, P. (1983) *Sociolinguistics: An Introduction to Language and Society*. Penguin.

Trudgill, P. (1990) *The Dialects of England*. Blackwell.

Trudgill, P. and J. K. Chambers (eds) (1991) *Dialects of English*. Longman.

Trudgill, P. and J. Hannah (1984) *International English* (revised edition). Arnold.

Wakelin, M. (1988) *The Archaeology of English*. Batsford.

Wardhaugh, R. (1992) *An Introduction to Sociolinguistics* (second edition). Blackwell.

Wells, G. (1985) *Language Development in the Preschool Years*. Cambridge University Press.

Wells, J. C. (1982) *Accents of English* (volumes 1 and 2). Cambridge University Press.

Whitelock, D. (1965) *The Beginnings of English Society* (revised edition). Pelican.

Wilkinson, J. (1993) *Introducing Standard English*. Penguin.

Wood, H. H. (ed.) (1978) *Poems and Fables by Robert Henryson*. James Thin/Mercat Press.

Glossary

This glossary contains details of the terms that are highlighted in **<u>bold underlined</u>** type in the text.

accent   The characteristic pronunciation of a geographical area or a social group. (Sections 1.2.2, 2.1.8)

acronym   A word formed from the initial letters of a **phrase**, sometimes spelt out letter by letter (for example, *BBC*) and sometimes pronounced as a word (for example, *NATO*). (Section 3.5.2)

adjectival clause   A **clause** that functions like an **adjective** to modify a **noun**; for example, a **relative** clause. (Section 2.3.5)

adjective   A class of words used to modify **nouns**; for example, *tall, round, pretty*. Some adjectives are gradable and may have comparative and superlative forms; for example, *short, shorter, shortest; cautious, more cautious, most cautious*. (Section 2.2.2)

adverb   A class of words used to specify the circumstances of an action or event; for example, the manner (*slowly*), the time (*soon*) and the place (*here*). It also includes conjunctive adverbs (*however*) and adverb **particles** (*up, out*). (Section 2.2.2)

adverbial   A type of element in **sentence** structure, referring to the circumstances of the sentence, often expressed by an **adverb**, **prepositional phrase** or **adverbial clause**. (Section 2.3.4)

adverbial clause   A **clause**, often introduced by a subordinating **conjunction** (*if, because, although*) that functions as an **adverbial** in **sentence** structure. (Section 2.3.5)

affix   A part of a word that is added to a **root**, either in front (**prefix**) or behind (**suffix**). (Section 2.2.3)

allophone   A variant pronunciation of a **phoneme**; for example, the 'clear' [l] of *lip* and the 'dark' [ɫ] of *pill*. (Section 2.1.4)

antonym   A word that is opposite in meaning to another word; for example, *dark* and *light*. (Section 2.2.6)

approximant   A type of **consonant** that is articulated without restriction to the airflow, /w r j/ in English. (Section 2.1.2)

article   A subclass of the **word class** of **determiners**, including the definite article *the* and the indefinite article *a*. (Section 2.2.2)

articulation, manner of   The way in which the airflow is modified in the pronunciation of a **consonant**; for example, **stop/plosive** and **fricative**. (Section 2.1.2)

articulation, place of   The articulators in the mouth involved in the pronunciation of a **consonant**; for example, bilabial and velar. (Section 2.1.2)

aspiration   The puff of air that accompanies the **articulation** of voiceless **stops** in English, especially when they occur initially in a word; for example, *pot* [pʰot], *can* [kʰan]. (Section 2.1.4)

assimilation   The alteration in the **articulation** of a sound in the direction of a neighbouring, usually following, sound; for example, *fun park* – /fʌm pɑːk/. (Section 2.1.4)

auxiliary verb   A small set of **verbs**, including the modal verbs, *be*, *have* and *do*, which accompany lexical verbs and indicate modality, **progressive** and **perfect aspects**, and **passive voice**; or which act as a dummy auxiliary (*do*) for negative and interrogative verbs. (Section 2.3.3)

babbling period   The time, from around three months old, when babies seem to be trying out the **articulation** of speech sounds. (Section 4.2.1)

bilingual   Being able to speak two languages with reasonable fluency. An infant bilingual acquires two languages from birth, while a child bilingual begins to acquire the second language a little later in childhood. (Section 4.8)

case   A grammatical category that applies to **nouns** and **pronouns** and that signals the syntactic function (as **subject**, **object** or possessor) of the noun/pronoun; cases in English nouns are **genitive** and common, and in pronouns, subjective, objective and genitive. (Section 2.2.2)

classical compound   A word formed from two elements (called **combining forms**) that were **roots** in Latin or Greek, combined to make a modern English word; for example, *bibliography*, *xenophobia*. (Section 2.2.4)

class stratification   The division of society into a hierarchy of classes (usually from the Registrar General's classification) for the purpose of sociolinguistic investigation. (Section 5.2.4)

clause   A syntactic unit having the essential structure of a **sentence** but embedded in (functioning as part of) a sentence or sentence element. (Section 2.3.5)

cohesion   The grammatical and lexical devices that serve to make a **text** hold together; for example, **pronouns**, conjunctive **adverbs** and lexical repetition. (Section 2.4.2)

collocation   A lexical feature relating to the mutual attraction of words. If two words are collocates, then there is a greater than chance likelihood of them both occurring; for example, *dark* and *night*. (Section 2.2.7)

combining form   An element in a **classical compound**, either as initial combining form (for example, *astro-*, *biblio-*, *xeno-*) or as final combining form (for example, *-cide*, *-naut*, *-graphy*). (Section 2.2.4)

comparative   A form of an **adjective**, indicated by the *-er* **suffix** (*taller*) or by the **adverb** *more* (*more surprising*), used for making comparisons between things. (Section 2.2.2)

complement   An element of **sentence** structure, usually an **adjective** or a **noun phrase**, which describes a **subject** (in subject + verb + complement structures), typically after the **verb** *be*, or an **object** (in subject + verb + object + complement structures), typically after verbs such as *consider* and *regard*. (Section 2.3.1)

compound   A word made up of the combination of two independent words; for example, *rainfall, see-through*. (Section 2.2.4)

conjunction   A class of words used for joining **sentences** or **clauses**; coordinating conjunctions (*and, but, or*) provide **coordination**; subordinating conjunctions (for example, *because, if, when, although*) join subordinate (embedded) **adverbial clauses** to a sentence. (Section 2.2.2)

consonant   A speech sound articulated with some restriction to the airflow through the mouth, occurring at the periphery of **syllables**; not a **vowel**. (Section 2.1.2)

coordination   The joining together of sentences, phrases or words by means of *and, but* and *or*. (Section 2.3.5)

corpus   A collection of **texts** or **discourses**, providing the raw data of linguistic analysis, usually held on a computer. (Section 1.4.3)

declension   The **inflectional** forms of a **noun**, showing **gender**, **case** and **number**. (Section 3.2.1)

demonstrative   A subclass of **determiners** and **pronouns**, comprising the words *this/these* and *that/those*. (Section 2.2.2)

derivation   The creation of new words by means of **prefixes** and **suffixes**; for example, *re-try, entertain-ment*. (Section 2.2.3)

determiner   A class of words that accompany **nouns** in **noun phrases**, including **identifiers** and **quantifiers**. (Section 2.2.2)

dialect   The regional and social variations of a language, especially in respect of grammar and vocabulary. (Sections 1.2.2, 2.5.1).

digraph   Two letters in writing, used to represent a single sound; for example, ea in *lead* /liːd/ or /led/. (Section 2.1.5)

diphthong   A type of **vowel** sound that involves movement towards /i/, /ə/ or /u/. (Section 2.1.1)

discourse   A sequence of spoken utterances making up a coherent dialogue or monologue. (Sections 1.1.2, 1.3.4, 2.4)

elicitation   The use of an experiment or questionnaire to obtain information about language use from a sample of subjects. (Sections 1.4.2, 4.7)

elision   The omission of a sound in connected speech; for example, /t/ when preceded and followed by a **consonant**, as in *las(t)night*. (Section 2.1.4)

ellipsis   A device of **cohesion** in **discourse** in which items are omitted – for example, from replies to questions – so that a structural gap appears, which can be filled by referring back in the discourse. (Section 2.4.2)

ESP   English for Special Purposes; for example, English for Engineers or English for Academic Purposes. (Section 5.3.2)

finite/non-finite   Forms of **verbs** (and **clauses** containing them): non-finite forms include the **infinitive** and present and past **participles**; finite forms are marked for **tense** (present/past) and include the two present-tense forms and the past-tense form. (Section 2.2.2)

formality   A scale from informal or colloquial to formal, describing the stylistic level of language use appropriate in different situational contexts. (Section 1.2.3)

fricative   A type of **consonant** sound, made by a narrow constriction in the mouth through which the air can pass, and causing friction as it does so. (Section 2.1.2)

fronting   The promotion of a **sentence** element to the initial position for the purposes of information structuring in **texts**; *see also* **postponement**. (Section 2.4.3)

gender   A grammatical category applying only to third-person singular **pronouns** and signalling the distinction between masculine, feminine and neuter. (Section 2.2.2)

genitive   A type of **case**, typically signalling possession, marked in **nouns** by 's. (Section 2.2.2)

homograph   Two words that are spelt the same, even though pronounced differently, are homographs; for example, *wind* (air movement) and *wind* (turn a handle). (Section 2.2.1)

homonym   Two words that are spelt and pronounced the same, but have a different etymology, are homonyms; for example, *skate* (on ice) and *skate* (fish). (Section 2.2.1)

homophone   Two words that are pronounced the same but spelt differently are homophones; for example, *scent* and *sent*. (Section 2.2.1)

hyponymy   A semantic relation between words, in which the meaning of the hyponym is included in the meaning of the superordinate word; for example, *knife, fork, spoon* are hyponyms of *cutlery*. (Section 2.2.6)

identifier   A subclass of **determiners**, including the **articles**, **possessive** identifiers (*my*, and so on) and **demonstrative** identifiers (*this*, and so on). (Section 2.2.2)

idiolect   The characteristic speech of an individual person, including their idiosyncratic features of pronunciation, grammar and vocabulary. (Sections 1.2, 2.5.1)

idiom   A fixed expression in which the meaning of the sum is other than the meaning of the parts; for example, *pull someone's leg, a storm in a teacup*. (Section 2.2.7)

infinitive   A **non-finite** form of a **verb**, typically marked by *to*; for example, *to swim*. In a bare infinitive, the *to* is omitted. (Section 2.2.2)

inflection   A **suffix** added to a **noun**, **verb** or **adjective** to signal a grammatical category, such as **plural**, past **tense** or **comparative**. (Sections 1.3.2, 2.2.3)

interactional   A type of spoken **discourse** in which the focus is not on the content of what is said, but rather than on the social relationships between the participants; *see also* **transactional**. (Section 1.2.4)

interrogative   A word that is used for asking a question – for example, *Why? Who? Where?* – or a type of **sentence** typically used for asking a question or making a request. (Section 2.2.2)

intonation   Variations in pitch and rhythm that accompany speech and convey a speaker's attitude, as well as structuring a **discourse**. (Sections 1.1.1, 2.1.6)

intransitive   A type of **verb** that is not followed by an **object** in **sentence** structure – it is also used of such a sentence; *see also* **transitive**. (Section 2.3.1)

language acquisition   The spontaneous development of language in a child from birth, in contrast to the learning of a second or subsequent language later in life. (Chapter 4)

lateral   A type of **consonant** sound, made with a complete restriction in the mouth, but with the air escaping over the sides of the tongue, so laterally; in English, /l/. (Section 2.1.2)

lexeme   A word viewed as a dictionary entry, as a unit of grammar and meaning. (Section 2.2.1)

lexicology   The study of words, their formation, meaning, structure and use. (Section 1.3.2)

manner of articulation   *See* **articulation, manner of**.

maxim   A convention of spoken **discourse** relating to the quality, quantity, manner and relevance of what is said. (Section 6.1.1)

medium (of language)   The means by which language is expressed, either speech or writing. (Section 1.1.1)

metalinguistic   About language: metalinguistic statements are descriptions of language; metalinguistic knowledge is knowledge about language. (Sections 1.2.1, 6.2.2)

modal auxiliary verb   A subclass of **auxiliary verbs**, including *may/might, can/could, shall/should, will/would* and *must*, used to signal possibility, certainty, permission, obligation, ability and so on. (Section 2.3.3)

monosyllabic   A word having a single **syllable**; for example, *bring, plinth, straight*. (Section 2.1.3)

morpheme   A meaningful part of a word; including **roots** and **affixes** (**prefix**, **suffix**). (Section 2.2.3)

morphology   The study of the forms of words, including **inflections**, **derivations** and **compounds**. (Section 1.3.2)

motherese   *See* **parentese**.

nasal A type of **consonant** sound, formed by a complete constriction in the mouth, but with air allowed to escape through the nose. (Section 2.1.2)

neologism A newly coined word. (Section 3.5.2)

nominal clause A **clause** that functions in place of a **noun phrase**; for example, as **subject**, **object** or **complement** of a **sentence**. (Section 2.3.5)

non-finite *See* **finite**.

noun The largest class of words, referring to 'things' and typically having **plural** and **genitive inflections**. (Section 2.2.2)

noun phrase A group of words consisting of a **noun** as head, with accompanying modifiers, such as **determiners**, **adjectives** and **prepositional phrases**. (Section 2.3.2)

number A grammatical category associated with **nouns** and **pronouns**, having the terms singular (referring to one person/thing) and **plural** (referring to more than one person/thing). (Section 2.2.2)

numeral A subclass of **quantifiers**, including the cardinal numerals (*one, two, three, ...*) and the ordinal numerals (*first, second, third, ...*). (Section 2.2.2)

object An element of **sentence** structure, usually a **noun phrase** or **nominal clause**, occurring with a **transitive verb** and representing the thing affected by the action of the verb. (Section 2.3.1)

parentese (formerly motherese) The form of language that parents use when talking to babies and very young children. (Section 4.5)

participle One of two **non-finite** forms of a **verb**, either present participle, with *-ing* **suffix** (for example, *laughing*), or past participle, usually with *-ed* suffix (for example, *laughed*). (Section 2.2.2)

particle A subclass of **adverbs** (for example, *up, off, out*), used to form **phrasal verbs**; for example, *give up, take off, turn out*. (Section 2.2.2)

part of speech *See* **word class**.

passive voice The counterpart to active voice, where an active **sentence** is rearranged by making the **verb** passive (with *be* + past **participle**, bringing the **object** of the active sentence to **subject** position in the passive sentence, and optionally putting the subject of the active sentence into a *by*-phrase in the passive; for example, *The judge sentenced the prisoner to life imprisonment* (active) – *The prisoner was sentence to life imprisonment (by the judge)* (passive). (Section 2.3.3)

perfect aspect In the **verb phrase**, formed with *have* + past **participle** (for example, *they have arrived*), used to express happenings immediately prior to the present moment (present perfect) or a past moment (past perfect). (Section 2.3.3)

person A grammatical category associated with **pronouns**, having the terms first person (referring to the speaker/writer), second person (referring to the addressee) and third person (referring to people or things talked about). (Section 2.2.2)

phoneme   A speech sound, which when substituted for another phoneme, alters the word; for example, /sit/ – /sil/ – /mil/. (Section 2.1.4)

phonetics   The study of speech sounds, their **articulation**, acoustics and auditory perception. (Section 1.3.1)

phonology   The study of speech sounds with reference to a particular language; for example, English. (Section 1.3.1)

phrasal verb   A **verb** consisting of a verb word and an adverb **particle**; for example, *give up, make out, take off*. (Section 2.2.2)

phrase   A group of words that form a unit in the structure of **sentences, clauses** or other phrases, usually with a head word and accompanying modifying words; for example, **noun phrase** and **verb phrase**. (Sections 2.3.2, 2.3.3)

place of articulation   *See* **articulation, place of**.

plosive   *See* **stop**.

plural   A term in the grammatical category of **number**, counterpart to singular, signalling 'more than one', especially of **nouns**, usually marked with the **suffix** *-(e)s*. (Section 2.2.2)

polysyllabic   In reference to the phonological structure of a **word**, having more than one **syllable**; for example, *packet* /pa-kit/. (Section 2.1.3)

possessive   Relating to possession, marked by the **genitive case** in **nouns** and **pronouns**. (Section 2.2.2)

postponement   The delaying of an element of **sentence** structure to final position in the interests of information structure in a **text**; *see also* **fronting**. (Section 2.4.3)

pragmatics   The study of language in use. (Section 1.3.8)

prefix   A bound **morpheme** that is attached to the front of a **root**, used to derive new words; for example, *re-apply, anti-nuclear*. (Sections 1.3.2, 2.2.3)

preposition   A small class of words, including *along, from, in, of, on*, used for joining **noun phrases** to other elements of **sentence** structure. (Section 2.2.2)

progressive aspect   In the **verb phrase** formed with *be* + present **participle**, used to express an action/event that is in progress or of limited duration. (Section 2.3.3)

pronoun   A class of words that function in place of **nouns**, including the personal pronouns (*I, you, he, she* and so on). (Section 2.2.2)

psycholinguistics   The study of language in reference to the individual's mind and behaviour, including how we acquire language, the relation between language and personal identity, and language and mind. (Section 1.3.6, Chapter 4)

punctuation   The system of marks in writing used to indicate the structure of **sentences**, including the comma, semi-colon, full stop and question mark. (Sections 1.1.1, 2.1.7)

quantifier   A subclass of **determiners**, including the **numerals** and indefinite quantifiers such as *many, few, several* and so on. (Section 2.2.2)

reference   The semantic relation between a word and the entity it relates to in the world of our experience. (Section 2.2.5)

reflexive   A type of **pronoun**, including *myself*, *yourself* and *themselves*, used for emphasis (*She did it herself*) or for self-reference (*She has cut herself*). (Section 2.2.2)

relative   Used of relative **pronouns** (for example, *who, which, whose*), which introduce relative clauses that function as postmodifiers in **noun phrases**. (Section 2.2.2)

rheme   *See* **theme**.

root   In **morphology**, the part of a **word** when all **affixes** have been removed, usually itself an independent word in English; for example, *state* in *re-state-ment-s*. (Section 2.2.3)

semantics   The study of meaning in all its aspects, especially in relation to **words** and **sentences**. (Section 1.3.5)

sense relation   Relations of meaning between **lexemes**, such as synonymy, antonymy and **hyponymy**. (Section 2.2.6)

sentence   A syntactic structure, consisting minimally of a **subject** and a **verb**, but also possibly containing a **complement**, **objects** and **adverbials**. (Sections 1.1.2, 2.3, 2.3.6)

sociolinguistics   The study of language in relation to society, especially of the ways in which language varies according to social factors. (Section 1.3.7)

speech act   The communicative force which is enacted by an utterance. Types of speech act include locutionary, illocutionary and performative acts. (Section 6.1.1)

stop (consonant)   Also called 'plosive', a consonant articulated with complete constriction of the airflow in the mouth, which is subsequently released with plosion. (Section 2.1.2)

stress   The relative prominence given to **syllables** in speech; for example, in *certain* the first syllable is stressed while the second is unstressed. (Section 2.1.6)

subject   An obligatory element of **sentence** structure, which precedes the **verb** in the neutral form of declarative sentences. (Section 2.3.1)

subordination   When a **clause** is introduced by a subordinating **conjunction** (for example, *because, if, since, when*), usually an **adverbial clause**, but also used of all kinds of embedded clause. (Section 2.3.5)

suffix   A bound **morpheme** that is added to the end of **roots**, either to derive a new word (for example, *pur-ify, fair-ness*) or as an **inflection** (for example, *paper-s, wait-ing*). (Sections 1.3.2, 2.2.3)

superlative   A form of a gradable **adjective**, expressing the highest degree, formed with the *-est* **inflection** or the **adverb** *most*. (Section 2.2.2)

syllable   A phonological structure consisting of a **vowel** as nucleus and **consonants** as peripheral sounds; **words** may consist of one or more syllables; for example, *can* /kan/, *canteen* /kan-ti:n/. (Section 2.1.3)

synonym   Two words that mean substantially the same are synonyms; for example, *owner* and *possessor*. (Section 2.2.6)

syntax   (The study of) the structure of **sentences**. (Section 1.3.3)

tense   The grammatical category that relates to real-world time; in English only the past and present tenses are marked by **inflections**. (Section 2.2.2)

text   A sequence of written **sentences** marked by **cohesion** and coherence; *see also* **discourse**. (Sections 1.1.2, 1.3.4, 2.4)

text type   **Texts** classified according to purpose and structural features; for example, narrative, descriptive, expository. (Section 2.4.4)

theme/rheme   A division of a **sentence** into an initial 'theme' (what the sentence is about) and the 'rheme' (what is said about the theme); also called 'topic' and 'comment'. (Section 6.3.2)

transactional   A type of spoken **discourse** in which the focus is on the content of what is said, the business that the discourse transacts; *see also* **interactional**. (Section 1.2.4)

transitive   A type of **verb** that takes an **object** in **sentence** structure – it is also used of the sentence structure itself; *see also* **intransitive**. (Section 2.3.1)

verb   A class of words that refer to actions, events and states; subdivided into **auxiliary verbs** and lexical or main verbs. (Section 2.2.2)

verb phrase   A group of words with a lexical **verb** as head and optionally preceded by **auxiliary verbs** and the negative *not*. (Section 2.3.3)

voice   A grammatical category, with the terms active and passive; for example, *The opposition proposed an amendment to the bill* (active) – *An amendment to the bill was proposed by the opposition* (passive). (Section 2.3.3)

voicing   In the **articulation** of a speech sound, whether the vocal cords are vibrating (voiced sound) or not vibrating (unvoiced sound). (Section 2.1.2)

vowel   A type of speech sound, articulated without any restriction to the airflow in the mouth and formed by modifications to the shape of the mouth, composing the nucleus of **syllables**; *see also* **consonant**. (Section 2.1.1)

word   A basic unit of **syntax**, entering into the structure of **phrases** and **sentences**, composed of **morphemes**. (Sections 1.1.2, 2.2)

word class   A grouping of words according to shared features of **reference**, **morphology** and **syntax**; such as **nouns**, **verbs**, **adjectives** and **prepositions**. (Section 2.2.2)

INDEX